EDGE OF APOCALYPSE

Also by Tim LaHaye

Revelation Unveiled

Finding the Will of God in a Crazy, Mixed-Up World

How to Win over Depression

Anger Is a Choice
(Tim LaHaye and Bob Phillips)

The Act of Marriage: The Beauty of Sexual Love
(Tim and Beverly LaHaye)

TIM LaHAYE
& CRAIG PARSHALL

EDGE OF
APOCALYPSE

THE END SERIES

ZONDERVAN®
.com

ZONDERVAN.com/
AUTHORTRACKER
follow your favorite authors

ZONDERVAN

Edge of Apocalypse
Copyright © 2010 by Tim LaHaye

This title is also available as a Zondervan ebook.
Visit www.zondervan.com/ebooks.

This title is also available in a Zondervan audio edition.
Visit www.zondervan.fm.

Requests for information should be addressed to:

Zondervan, *Grand Rapids, Michigan* 49530

This edition: ISBN 978-0-310-33171-1 (softcover)

The Library of Congress has cataloged the hardcover edition as follows:

LaHaye, Tim F.
  Edge of Apocalypse / Tim LaHaye and Craig Parshall.
   p. cm. — (The end series)
  ISBN 978-0-310-32628-1 (hardcover)
   1. End of the world — Fiction. I. Parshall, Craig, 1950- II. Title.
 PS3562.A315—E34 2010
  813'.54 — dc22   2010002106

Published in association with the literary agency of WordServe Literary Group, Ltd., 10152 S. Knoll Circle, Highlands Ranch, CO 80130.

Cover design: Curt Diepenhorst
Cover photography: Shutterstock
Interior design: Christine Orejuela-Winkelman

Printed in the United States of America

11 12 13 14 15 16 17 /DCI/ 24 23 22 21 20 19 18 17 16 15 14 13 12 11 10 9 8 7 6 5 4 3 2 1

To those who believe that out of the chaos
of our rapidly changing world something momentous
is about to happen ...

To those who wish to face the uncertainties of the
End of the Age with an understanding of Biblical prophecy ...

And to those who want to enjoy
God's wonderful plan for our future ...

EDGE OF
APOCALYPSE

PART ONE
Under the Nuclear Shadow

Richard Garwin, a designer of the hydrogen bomb, was called by Nobel Laureate Enrico Fermi "the only true genius I had ever met." Testifying to Congress in March 2007, Mr. Garwin estimated a "20 percent per year probability of a nuclear explosion with American cities and European cities included."... My Harvard Colleague, Matthew Bunn, created a model that estimates the probability of a terrorist nuclear attack over a ten year period at 29 percent.

Graham Allison, director of the Belfer Center for Science and International Affairs, Kennedy School of Government, and former assistant Secretary of Defense (*Washington Times*, April 23, 2008)

Return to sender,
Address unknown.
No such number,
No such zone.

Winfield Scott and Otis Blackwell, 1962

Blessed is he who reads and those who hear the words of the prophecy,

and heeds the things which are written in it; for the time is near.

Revelation 1:3

ONE

In the Not-Too-Distant Future

At twelve thousand feet, alarm bells started going off all over the cockpit of the Navy EA-6B Prowler. At first Captain Louder thought they'd run into a flock of birds, but they were much too high up.

"Captain," shouted his lead ECM officer, Lieutenant Emmit Wilson, "on-board computers have crashed."

"Avionics?"

"Screwed up, sir."

"Navigation?"

"Everything's bugging out, sir," said his navigation officer, Lieutenant Jim Stewart, a bespectacled electronics nerd from the Naval Communications School at Pensacola.

"Were we hit?"

"Not that I can see, sir."

Captain Louder glanced quickly at the jet engine to his left. No smoke, no oil. He glanced to his right. The other engine appeared equally sound. Everything seemed normal, but the instruments said otherwise: pressure dropping, fuel gauge empty, altimeter and directional indicators completely out of whack.

"I need answers, men."

Though the crew was good at their jobs, they were young, and the person they usually looked to for answers was Captain Louder.

"That's an order!"

"Sir," said Lieutenant Wilson hesitantly, "all I can think of is that we were hit with some kind of massive electromagnetic charge, either internal or external, fried all our instruments or ..."

"Or ...?"

"Or the Koreans have some new kind of sophisticated jamming system."

"We're supposed to be doing the jamming, not them."

The Prowler's chief mission was reconnaissance and radar suppression, its weapons sophisticated electronic jamming equipment and a single HARM — high-speed anti-radiation missile — that could seek out and destroy enemy radar defenses all on its own.

"What about sunspots, sir?" suggested Lieutenant Stewart.

"More likely we ran into Santa Claus," growled Captain Louder as he fought to maintain control of the stick and keep the aircraft steady, "but it's only September." He didn't need guesses now; he needed solutions — and fast.

"HQ Foxfire, this is Looking Glass, over," he yelled into the radio. "HQ Foxfire, this is Looking Glass, do you read me, over."

"We're twenty minutes early on our verbal, sir. They're not going to respond," said Lieutenant Stewart.

"Or else the radio's dead too. Anything still work on this plane?"

The youngest of the three ECMOs, Lieutenant Derrick Milius, a pimply faced twenty-one-year-old from Lubbock, Texas, shyly pulled an iPod out of his shirt pocket. He plugged it into the aircraft's intercom. The twangy strains of Hank Williams Jr. filled the cockpit.

"A little inspiration, sir."

□□□

"HQ Foxfire, this is Looking Glass, over ... HQ Foxfire, this is Looking Glass, do you read me, over." The voice of Captain Louder crackled over the speakers in the Tactical Communications Bunker at Osan Air Base, just forty-eight miles south of the DMZ.

"Do we respond, sir?"

Wing Commander Charles Stamper chomped down on another stick of Nicorette gum. What he really needed was a cigarette, but the base had recently gone smoke-free, and he had to lead by example.

"No. We have strict orders to maintain radio silence all along the parallel."

A tinny version of Hank Williams Jr.'s "Born to Boogie" seeped through the speakers followed by, "HQ Foxfire, this is Looking Glass; we have a situation up here; request permission to break off current flight path and return to base, over."

No one in the communications bunker said a word, waiting for the commander to speak; the only sound now his obsessive gum chewing.

Hank Williams Jr.'s warble returned, then, "HQ Foxfire, this is Looking Glass, breaking off current flight path, requesting secondary landing site, do you copy, over."

"Do we respond *now*, sir?

Commander Stamper bit his tongue accidentally. The orders were explicit. No radio contact with planes over the DMZ. But he knew Captain Louder personally, probably owed him a few bucks from a poker game or two, and he knew he wouldn't break radio silence unless he had to. He also knew the captain wouldn't want to give out too much information over the radio. They both knew that the North Korean military, known as the Korean People's Army, or the KPA, were always listening, looking to turn every situation to their advantage. But still. Captain Louder was listening to music in the cockpit. Country music. Was that code for something? He wracked his brain but came up with nothing.

"Give them a couple clicks of the hand mic to let them know we heard." The commander turned to his flight officer. "Send up a couple fighters to check it out. Tell them to stay high and out of sight. Make visual contact if they can, but no radio under any circumstance."

He'd picked a bad week to give up smoking.

ㅁㅁㅁ

Captain Louder knew from the silence on the radio that he was on his own — at least until he cleared the DMZ. His flight plan called for him to stay on this heading until he reached international waters over the Sea of Japan, but he didn't think his plane had enough in her to get that far. Whatever had attacked the electronics had done a number on the systems. Nothing was responding. It was like being back in an old T-2 Buckeye trainer where muscle and moxie were as important as avionics. Strictly stick-and-rudder stuff now.

"We're going to try and glide this beast in," Captain Louder informed his crew. "We're starting to lose thrust and trim, and the hydraulics are gone. Maintaining altitude and velocity will be impossible. I need work-arounds for navigation and pitch control so we don't just find ourselves floating over on the other side of the Bamboo Curtain."

His young crew dug into their task, fueled by adrenaline and Hank Williams Jr.'s bluesy ramblings. He knew he was going to get into a rash of trouble about the music when he got back to base, but it seemed to focus his crew, so what the ...

Captain Louder saw them first — two North Korean fighters coming directly out of the rising sun at Mach 2.

"We got company, and they don't look happy to see us."

The two North Korean birds streaked past and started a long loop to maneuver behind the crippled American plane.

"I'm taking evasive action," Captain Louder barked. "We don't need any more surprises." He tried to maneuver the plane, but it was like walking in wet cement, each step getting harder and harder. He knew they were sitting ducks, but he couldn't worry about that now. He had to work with what he had. Besides, why would they fire on him and risk World War III?

"Their radar just painted us, sir," screamed Lieutenant Milius.

"What?"

Captain Louder was rocked. *They're targeting us? Why? Had we strayed so far off course when our navigation controls went down?*

"Missile away, sir!"

A white trail of smoke corkscrewed out from behind the heat-seeking missile a mile back as it left the lead North Korean jet.

"Set the auto countermeasures!"

Lieutenant Wilson pushed the auto-set button. "Auto countermeasures failed to launch."

"Fire manually."

Wilson flipped the directional IR countermeasure switch. Then he flipped the second switch for high-heat flares to launch and hopefully detract the incoming heat-seeking missile.

"Second missile away, sir!" Lieutenant Milius's voice raised a few octaves as a second rocket streaked away from the wingtip of the Korean jet.

"Let's see if this old bucket still has a few tricks in it." Captain Louder jammed the stick as far forward as he could. The plane went into an immediate free fall as the first missile sailed harmlessly overhead.

"Second missile still tracking, sir."

The second missile was closing in on the plane's jet engines almost as quickly as the earth was coming up to meet it.

"Shutting down engines!" It was a highly risky maneuver — he may never get them started again — but he was running out of options.

"Just a few more seconds ..." The captain wrenched back on the rudder trying to pull the plane out of its headlong nosedive. "I need some flaps; I need power!"

Lieutenant Wilson was furiously working over his console, trying to reroute any active circuits to give the plane one last chance to avoid a fiery collision.

"Now!" screamed the captain. Suddenly the rudder came free, slamming back hard into the captain's chest as the plane looped straight back up into the sky with a sudden burst of power from the twin jet engines.

The missile tried to correct itself, but ran out of altitude, slamming into the earth in a fiery inferno.

As the cheering died down inside the cockpit, Louder realized they had dodged one bullet only to cause a new threat. Lieutenant Wilson had managed to overload the circuitry in the fuel cells to give the engines the necessary boost they needed to restart, pulling the plane out of its free fall. But now he was out of tricks as the right turbojet belched smoke and flames.

"The electrical surge must have caused a short."

"Can you shut it down?"

"Don't think so, sir. Nothing's responding."

"How's our altitude?"

"We're not going straight down anymore, if that's what you mean, sir," said Lieutenant Milius with his characteristic dry West Texas drawl. "I guess that's a plus, sir."

Captain Louder looked at his crew. All eyes were on him waiting for inspiration. But he had none to give. He'd never lost a plane before, and he wasn't too happy about the prospect of losing this one. But he knew there was nothing else to do if they wanted to stay alive. Those two MiGs were still out there hunting them.

"We better scuttle her; not much to salvage anyway."

"The HARM might still be operational, sir," piped up Lieutenant Stewart as a sort of consolation. "Might just get lucky and hit whatever the Koreans were using to jam our electronics."

Captain Louder considered this for a second, then picked up the radio.

"Mayday! Mayday!" Captain Louder's voice crackled over the Navy fighter jets' radios; then one, two, three parachutes blossomed out from the cockpit of the crippled Prowler and floated slowly to earth.

Half a mile away, the fighter pilots looked at each other over the narrow space of air that separated their two Lightning Stealth fighters. Where was the fourth parachute? Where was the pilot?

Then they saw the MiGs coming back, circling like jackals scavenging a carcass.

One of the Korean jets pulled behind the limping American recon plane, lining up for its kill shot. Alarms started to go off inside the cockpit. The Korean pilot looked up. Too late. He never saw the Lightning Stealth or the missile that took him out.

Captain Louder saw the flash of the explosion behind him. Were the Koreans making another pass? He just needed a little more altitude to get the maximum range for the HARM to find pay dirt. He knew his own plane was history. He'd gotten his crew out, to safety, he hoped, but now he was going to get a little bit of revenge. He just needed time for one shot ...

A MiG streaked overhead, twisting and turning in the morning light. Captain Louder ducked involuntarily. Then he saw what was causing all the aerial acrobatics. Two American jets screamed past. He roared in triumph, letting fly the HARM as he pulled the ejection cord.

Louder's parachute opened and suddenly everything was quiet. He watched as the HARM sped away toward the horizon seeking an unseen enemy jamming beacon somewhere on the northern edge of the demilitarized frontier. His plane disappeared over a small rise and then exploded in a muted concussion of jet fuel. The last thing he saw were twin missile plumes from the two American fighters as they homed in on the desperate North Korean fighter.

TWO

Captain Han Suk knew something was wrong even before he reached the bridge of his ship. The *Daedong* was a sleek long-range North Korean missile launcher. It was everything he had dreamed of as he went through the rigors of the Democratic People's Republic of Korea's Military Naval Academy. When he'd been a young seaman coming up through the ranks, the Korean People's Navy was considered a "brown-water navy," its ships few and small with no long-range ability, operating mainly in coastal waters and inland rivers. But with the advent of the great nuclear reawakening at the hands of their new "supreme leader," Kim Jong-un, the nation had turned its energies back to repelling the American threat and had embarked on several ambitious military enterprises. Yet unlike the other missile-launching destroyers in the North Korean navy, the *Daedong* was different in one spectacular aspect: it was designed to launch weapons of mass destruction.

The financial drain on the country, already suffering from shortages and the rumored starvation in the northern provinces, was enormous, but the benefits were incalculable. The nation's prestige as an international military power soared. After all, the imperial American menace would soon be cowed by the sight of dozens of ships along their coastlines flying the red star of North Korea.

That was the glorious future as Captain Han Suk saw it. But for now, the *Daedong* was the first that was tasked to patrol the eastern coastline of the hated United States, and he was honored to be given the task of bringing its fearsome might to the teeth of the enemy.

Still, he had reservations. Reservations he would never raise to any of his superiors, reservations he allowed himself to consider only in the few moments he had to himself, between sleep and duty.

The ship, a beautiful, fast, seaworthy triumph of Korean naval expertise, had been rushed through assembly, its production goals set to meet the date of the great leader's anniversary celebration. Though completed on time, shortcuts had been taken and materials shortchanged. The time for proper testing had been limited to get the ship into the Atlantic before the winter freeze of the Northern Arctic passage.

The captain had been able to catalogue some of the ship's shortcomings. Most pressing of which were its communication systems. The Americans had a vast array of satellite and ground station receivers utilizing the latest VLF, microwave, and laser technology to quickly communicate from anywhere in the world. For the Koreans, being out of their own territorial waters was a new experience, and no system yet existed to ensure safe, secure, consistent communication. From the moment the ship had entered the Atlantic, the Americans had been jamming its radar.

The captain was also concerned by the isolation he felt, alone in enemy waters. The *Daedong's* sister ship wouldn't be ready for another six months, so he had been tasked with the maiden voyage on his own. He knew the strict coastal territorial limits of each nation and had been sure to steer clear of any hostile shores, but he still felt vulnerable to an enemy that had occupied Korea's sovereign territory to the south for over sixty oppressive years.

All this the captain kept to himself. It was his duty to honor the flag of his beloved North Korea and to bring glory to his grateful nation and leader. It was especially important since Supreme Naval

Commander Admiral Sun Tak Jeong was himself on board, to report, firsthand, on the glorious news of their triumphant voyage.

As the captain climbed the exterior gangway to the glassed-in bridge, most of the crew was down in the mess hall. As he entered the bridge he could sense something unusual, an increased agitation among the small group manning the ship's radar and controls. The normal military efficiency of his handpicked deck officers had been replaced by something he couldn't quite put his finger on. As he stepped onto the bridge, everyone snapped to attention. He let them stand there for an extra second as he took the temperature of the room. What he sensed did not reassure him. Fear.

"Back to your stations, men."

"Captain." The XO immediately stepped forward.

"Captain." The second voice came from Admiral Jeong, who emerged from the shadows at the back of the octagonal structure. The captain hadn't seen him when he came in, and his presence on the bridge this early in the morning only confirmed his worst misgivings.

"Captain, we received a coded message." The admiral held out a slip of paper for him to read. The text was brief but chilling:

2 KPA jets ambushed and shot down over sovereign Northern territory by overwhelming American occupying air forces. No provocation. No warning. Missiles launched . . .

"Why wasn't I told of this immediately?"

"Because I received it first," enunciated the admiral. The implications were clear. He scanned his men for a hint of betrayal. No one met his gaze.

The captain wanted to know more. "Is there any more to the message?"

"The Americans jammed our communications," volunteered the XO. "We haven't been able to reach Pyongyang since."

"If it's still there." The admiral's statement sent a shiver down the captain's spine.

"We must turn around and return home immediately to defend our beloved country and leader," said the captain.

"Isn't that what he sent us *here* to do?" Again the admiral's words shot a sickening chill through the captain.

"Admiral, no one is more aware than I of the wisdom of your long experience and knowledge. But I believe we can serve our country and our leader best by returning to join the battle at home ... to repel the American invader from our beloved shores."

"I disagree."

Everyone on the bridge froze.

"The message said, 'Missiles launched,'" the admiral barked, making sure his meaning wasn't lost on anyone in the room, especially the captain.

"The message was interrupted, sir; we can't just leap to conclusions."

"The interruption wasn't here, Captain; it was in Pyongyang."

The captain felt a sting of rage, blindsided, as he turned to his XO. The XO blurted out, "I don't know, sir; we cannot confirm one way or the other yet."

"Then get me a confirmation!"

"We don't need a confirmation, Captain; we need to act."

"We *are* acting, sir."

"Like cowards with our tails between our legs!" The admiral's words echoed through the bridge.

"Do you have an order, sir?" Han Suk retorted.

"Do you need an order, Captain?" The captain remained silent. The admiral quickly turned to the firing officer. "Then here's an order. Proceed to commence prelaunch procedures ..."

"Admiral?" shouted the captain.

The admiral continued, "I will transmit the nuclear authorization code — "

"Admiral!" The captain's voice was steadily rising.

The admiral snapped open a hard plastic stick revealing a coded set of numbers, then turned coldly to the captain. "I need your key, sir."

The captain stepped back.

"That *is* an order, Captain."

The captain continued to back away.

The admiral turned to the XO and said, "Give me your firearm."

The XO hesitated.

"Give me your firearm!"

The XO unholstered his weapon and handed it to the admiral. The admiral raised it and aimed it at the captain's head.

"Are you going to give me the key now, Captain?"

"Admiral, I beg you, we don't know what's happened yet ..."

The sound of the gun going off in the closed space was much louder than the admiral had expected. The bullet entered the captain's right cheekbone and exited the back of his skull, spattering the steel panel behind him with blood and brain matter.

The admiral's hand was shaking as he reached down to retrieve the firing key from around the captain's neck, where he had slumped dead onto the corrugated metal floor.

No one said a word as the admiral, with the gun still in his trembling hand, passed the bloody key to the XO.

The admiral stared out at the sea for a moment, then smiled with an air of manufactured confidence. "They'll write stories about us someday." He turned slowly to the XO and nodded. "The ship is yours now, *Captain*. Make us proud."

A phone rang in the office of the chairman of the Joint Chiefs of Staff. It was 7:00 at night, but the chairman was still there. He liked to use the early evening hours, when the rest of the staff was gone, to think over the next day's agenda. His secretary had gone, so he picked up the phone. "This is —"

The voice on the other end of the phone didn't let him finish. "General, we have a status red, repeat, a confirmed status red."

The general's body shot up in his chair. "What and where!?"

"Two birds incoming, U.S. East Coast," intoned the voice on the phone.

"Specify!" roared the General. "Where?!"

"New York City."

THREE

There was one unusual thing about that night for Abigail Jordan. At long last she and her nineteen-year-old daughter, Deborah, had managed to book tickets for an opera at the Met. Puccini's *Madame Butterfly*. Abigail tried to arm-twist her husband, Joshua, into going, but she had to laugh at the improbability of that. Besides, Joshua was scheduled to fly back to New York from a meeting with some military brass in Washington. He was taking the shuttle to JFK and would then, in his private helicopter, go directly to his Manhattan office to do some late-night work with his research and development team. Which meant Joshua Jordan had a built-in excuse to miss the opera. *Much to his relief,* Abigail figured.

Still, Abigail had applied her powers of persuasion. Clever arguments came easy for her. She'd been trained as a lawyer. "Look, Josh," she'd said to him on her cell phone earlier, "I know you don't like the opera, but *Madame Butterfly* is actually a story about a lieutenant in the Navy who has this conflict —" Her husband chuckled and cut her off. He even managed to say it with a straight face: "Navy? You got to be kidding. Abby, honey, even if I didn't have to work late, let's remember that I retired from active duty as a colonel in the Air Force. The *Air Force.* Sitting through an opera about a sailor, hey, that'd be a betrayal to all my flying buddies ..."

She'd tried not to laugh at his sly comeback, but it was hard. At least this way she would have some private time with Deborah — first a wonderful dinner together, and now they were looking for a cab to whisk them to the Met before curtain time. In some ways her daughter was so much like her dad. A cadet at West Point, Deborah was heading for a career in the military. Yet Abigail was delighted that she still loved *girly* things. A good love story, even in Italian, would be right up their alley.

As the two of them walked quickly through Times Square looking for a taxi, she glanced at Deborah. She had Joshua's dark, penetrating eyes and a softer, pretty version of his square-jawed face. Like her mother, Deborah was tall, thin, and athletic. Abigail had missed her, even though West Point wasn't that far from their penthouse in New York City, and she and Joshua had seen her several times during her third year at the academy. It was still so good to have her around, even if only for a weekend.

The two of them crossed Broadway, underneath the brazen illumination of the giant three-hundred-foot-high LED screens, neon signs, and flashing JumboTrons of Times Square. Abigail and Deborah were almost to the island in the middle of the street that housed the large glass-encased TKTS discount tickets booth. They would have to get off of Broadway to find a cab. For many years traffic had been banned from Times Square, so Abigail and Deborah were about to head to a side street to hail a taxi.

But just then they heard the awful sound. A sickening metallic crash.

Abigail and Deborah quickly whipped their heads around. A cab had just smashed into a vendor's hot dog cart.

Abigail was stunned. *What's a cab doing in Times Square?*

Unbelievably, the taxi didn't stop. The cabbie continued to gun his engine down 47th Street, first dodging around pedestrians and then hopping the curb onto the sidewalk at full speed, toppling pedestrians like bowling pins. Several theater lovers, waiting in line at the TKTS booth, started to race across the street to get to the fallen pedestrians.

Deborah turned to sprint after them. "Come on, Mom; they need help!"

But Abigail saw something and grabbed her daughter's arm. "Look out!"

A large black limo and then a minivan streaked into Times Square and almost mowed down the good Samaritans. A second cab attempted to veer around the crowds and jumped the curb, this one slamming through the foldout tables where hawkers had been selling Yankees and Mets memorabilia moments before.

Abigail stared in shock. She couldn't compute the odds. Almost as if orchestrated, vehicles were racing into the no-traffic zone of Times Square. Two taxi drivers had jumped curbs, committing the same insane act in the same place within seconds of each other. What was going on?

Suddenly cell phones started to ring all around her. For a moment it was as if the world encompassed in that twenty blocks of Times Square had stopped to answer the same communal phone call. Abigail had her cell with her, but it was turned off on purpose. She cherished her alone-time with Deborah.

Deborah looked as if she was trying hard to figure it all out. Trying to make sense of it. "Something big's going down, Mom."

Abigail grabbed for her Allfone, the new generation multifunctional cell phone, to turn it on. Every person around her with a cell phone, as if on cue, was moving now — some running, others crying, some screaming wildly. Everyone else simply stood there with bewildered faces.

Abigail punched the speed dial for her husband. By then Joshua would be up in the chopper high over Manhattan, heading to his office. But a homeless man in a dingy Knicks hoodie stumbled past her and knocked her Allfone out of her hand.

He was yelling, "It's the end, man; it's the end!"

Abigail reached down to snatch up the phone, but another reckless vehicle, an airport van, came speeding toward her. She jumped back as it brushed past, but it slammed into the homeless man from behind. He flew over the top of the van and landed several yards behind it in the gutter. The driver never slowed down. More cars and trucks began careening into Times Square at breakneck speed.

"What's happening?" a woman with shopping bags screamed out to no one in particular. No one stopped to answer. From Abigail's vantage point on the traffic island, people were swirling madly around her, running in all directions. The sidewalks had become deadly speedways for taxis and cars, smashing into anyone and anything, trying to get around the intersection crowded with scrambling pedestrians and out-of-control traffic.

Abigail could not imagine what chaos had just been loosed. Cars and buses were colliding, creating bottlenecks, forcing more people to spill onto the streets on foot. Subway entrances were jammed with people trying to escape the mayhem above ground. People pushed and shoved, knocking others to the pavement in a mad exodus to nowhere. The plate-glass window at the empty Nike store was shattered by looters who had already grabbed overpriced shoes, jerseys, and anything else they could get their hands on.

A few confused souls had taken refuge with Abigail and Deborah on the traffic island — a relatively calm eye in the middle of the storm. Most simply stood and watched in horrified confusion. Others cried. Some prayed.

Deborah was circling around helplessly, watching, and shaking her head. "We've got to do something ..."

But Abigail's mind was whirling. She shouted back. "Have to figure out where it's safe. Where the danger is ..."

Just then she noticed people looking up at the sky, mesmerized, as if waiting for something beyond their control, something catastrophic to fall on them.

An elderly man behind Abigail pleaded, "I need to get to my granddaughter's. Can anyone tell me what's going on?"

Then Abigail noticed something on one of the largest of the building-sized electronic billboards. Instead of the usual glitzy ads for the latest designer jeans and blockbuster movie was a simple aerial shot of the sparkling Manhattan skyline, an eerie reflection of the skyscrapers towering around them.

"I don't understand," said someone in the crowd, pointing to the looming video feed.

Then Abigail saw it. She pointed down the street to a giant ribbon of digital text wrapping around a building. The breaking news headline scrolling high above Times Square was too outrageous to make sense of. Then it sank in. The digital words were announcing a headline that was too horrible to comprehend:

Two nuclear warheads have been launched from a N. Korean ship off the coast of Greenland ... Target: Manhattan

Involuntary sobs escaped from the woman with the shopping bags. People screamed in terror.

Deborah shouted, "Got to find a bomb shelter ..."

Abigail grabbed her hand. "Stay with me. Let's run to the Crowne Plaza. Maybe they've got a basement level ..."

The two women began to sprint together across Broadway toward the hotel. A human flood of screaming pedestrians were scattering in all directions.

Deborah yelled as they ran, "The sign said nukes. *Nukes*, Mom! A basement won't save us. We're ground zero!"

"Maybe they're wrong. Maybe they're not nukes."

"But what if they are?"

They were at a full sprint now, blowing through the chaotic crowds. But Abigail knew something that even Deborah didn't know. A few details about her husband's top-secret project. Joshua ought to be very close to his office by now. His R&D team was supposed to be waiting for him. Maybe. Just maybe ...

Abigail yelled over to her daughter as they were locked into matching strides, "If they're nukes, we have to pray that Dad can stop them ..."

"Dad?"

Without breaking her stride, Abigail started to pray. Tears were starting to come. But it didn't stop her voice as she shouted out a prayer.

"Heavenly Father, oh, please, God, please save us ... and help Josh ... help him, Lord!"

FOUR

The private executive helicopter glided high in the night sky over the glittering lights of New York City. Joshua Jordan, the lone passenger, was in the back. Forty-three, square shouldered, athletic, and dressed in an expensive Italian suit, he looked like a man on top of the world. But he didn't feel that way.

On a normal evening, heading to his office for late-night work, he'd be paging through his Allfone — checking emails and tabbing through a variety of documents that had been scanned-in for him to review. The digital revolution had finally merged all the major information, communication, and entertainment functions into one platform: a small handheld device that became all things — cell phone, fax sender, two-way Skype video camera, television, radio, and, of course, Internet-accessible computer. The big versions replaced TV sets in the entertainment cabinets of homes across the country. But it was the small handheld units, the top-of-the-line Allfone and its cheaper imitators, that had become the primary personal communication link for the public.

Ordinarily Joshua would have been accessing Fox News, CNN International, GlobalNetNews, BusinessNetwork — anything he needed to stay on top of the economy, politics, business, and world affairs.

On his mini-laptop-sized Allfone, he would be reviewing the headlines from four key publications: *The Wall Street Journal*, *Barons*, *International Financial Times*, and the *Daily Economic Forum*, while keeping an eye on a second Allfone laptop opened to a graphic of the world, where charts would appear in the four corners and updated data would scroll under the banner "Global Risk and Security Assessment."

Then again, if this were an ordinary evening he'd be mulling over disturbing new developments that were gutting the nation that he loved. He had served America as an Air Force test pilot and secret reconnaissance officer flying in some of the world's hottest spots. Now he was serving the U.S. as a defense contractor. But in the light of catastrophic current events, that wasn't enough for Joshua. So he and several others had begun an audacious new venture. Under normal conditions all of that would have been bouncing around his head like a pinball.

But this wasn't a normal evening. Joshua couldn't get yesterday's conversation with his son, Cal, out of his head. Why did he have to blast his son like that? All Cal wanted was to talk about changing his college major. What was the big deal? He'd already accepted the fact that Cal wanted to go to Liberty University; after all it was a good school, and maybe Cal wasn't cut out for the military. Joshua's own father had been a military man. Joshua himself had spent almost twenty years in the Air Force. Even Debbie, his precious little girl, was at West Point now. But Cal was different. He'd turned down the military academy and said he wanted to go to a Christian college. So there was also that religious issue that Joshua had to deal with. Cal, like his mother, Abigail, and even Debbie, had all said at different times that they had become "born again Christians." Joshua just couldn't see the whole Christian thing, at least not for himself. But he had worked hard at trying to support Cal's decision about college. Now that Cal was in his second year at Liberty, Joshua had settled into the idea.

That was until this morning when Cal told him he was switching majors. From engineering to art. Just one more of his son's decisions that seemed to collide with common sense.

Joshua loved his son more than anything, more than life itself. He just didn't understand him. Cal was so much like his mother, and, yes, Joshua envied him for that. Was that it? Was it envy? That even though Cal, like his father, believed that flag and country were important, what he really wanted was to bury himself in oil paints and canvas and shut out the world? It was one of the things he loved about Abby. She had been a brilliant lawyer, and yet she could also turn off the analytical side, the duty and legal side, and bury herself in a book or an art gallery, losing herself in the nuances of color and texture and light.

Why did he have to get so angry about it? He'd promised himself that when he had kids he wouldn't be like his father — strict, demanding, perfectionistic — yet here he was, doing the same thing, making the same demands that had been made of him. Now Cal was gone, heading back to school with the echo of his father's disappointment in his ears. Joshua ached for his son and, in a strange way, ached for himself.

The ring of a cell phone suddenly broke Joshua's train of thought. He checked the personal phone function on his handheld Allfone. But it wasn't ringing and showed no incoming calls. He realized that this ring tone was the heavy metallic one.

He thrust his hand into his suit-coat pocket and retrieved another phone. This one was flat and wide, colored a deep shade of blue. It was a specially encrypted satellite phone designed only for high-level secure conversations. It didn't ring often. But when it did there was an emergency. The scramble-your-jets kind.

Joshua hit the encryption filter button and answered. "Joshua Jordan."

"Colonel Jordan," said a voice after a half second of descrambling. "This is Major Black, adjunct to the Joint Chiefs, sir, in R&D at the Pentagon. We've talked before."

"Yes, Major."

"We have a status red."

Joshua paused for a millisecond as he felt his chest tighten.

"How can I help?"

"We've got two birds incoming, most likely nuclear," the major snapped.

"Make and model?"

"North Korean. Taepo Dong missiles. Which means they should have a guidance system compatible with your RTS-RGS protocol."

The RTS-RGS system, formally known as the Return-to-Sender – Reconfigured-Guidance System, was the antiballistic laser system Joshua and his team had been developing for the better part of ten years. It was still considered experimental and scheduled for its first real-world test next month.

"We're going to have to move that test up, Colonel," said the major, reading Joshua's mind.

Joshua leaned forward toward the helicopter pilot and yelled, "Bert, drop us back down. And call ahead to get the team assembled — ASAP!"

Joshua turned back to the SAT phone. He almost couldn't get out his next words. "What's the target?"

"New York City."

Joshua felt his heart stop. Cal should be clear of New York by now. He should be sitting on a train on his way back to college. But Abigail and Deb were in the city. Maybe they could still get to safety ...

"How much time?" he choked out the words.

"Estimated detonation over Manhattan is fourteen minutes."

Joshua's mouth dried up as though he'd swallowed sand. "Please tell me we've got back-up options to interdict those missiles."

"We've scrambled our jets, but they may not make it in time. The rest of our Eastern Seaboard missile system has been handicapped since the White House tied us to the Six-Party Missile-Defense Treaty. You and your system may be our last hope. So let's just pray your little jammer can kick those two footballs back where they came from. If not, God help us all."

F1VE

Grand Central Station was warm, crowded, and noisy, a wonderful place to feel anonymous, to escape, to be alone. At least that's what Cal Jordan was thinking as he slung his backpack onto a bench and flopped down beside it. He couldn't wait to get out of the city and back to school, couldn't wait to get away from his family, particularly his father, but he especially couldn't wait to get back to Karen. The two of them had just spent a day and a half together in New York, but he missed her already. She'd left ahead of him, taking a flight out that afternoon, heading home for a cousin's wedding before returning to Liberty University. The thought of her made him smile. He'd met Karen Hester at Liberty last year when they were both freshmen, but it was a miracle they'd met at all.

Cal was painfully shy when he'd arrived at school. He didn't go to many campus events, except for hockey games. Cal loved hockey, ever since his father took him to an Avalanche game as a young boy in Colorado. He loved the speed and precision and grace, and envied the players their confidence and unchecked aggression, qualities he knew he lacked. At Liberty home games he would wear his Avalanche jersey and sit by himself high up in the stands to watch.

One night a cute girl wearing a Minnesota Wild shirt came up to Cal as he sat alone. She nudged his foot.

"You're in my seat."

Cal looked around. There wasn't anyone seated within a dozen rows of them.

She nudged him again, insisting, "You're in my seat."

He got up to move.

As he was walking away, she laughed, "Just like an Avalanche fan to roll over without a fight."

She smiled a big, beautiful warm smile. That was how he met Karen.

He probably fell in love with her that first instant, but it took him three months to admit it to himself and another three months to finally tell her how he felt. All she could do was smile and say, "What took you so long?"

He loved her unpretentious way and how she made him feel safe and confident. And of course, they both shared a faith in Christ. Beyond all that she supported his desire to be an artist. She wanted to be a performer herself, either an actress or a singer. But she said she wanted to do more with her talent than just get famous and rich.

Cal had only told his parents a little about Karen, but it had taken him all summer just to get up the courage to tell them he was changing majors. He didn't want them to think she had had anything to do with his decision. And the truth was, she hadn't. She'd just given him the confidence he needed to realize what he really wanted to do. If only his father could see him the way she did, then he'd understand, then he wouldn't be so angry and disappointed.

Cal pulled his ticket from his shirt pocket to check the train time. Fifteen minutes. Fifteen more minutes, and then he could leave all this behind. All the harsh words, the long looks, the cold silences.

Then he heard the first scream.

He looked up to see a woman across the train station. She was white as a ghost, staring at a TV monitor on the opposite platform. Everyone around her was doing the same. Cal turned to the nearest monitor. He couldn't hear the sound, but he could see on the screen a reporter in Times Square pointing up at the sky. The text below him read, "NY City in Panic, Nuclear Attack Imminent."

Cal stared at the words as if in a nightmare. They made no sense. He could feel his hands going cold and clammy. He turned to survey the crowd and realized people had started to pour into the station from every entrance — pushing, shoving, full of panic.

From what he could see on the TV monitors, New York was in pandemonium. Drivers were trying to get out of the city any way possible, careening down sidewalks, scattering screaming pedestrians, knocking over display signs, newspaper racks, and hot dog carts.

New Yorkers on foot were running for their lives past stalled cars and traffic jams. Bridges were filled with panicking people, fleeing. Riots developed at subway stops as escapees fought for seats on the next subway out.

As Cal's senses slowly came back to him, the noise in the cavernous main concourse grew unbearable. He covered his ears, but the horrible din of a thousand people trying to flee certain death still filtered through.

He looked up and saw a woman shoved to the ground by the crush of people running to reach the train tunnels. Cal was standing only a few feet away, pressed up flat against the marble walls to avoid being swept away in the human flood. She reached out to him for help, out from the tangled mob of feet that were trampling her, but Cal was frozen, unable to move. Fear gripped him like a vise, squeezing his chest and turning his stomach to knots, his breath coming in short, panicked gulps. He stared at the woman, her hand outstretched, eyes pleading. What if this was Karen? But Cal couldn't move, couldn't reach out to help her. His legs were like rubber as he found himself slipping to the floor, shaking uncontrollably.

His cell phone rang. He didn't hear it so much as he felt it vibrating in his pocket. Maybe it was Karen. He fumbled it from his jacket. The screen read "Mom calling." He tried to push the button to answer but couldn't make his finger work. The cell slipped out of his hand to the marble floor and slid away into the mass of rushing humanity. Cal looked across at the lifeless body of the woman. The mob had crushed her underfoot.

Flooded with feelings of guilt and helplessness, Cal could feel the sobs starting to well up inside his throat.

SIX

Joshua burst into the glass-lined corridor of his penthouse office and waved off the private security guards. As he dashed through the lobby, his frantic receptionist jumped to her feet, yelling something about an announcement on the radio.

"Ignore it," Joshua ordered. "It's under control."

"Abigail's been trying to reach you," she yelled back.

"Is the team in my office?" he barked.

"Yes, but—"

Just then his personal cell phone rang. He clicked the answer function on his Allfone as he headed for the executive suite.

"Josh!" Abigail shouted on the other end. "I just saw the headline on the crawler in Times Square—"

"I already heard ... I'm at the office ... we're doing everything we can to stop it. Where are you?"

"In the basement of a hotel just off the Square. Deb's with me. Josh, is it true?"

"Yes. But I'm counting on the Return-to-Sender, the jammer. I've got to believe we're ready for this," Joshua said, trying to sound upbeat.

The phone went quiet for a second.

"Tell me that I'll see you again," his wife said with a catch in her throat.

"Darling, we're going to stop this thing," he said as he sprinted toward his office. "Did Cal get away?"

"I think so; he didn't answer his cell."

Joshua could only hope that was because he was on a train right now speeding away to safety.

"Kiss Deb for me."

"I will," she said in a voice that was struggling for control.

"I'll see you tonight — you understand me? I promise ... Abby ... I love you ...," Joshua assured as he burst into his office, his team already waiting.

"I love you too," she said. "So much ... so much ... oh, Josh, I'll pray for you that God protects ... all of us ..."

He hung up and glanced around the room. These were the best and brightest research and weapons-design engineers in the world. He focused past them to the floor-to-ceiling views of the tops of New York City skyscrapers looking all the way out to Ellis Island and to Liberty Island where the Statue of Liberty stood. Could this all end today? The RTS-RGS system simply had to work — for all of them there, for his wife and children, for New York, for the country, for the whole world. He snapped back to reality. His team stared, waiting for direction. He took a breath and steadied himself.

"I need an answer — concise and within the high range of probability," he began. "Can a single one of our jammers redirect not just one, but two nuclear warheads where their trajectory suggests a common target?"

After less than ten seconds of reflection, Ted, the senior engineer spoke up. "We tested those protocols. We have all the calibrations to make that happen — "

"But we've never fired a dual redirection system," Carolyn, the weapons physicist blurted out. "Not in a real-world test."

"Fine, but either our protocols are correct or they aren't ...," another engineer shouted.

"And if they aren't — ," a second engineer started to say.

But Joshua jumped in.

"If our calculations are wrong," he said, "then we're all in trouble, along with several million Americans. Anyone here have any suggestions to increase the likelihood of success?

Silence. Ted shook his head.

"Then I'm making the call," Joshua snapped, and he reached down to a locked desk, tapped in a code, and a titanium steel drawer opened, revealing a red-white-and-blue phone. He dialed a number on a keypad, then waited.

Three seconds later it rang.

The phone emitted a heavy metallic ring that made everyone jump. The team may have looked cool and calm, but their nerves were on the very edge.

Joshua picked up the receiver.

"This is Major General Zepak, calling on behalf of Vice Chairman Bolthauer from the Joint Chiefs. Who am I speaking to?"

"Joshua Jordan here, along with my primary systems design team ..."

"What's the verdict?" the Pentagon officer snapped.

Joshua was resolute. "We have a high degree of confidence that if we follow the protocols we developed for a multiple missile attack we'll be successful, sir."

"Okay. I'll patch you through to the USS *Tiger Shark*. You folks'll run the show from there, coordinating with the ship to get that jammer target-ready and airborne in the next ..." his voice paused, "seven minutes."

Then the Pentagon official added one more sobering thought.

"And I don't have to remind you, we only get one crack at this ..."

□□□

In the Atlantic, a few miles off Long Island, Commander Bradley of the USS *Tiger Shark* waited in the weapons launch room with a direct line to the security phone in Joshua's office. His naval weapons officer sat at a keyboard, typing in commands. As the officer hit each keystroke he called out the verbal cue. In Joshua's office the design team listened and watched on the secure videophone, comparing the seaman's verbal cues with the system protocol displayed on a large screen on one of the walls.

When he was done, Joshua started to type furiously on his laptop, setting the laser coordinates for the two nukes, using GPS data fed directly into his computer from defense satellites. With Ted and Carolyn looking over his shoulder, Joshua checked his work and leaned back. Then they reviewed his commands line by line.

"Are we go?" Joshua asked.

Ted answered, "We're go."

Joshua looked at Carolyn.

Carolyn nodded. "Yes. We're go."

Joshua turned back to the videophone.

"Commander, is the launch sequence complete?"

The commander turned to his weapons officer, nervous perspiration rolling down his face. "Yes, sir," said the officer, his voice cracking.

Joshua turned back to his laptop and punched a key. A red screen flashed "Protocols locked. Lasers armed. Ready to fire."

SEVEN

On the bridge of the *Daedong* the crew tried to go about their duties as if nothing had happened. The body of the captain had been dragged away, but his blood was still streaked across the area where he was shot.

The admiral huddled with the XO over the radar officer's station, the gun still clutched in his hands. He grimly cheered on the tiny green blips on the screen as the two nukes continued their trajectory toward Manhattan. The seventy-two-year-old man was beyond ecstatic. Even as a child he had never known a united Korea. He'd always lived with the hated enemy occupiers just to the south, so close you could almost reach across the DMZ and put your hands around their throats. He'd dreamed about driving the Americans from his sacred homeland since he was a boy, but the nuclear tripwire had always prevented each side from making the first move. But now they'd tripped that imaginary wire, and, as fate would have it, it had fallen to him to restore the honor of his people and his country. As for the captain, he had been weak. The weak needed to be exterminated when they stood in the way of valiant men of strength and courage like himself.

000

Exactly one minute had passed since the Joshua-I missile left the launch silo on the *Tiger Shark*. Sixty seconds, the longest sixty seconds in Joshua Jordan's life.

As with all launch-based missile-defense systems, there was a narrow range of time when the weapon could effectively engage its target and deploy its defense system. This was usually within the first thirty to sixty seconds of flight. But they were at seventy-five seconds now, and the Korean missiles were still tracking steadily toward Manhattan.

Several of his team members couldn't hold back their emotions any longer. Tears began streaming from their eyes.

Down in the *Tiger Shark*, the weapons officer, eyes fixed on his radar screen, was cursing under his breath, "Stop 'em, stop 'em, do it, do it..."

The commander standing over him was gritting his teeth hard. So hard that everyone on the weapons deck could hear the sickening, grinding sound.

On the top floor of the Jordon Building in New York, Joshua and his team stared in stunned silence at the videophone waiting for some change, some hope, some chance.

Nothing...

Joshua turned away and pulled out his Allfone. He punched up Abby's cell number. At least he still had time to say good-bye to his wife and daughter. Tell them he was sorry. Try to explain he had failed them, failed everyone. Maybe he could even get through to his son. He certainly owed him an apology. Actually, he owed him several. Where would he start?

Joshua couldn't believe he was about to say good-bye to his wife and family ... forever.

When his wife answered the phone, he could tell she had been crying.

"Abby ...," he started to say, but the words began to catch.

He couldn't go on, there was nothing more he could say, but just knowing she was there on the other end was something at least ... something to hang on to until everything exploded into a fiery hell for all of them.

"Colonel!" the voice was the commander's coming over the videophone.

Joshua wasn't used to being called by his former military rank. At first he didn't connect the voice to himself ... that the man on the other end was talking to him.

"Colonel Jordan!" the voice shouted again.

Joshua spun around and stared at the monitor.

"I think ..." But the commander didn't need to finish his sentence. The radar-tracking screen clearly showed the two North Korean missiles looping around in a perfect duet and heading in the opposite direction, back toward their point of origin.

The weapons officer couldn't control himself. "Li'l jammer got 'em!" he yelled out.

The entire office erupted in one tremendous unified roar, the cheer carrying down the hall like wildfire until the whole top floor was celebrating ... it was New Year's Eve, Mardi Gras, and the Super Bowl all rolled into one. People began hugging each other, jumping up on tables, laughing, weeping for joy, happy to be alive.

Then Joshua remembered Abby.

"Abby!" he yelled into his cell phone.

"Joshua?" There was still a question in her voice.

"I just wanted ... I wanted to tell you I love you so much," he shouted at the top of his lungs for all to hear. "So very, very much. We're going to be fine baby, fine, all of us, just fine!"

□□□

"Admiral ..." The XO spoke urgently, breaking into the admiral's thoughts of North Korean triumph.

He pointed down at the radar screen. Something was wrong, something incomprehensible.

"Is the radar broken?" the admiral asked as he stared at the two blips on the scope, the radar screen clearly showing the two Korean missiles heading back toward their ship.

The radar officer was too overwhelmed to answer.

"What does this mean?" demanded the admiral.

"They're coming back, sir," offered the XO.

"Coming back?"

"Yes, sir. The missiles are ... they're returning ..."

The two men were huddled over the radar officer's station, talking in hushed whispers. The rest of the crew was looking over their shoulders from their posts, not sure what to make of this strange anomaly. Within moments, however, they would come to understand that they had all stepped into a collective nightmare. And it was quickly unfolding in front of them.

"How can this be possible?" The admiral's voice was deeply distressed and guttural.

"I don't know, sir, but they're coming back. Very close ..."

"I don't understand ... when did your radar pick this up ..."

"Just now, sir. The Americans must have jammed our incoming radar detection system ..."

"What do we do?" The admiral queried with a tragic astonishment that was still rooted in denial.

The XO stood there, afraid to speak, he had no answer.

"What do we do?!"

This time the admiral yelled for the whole bridge to hear. Suddenly everything had grown very quiet with the only sound being the beeping of the radar as the green blips inched closer and closer to the digital image of their ship.

"What ... do ... we ... *do*?"

Still no one offered up an answer.

The admiral looked at the faces of the men surrounding him on the bridge. In their vacant stares and their look of shock, the admiral now understood something … he realized he was asking the wrong question.

"What have I done?"

The words fell from his mouth like an indictment.

The men didn't respond. They just stood at their stations, waiting for an answer that would never come.

The admiral straightened his uniform jacket and saluted crisply as he walked across the bridge. With eyes held high, gun still clutched in his hand, he moved past the bloodied area where the captain had been executed. Without a glance, he stepped out onto the upper deck. Once alone in the open sea air, he looked up into the sky as if to try and see the missiles as they headed back to their home.

"What have I done?" he said, now in a hoarse whisper, speaking only to himself.

He didn't wait for an answer this time. He immediately placed the gun's barrel into his mouth.

Whether the admiral saw the blinding white megaton flash before pulling the trigger was inconsequential, as it would have been only a matter of milliseconds. The twin nuclear explosions vaporized the ship and all its crew in a merciless tornado of fire and cataclysmic concussion.

□□□

By Sunday, the shock of that day, the nuclear attempt against New York City, and the stunned news reports about the nukes incinerating the North Korean ship, were starting to abate slightly, but only slightly.

Up in the pulpit of the Eternity Church in Manhattan, Pastor Paul Campbell was standing silent before his congregation. The sanctuary was packed. Overflow chairs had to be added. It was the first Sunday service following the near strike. A nervous anticipation rippled through the crowd, as all eyes where transfixed on the pulpit. Campbell knew why these people were here, some with fear, but all with expectation on their faces. Waiting for some word of comfort, some truth, or maybe both, about a world that seemed to be careening out of control.

Pastor Campbell looked over the crowd. He saw a number of new faces. But he also recognized some familiar ones. Abigail Jordan, a regular attender, was seated five rows from the front on the aisle seat.

Looking down at the open Bible on the pulpit stand, Campbell fixed his eyes on the verses he had marked there. The Gospel of Matthew, chapter twenty-four. His mind was weighted down with the immensity of the subject of his sermon. But more than that, his heart was pierced by the empty gazes of those who had wandered in from the street that morning to hear ... anything. Lost looks and vacant stares. Troubled souls.

He whispered a wordless prayer.

Then he began.

"Some of you have come here today for comfort. Others out of curiosity. Still others for a reason that is two thousand years old. Toward the end of His earthly ministry, Jesus gave a great lament over the city of Jerusalem, and then He made a startling prophecy about the destruction of the great Herodian Temple in that city, a prophecy that would be fulfilled in AD 70, just a few decades later. Leaving the Temple that day, Jesus went up to the Mount of Olives, overlooking Jerusalem, and He sat down with His disciples, perhaps under the shade of one of the trees, and they asked Him two questions. First, they wanted to know when the Temple would be destroyed. But they also asked Him another question, one that may be on your minds and hearts today. They wanted to know what the signs would be of Christ's second coming and what signs would mark the end of the age, that final chapter of the world as we know it."

Campbell laid his finger down on his Bible next to verses six through eight.

"Jesus said that nation will rise up against nation and kingdom against kingdom. That implies worldwide conflict. We have already seen two world wars in the last century. And just a few days ago we narrowly missed what could have been the beginning of yet another one. Jesus also said that there would be famines. In our nation alone, in the agricultural breadbasket of America, we are now seeing drought and pestilence far beyond anything we had during the dustbowl years of the Great Depression. Jesus said there would be earthquakes. Now friends, look at the last six months. An earthquake in Indonesia, a ten on the Mercalli scale, with twelve being the worst. Then an earthquake that ripped through Guatemala, an eleven on the scale. And finally an eleven-point-five earthquake in Turkey."

He closed his Bible. What he would say now had been imprinted on his heart.

"Some of you listening to me this morning don't know Jesus Christ. You haven't opened the door. You haven't allowed Him to come in, to change you, save you, and fill you with His presence. For you, images of the end of the age, the cracking open of the earth, the toppling of kingdoms, these things hold nothing for you but terrifying darkness, hopelessness, and fear. But it doesn't have to be that way. You can join the assembly of those who know and follow Jesus. And while none of us relishes the idea of the destruction that is destined to occur, we have something that sees far beyond the smoldering rubble that will last only a little while. A future kingdom that will be filled with light and peace and love. We have a living hope. And so can you. You too can join that chorus in the last book of the Bible, in the second to last verse, those who can boldly shout out, 'Amen. Come Lord Jesus!'"

Several people in the crowd shouted out amens. But most of those in their seats were silent. A few who were visiting for the first time had grimaces of disgust or even cynicism. Many were deep in thought. A few, wide-eyed, had the look of those who were waiting for something but didn't know exactly what it was.

Campbell finally directed himself to his listeners, sweeping his gaze across the sea of faces.

"So those were the questions of the disciples that day. As they sat up on the Mount of Olives, looking over the city of Jerusalem."

Then he asked something else, and when he did he leaned forward and took in row after row, face after face.

"Now it's time to get honest. As you look to the future, what is *your* reaction? Fear? Or faith?"

His question reverberated through the large sanctuary with the high vaulted, cathedral ceiling.

EIGHT

Two Weeks Later

After all the political speeches and public outpouring of support and relief, New York was beginning to get back to normal. Special Agent John Gallagher of the FBI cursed the traffic as he sat gridlocked on Broadway, trying to head uptown during the morning rush. Then he thought back to the terror they had all felt that morning, popped another Ho Ho into his mouth, and was grateful to be driving through Manhattan today.

Gallagher was part of an elite counterterrorism unit. On the evening of the attack, he'd taken the ferry out to Staten Island to conduct an investigation into chatter on a popular social networking site, chatter that seemed to be targeting the Statue of Liberty. It turned out it was just some kids trying to improve their rep at a local high school by co-opting the term *terrorist*, much like wanna-be rappers used to throw around the word *gangsta* to build their street cred. Still it was his job to check it out.

He was older than most of the other agents in his unit and probably exceeded them in weight by at least fifty pounds. That was the price of riding a desk for most of the last ten years. They kept him on the unit for his local expertise. But the truth was — and deep down he knew it — he was little more than glorified set dressing. It looked good to have a bona fide hero on the team.

The recent missile attack wasn't his first experience with real terror in New York. On the morning of 9/11, he'd taken the PATH train into the World Trade Center, with the intention of walking the few blocks up to 26 Federal Plaza, to the New York field office of the FBI. But just as he came out of the Port Authority train station, the first plane hit the North Tower. He spent the next hour trying to get as many of the injured to safety as he could.

By 9:59 a.m., he was crossing the plaza in front of the towers, helping an injured office worker, when the South Tower came down. That's the last thing he remembered of that day. But he was lucky. He woke up in a hospital bed with a broken back, a broken arm, and several cracked ribs, not to mention all the toxic dust he ingested. But he was alive, more than could be said for over three thousand souls.

He received the FBI's Medal of Meritorious Achievement and an honorary Citation of Valor from the New York City Fire Department and the City of New York.

After 9/11, when the FBI was looking to beef up its Counterterrorism Unit in New York, he was the first on the list. But after a couple of years his injuries began to get the better of him, and he had to curtail his fieldwork. Out of necessity he'd become somewhat of an expert in using the Internet to track terrorist cells since it didn't require him to leave his desk.

But every so often he would be called out from behind his desk, usually for something unusual, like this Statue of Liberty threat. He was en route to Staten Island when the news broke about the incoming nukes. Though there was panic on the boat at first, a semblance of calm came over the passengers when the captain headed out to sea — away from Manhattan — at full speed. Gallagher spent the whole time staring at the skyline from the back rail of the ferry, unable to help this time, wondering whether this would be the last time he'd ever see his beloved skyline.

The fact that America hadn't immediately leveled the entire country of North Korea in retaliation surprised Gallagher. The 9/11 attack on American soil had launched two wars. But this time the leader of the Free World was playing things more cautiously. Back when he was a senator from Iowa, Virgil Corland had tacitly supported the War on Terror. But now, as president, he was weighed down by indecision and a devastated economy that became more indebted to foreign nations each year.

The U.S. could have wiped out the little dictator with the push of a button, but President Corland hesitated, fearing it would plunge the world into a global conflagration. The United Nations counseled restraint, and after Kim Jung-un's government indirectly seemed to admit that the attack may have been caused by a communications error, the U.S. backed away from any type of action against North Korea.

Gallagher thought they should have at least tossed a couple of nukes over there for good measure, but the country had bowed to cries of "One World, One Peace" emanating from the new power centers of Europe and Asia. The time to act had been the first seventy-two hours, yet an ailing and increasingly ineffectual President Corland had faltered. And America had taken yet another giant step backward in the eyes of much of the world.

Within an hour after the destruction of the North Korean vessel, rumors began to spring up like mushrooms on the Internet that the Korean ship hadn't actually launched the two nuclear missiles at all but had been on the receiving end of a first strike by the United States. Most of this web chatter was silly ranting from the alien-abduction conspiracy crowd, but it kept the media bloodsuckers yakking and had the potential to fuel extremists around the world, feeding their hatred toward America.

As soon as the nukes had been deflected, Gallagher, still on the ferry, got a call from the field office on his cell phone. There would be a new assignment ... this one tailor-made for him. Dozens of people had been killed in the panic on the streets of New York that evening and nearly a thousand more injured. Someone high up in the government had leaked information to the media. That was tantamount to premeditated murder, or at the very least, reckless homicide — considering the resulting death and destruction it caused. One of the first rules everyone learns is you don't yell "fire!" in a crowded theater. Someone yelled fire, and now it was up to Gallagher to find out who.

The first person to go live with the news was a shock jock named Ivan Teretsky at WFQL Radio. "Esteemed" for his bombastic political pronouncements and on-air stunts, which once included the playing of a tape-recording of a prominent governor and a prostitute while they were going at it, he was best known to New Yorkers as "Ivan the Terrible."

Gallagher was now winding his way through miserable traffic to interview the radio host at his station on the Upper West Side of Manhattan. He steered through Columbus Circle and drove along the park to 66th, then pulled into an underground parking garage a block before the street turned onto Riverside Drive.

In the elevator, Gallagher steeled himself for the interview. He was well aware of the kind of stunts this nutcase could pull. Teretsky might try to put him on the air, turn the whole thing into one big joke. But Gallagher wasn't laughing. People had died, and somebody was responsible.

He gave his name to a pretty receptionist at the front desk and was told to wait. "Mr. Teretsky is just finishing up his show."

Good, thought Gallagher. *At least I know this interview won't be going out over the airwaves.* He sat down on the couch to wait. A television hanging from the ceiling played silently overhead. It was flashing images from Washington, D.C., with a heading underneath that read, "JOINT CONGRESSIONAL COMMITTEE PROBES RETURN-TO-SENDER WEAPON."

The camera landed briefly on Joshua Jordan and his wife, Abigail, as they made their way up the Capitol steps flanked by a swarming army of reporters. Gallagher was hit with a sudden wave of anger.

This guy was an American hero, and now these idiots on Capitol Hill were going to barbecue him for their own selfish political agendas. Why? Because he'd single-handedly saved New York with a weapons system they hadn't approved. Were they crazy? They should be giving him the Congressional Medal of Honor, a Nobel Peace Prize, an Academy Award, maybe even the Heisman Trophy — anything he wants.

Yes, Gallagher was ticked off. The receptionist told him to go in; Mr. Teretsky was ready for him. *No, he isn't*, thought Gallagher, *not even close*. He was in no mood for Teretsky now; in fact, he almost felt sorry for him. "Ivan the Terrible" was about to have a very bad day.

NINE

As Joshua Jordan strode through the halls of Congress on his way to the hearing, Abigail held tightly to his arm. For over twenty years she had been by his side, whether stationed at a military base in Europe, teaching at the Air Force Academy in Colorado Springs, working while he studied at MIT in Boston, or moving their young family to New York City to start a new life. Even when he was away flying missions in the Middle East during the war, she'd always been there after every flight, waiting for his call. Jordan knew she didn't have to choose this life. She'd been a highly successful attorney at a prestigious Washington law firm when they first met. He had been immediately taken by her beauty, dark hair, green eyes, and athlete's tall tanned body, but he was ultimately knocked out by her brains. She never forgot a face or a fact, could cite football stats, particularly for the Denver Broncos, her favorite team, with the same ease as citing Constitutional law cases or federal statutes. She never made a bet she didn't win and was an absolute killer at Scrabble.

Today, though, she wasn't going to be by his side the whole time. He was going into a closed-door hearing with only his wits and his attorney to help him take on the full power of the U.S. Congress. He'd wanted Abby to be there, but she convinced him it was better to have an objective advocate instead of a loving and biased spouse to counsel him. Besides, she added, she hadn't been in a courtroom, let alone a congressional hearing room, in years.

The lawyer she'd recommended was Harry Smythe, a mentor and colleague of hers from her Washington days. He was a legal fixture in D.C. and had made quite a name for himself advising a former president and arguing, and winning, several cases before the Supreme Court. Jordan glanced over at the balding, sixty-year-old man walking next to him. Impeccably dressed, with small round glasses, sporting his famous bowtie, he was vaguely reminiscent of the old silent screen comic Harold Lloyd, yet he had a reputation as a cobra. He wasn't Abby, but he'd have to do.

As they approached the final security checkpoint, only those going into the classified hearing could pass any farther. Joshua pulled Abby aside and gave her a hug. It was amazing, even after all this time, the charge he got just being near her.

"I wish you were going in with me."

"I know," she smiled, "you'll do fine, you always do." She gave his hand one last squeeze. "I'll be praying for you; don't forget that."

Joshua was going to say something back, but squeezed her hand in return and headed toward the hearing room door.

As Joshua disappeared beyond the door with his attorney, Abigail couldn't help but let a few doubts creep in. After the euphoria of that day when the missiles were turned back, questions had started to pop up. First it was just a low murmur in the background, but now that murmur had turned into a steady stream of acrimonious questions. Who authorized the use of an untested system like the RTS-RGS? Why were the bombs retargeted to a live target? Why weren't they destroyed harmlessly in midair over the Atlantic? Why weren't the intelligence and defense committees of Congress even aware of this system? Who did Joshua Jordan think he was to make these decisions? As a private military contractor, was he making national defense policy for the whole country?

Abigail had lived in this town long enough to know that it wasn't going to be a cakewalk for her husband today. Careers were made out of crushing the bones of honorable men like him. It was a zero-sum game. Any advantage you could take, any weakness you could find, any crack you could pry open and exploit was counted as a political notch on your belt. She'd tried to prepare her husband for what he might expect, but he seemed confident he had right on his side. And Harry Smythe. Thank goodness for Harry. He was an old hand who knew his way around the political cloakrooms and brass-railed bars where most of the work in Washington really gets done. He wouldn't let Joshua step on any landmines these senators and congressmen might strew in his path.

But the real question was whether he could save Joshua from himself. When Joshua got an idea in his head, he was like a dog with a bone; there was no getting it away from him. It's what made him so brilliant, so successful, but it could also make him infuriating. Joshua knew no compromise. It was the biggest problem between father and son. Joshua had expectations that Cal would never be able to meet.

Abigail hadn't told Joshua what really happened to Cal on the evening of the attack. She found out herself a few days later when Cal confided his terror to her. Joshua had assumed Cal was on a train, well out of New York City, when the panic hit; but he was right in the middle of it. She didn't like holding things back from her husband, but he was so preoccupied with the hearing in Washington. Besides, things had been touchy between him and Cal before he'd left for college. Now everything seemed better. The near tragedy had brought the family together. Debbie had been like a rock for her younger brother, and Joshua seemed at least to be trying to understand Cal's decision to study art at Liberty. She didn't want to take that away from them. Not now. Not yet.

But as she walked down the hall, she promised herself, after this was all over and things had died down, she'd tell her husband the truth. He deserved it and so did Cal.

TEN

The public was barred from the closed-door, high-level security hearing, but the press was allowed in to take photos for a few minutes before the session started. Joshua was seated at a long, green cloth-draped table, looking uncomfortable while cameras clicked and strobes flashed in his face. He didn't like having his picture taken, and he didn't try to hide it as he leaned over to his lawyer seated next to him.

"I'd take any amount of grilling from a senator over this form of torture."

With a wry smile the lawyer shot back, "I hope you still feel that way after the hearing."

Then, as if on some hidden cue, the photographers stopped, packed up their cameras, and walked out. Joshua wondered, chuckling to himself, if there had been some sort of high-pitched dog whistle calling them off that only the news hounds could hear. Whatever it was, he was happy to be spared any more embarrassing attention from the press.

He looked around the room. Even though the public wasn't allowed in, some pretty heavyweight bystanders sat in the mostly vacant audience section behind him: the president's national security advisor, the chief of staff to the vice president, an aide to the Joint Chiefs of Staff he'd met once but whose name he couldn't remember, and various other high-level advisors and military personnel. It was a pretty heady peanut gallery.

The senators and representatives began to file into the chamber in ones and twos, taking their places at the raised dais at the front. A few came over to shake Joshua's hand enthusiastically, but most just took their seats and looked over their notes or conferred with their aides. They were a select group of experienced lawmakers, the so-called gang-of-eight, as they were commonly referred to in Washington political parlance: those members of Congress with whom the president traditionally conferred in times of grave national security, the Democratic and Republican leaders in the House and Senate, and the chairs and ranking members of their respective intelligence committees.

The chairman of this select committee, Senator Wendell Straworth, was a powerful veteran of Washington politics. He was seated in the middle of the dais in a high-backed chair that set him apart from the others. A large, imposing man, with a shiny bald head and thick, tangled eyebrows, he took a minute to survey the room, peeking out over the reading glasses perched at the end of his nose.

"Ladies and gentlemen," the senator began, "this will be a closed and confidential session of this special committee … created to investigate what I consider to be one of the most shocking and disturbing national security events in the history of this great nation,"

Senator Straworth took a long pause before he continued. "Now we are all painfully aware that this committee has issued letter requests for various documents pertinent to this investigation. Letter requests sent to Mr. Joshua Jordan, a private weapons contractor, as well as to his counsel. To date, Mr. Jordan has refused to produce a single document. I note that Mr. Jordan is present in this hearing room, along with his counsel, Mr. Harry Smythe."

Senator Straworth slowly turned his gaze to Joshua. "This committee," he announced with a booming voice, "calls as its first witness Mr. Joshua Jordan."

Joshua stood up from the table and raised his right hand. He then took the oath and swore to tell the truth under the federal penalties of perjury. "... So help me God."

Then he sat down.

Joshua was not a religious man, not in the way Abigail was. But just then, as he looked out over the congressional panel assembled in front of him, knowing as he did, the political and legal quicksand that lay all around him, he was happy about one thing: he knew Abigail was praying for him.

ELEVEN

Senator Straworth was anxious to rip into Joshua Jordan. The North Korean nuke incident and Jordan's RTS antimissile system had spawned a growing media storm. There were allegations that the experimental system was too risky to have been tried and that the missiles could have been disarmed by conventional means that were already at the Pentagon's disposal. Several major media outlets were beginning to call the incident "lasergate," and the blogosphere was spinning out of control with an avalanche of conspiracy theories.

In the midst of this media firefight, Senator Straworth had maintained a public face of disturbed concern mixed with strained neutrality. After all, it was an undeniable political reality that the City of New York and its residents had been saved.

But those who knew the senator understood that beneath his cautiously managed exterior was an attack dog straining at its leash. In the congressional cloakrooms he had made his position clear. The North Korean incident had been mishandled by the Pentagon. White House policy and usual Pentagon procedures had been, in his view, arrogantly disregarded. Not to mention the question of whether the military's choice of antimissile response, lobbing the two nukes back where they had come from, had actually violated international antimissile defense treaties. Because Straworth had personally championed those treaties in the Senate, the use of Joshua's RTS weapons technology was viewed by the senator as a political knife in his own back.

But Straworth had to follow senatorial protocol first. After that, he could start his well-honed political grandstanding.

Straworth smiled, turning to the man seated next to him. "First order of business, the chair will recognize the honorable senator from Wyoming. Now, I understand, Senator Hewbright, that you have some other business you must attend to in another committee you chair. So, Senator, as ranking member, I'll yield, and you may proceed first today."

"Thank you, Mr. Chairman." Senator Hewbright, a square-faced man with his dark hair cut short, almost military-short, turned to face the witness, Joshua Jordan. "Colonel Jordan, let me say, sir, that I consider you a true American hero. I know your stellar military record as an Air Force pilot. I'm aware of the great risks you took to fly secret intel missions over Iran to help us determine the extent of their nuclear ambitions. We all have a copy of your impressive resumé: your activities after leaving active military duty, your graduate degree from MIT in applied physics, and your brilliant work as a defense contractor. So let me say thank you, sir, for your courage and your service to this nation."

Joshua nodded politely, bent forward slightly to the microphone, and answered with a simple "Thank you."

Senator Hewbright continued, but as he did, his tone changed. "However, not everyone is as enthusiastic about your recent weapons achievements as I am. As I see it, this special committee is tasked to address several questions. First, there's concern about the use of so-called Return-to-Sender weapons technology, especially when it involves reversing the trajectory of a nuclear warhead, and whether that violates the Six-Party Missile-Defense Treaty, a treaty I personally opposed, and vehemently, I might add. The treaty *didn't* include, as signers, the world's biggest nuclear threats, namely North Korea, Iran,

India, and Pakistan. On the other hand, it *did* include nonstate entities like the United Nations and the European Union, which I didn't think was appropriate. But worse yet, to me that treaty represents just one more major erosion of American national sovereignty — "

"With all due respect," Senator Straworth interjected with only a thin veneer of restraint, "I'm going to ask the senator to stick to the issue at hand. Namely, the use of Mr. Jordan's weapons technology, which was unauthorized by the White House on the day it was used, and which had *not* been properly approved through the appropriate congressional channels or through the Defense Department's own vetting. In short it was completely untested and frankly dangerous — "

"Mr. Chairman," Senator Hewbright shot back, "this man's technology saved the City of New York and its inhabitants from a nuclear holocaust — "

"Senator," Straworth cut in, "I believe that this hearing is going to show that the Air Force jets dispatched that day were quite capable of stopping those warheads in midair, without detonating them, without using Mr. Jordan's highly experimental Return-to-Sender laser weapon, without *any* loss of life, I might add, and without creating an international crisis — "

"May I continue?" Senator Hewbright stopped Straworth's speech dead in its tracks. "I was under the assumption I had the floor ..."

Straworth's eyes flashed, and he squared his shoulders like a boxer. "You do, provided that you give deference to this committee by staying on track."

Senator Hewbright had won that round but just barely. His voice was firm but measured. "As I was saying, I'm concerned less about any perceived chain-of-command issues and more about our loss of national sovereignty, and with it, a large measure of our national defense. This incident with the North Koreans should force us to evaluate where our nation is right now. How did we find ourselves in such dire straits? How? Well, I have a pretty good idea, and it didn't start with foreign policy or military defense. No. It began as a matter of simple economics. When OPEC decided to cut our oil imports so that India and China could get increased allotments, we all know how that caused an energy crisis here at home. We had failed to make sufficient gains in alternate energy sources so we had to go crawling on our knees around the globe searching for other sources from equally unsavory providers: Russia, Venezuela, Brazil. Now I suppose we could have weathered all of that, but the fates, or the hand of Providence, or Mother Nature, whatever you want to call it, had other plans. A two-year drought in the Midwest, together with devastating livestock diseases, have had a catastrophic impact on our agriculture. And we've all seen the Dow, the tumbling numbers on the Standard & Poor's index, the closest thing to a stock-market crash since the Great Crash of—"

"Senator," Chairman Straworth interrupted, "I've extended you the courtesy of being taken out of order for your comments; now, do me the same favor by concluding your speech on the United States economy and *please* get back to the point at hand."

Senator Hewbright's face was slightly scarlet now. "The *point*, ladies and gentlemen, is that America's catastrophic financial problems, the ruined dollar on the international monetary market, our loss of credit globally, the fifteen percent domestic unemployment rate—all of this, if I can put it bluntly, simply scared us stupid—stupid enough to sign off on disastrous treaties in exchange for the promise of more favorable trading and credit terms with the European Union, China, and other nations who are now holding us economically hostage. Our freedom and security in exchange for a little more cash in our pocket, a little more oil, and a whole lot more debt—"

"Senator!" Chairman Straworth implored.

But the ranking member kept talking. "I'm not talking *just* about that ill-conceived missile-defense treaty that is involved in this hearing." Senator Hewbright had his arms outstretched in front of him as he addressed the other senators and representatives on the dais. "A missile-defense treaty we negotiated out of our financial fear. I'm also talking about that United Nations Covenant of Tolerance and Human Rights that, I'm ashamed to say, the United States Senate also ratified. And what's the result? We now have permanent U.N. monitors being placed in many of our major cities. U.N. monitors on American soil — giving us advice on how to administer our own civil liberties and our own laws!"

Chairman Straworth was on the verge of censuring his colleague. But Hewbright saw it coming and backed off just in time. "However, all that is simply prelude. What I've given you is merely an introduction to my first question of Colonel Jordan."

Straworth leaned back, satisfied that he had reined in his political opponent.

"Colonel Jordan," Hewbright said, "I have great respect for the innovation that your RTS defense system employs. Please know that. But on the other hand, this body has requested all your documents on this experimental project. Your attorney has responded on your behalf, indicating that you won't produce them. Please help us understand your reluctance to comply with this demand. Explain it to us in as much detail as you can. Because I, for one, want to give you every benefit of the doubt."

Joshua Jordan took a moment to collect his thoughts. Then he leaned toward the microphone, his hands folded on the table in front of him, and began. "Senator, my lawyer, Mr. Smythe, in his letter, has already explained our legal objections to the request of this committee. So let me try to explain the practical problems. The RTS technology my company developed, and which was successfully used during this North Korean crisis, is highly unique and proprietary in nature. Frankly, we believe we should not be sharing this information with anyone but the Pentagon."

"I agree. But you haven't even done that yet fully."

"No, because this committee has not given us their full assurances that they would keep my technology classified and not pass it on to third parties."

"Mr. Jordan, is there a reason you don't trust this committee?"

"Sir, with all due respect, I don't believe the complex technical details of any weapons system is within the province of any congressional committee. The highly classified inner workings of our most secret technology should stay that way — secret."

"What if this committee ends up serving you with a subpoena, Colonel Jordan? What then?" Senator Hewbright's face revealed a deep desire to try to help Joshua to extricate himself. "I would hate to see it come to that. And besides, isn't some of the technology you're trying to keep secret already out in the marketplace, which means it really isn't that unique? Which would mean that your legal grounds for refusing to comply with our request, frankly, would look pretty shaky."

Joshua nodded. "In one sense, you're right. The use of lasers to transmit data has been used recently in other limited applications. You know, in the old days lasers were used to simply destroy things. Like high-energy bullets. Blunt instruments. Then those of us working in this area started to see other possibilities. A number of years ago the wires connecting circuits in computers were replaced with tiny lasers, which could then shoot data back and forth from the chips at higher speeds than wires could. Then there was the successful test where a German satellite and a satellite from our U.S. Missile Defense Agency communicated information back and forth over three thousand miles using only lasers. What we did at Jordan Technologies was to refine those concepts considerably, and with a revolutionary application. As a result, our RTS is capable of sending a laser message to the computer in the nose cone of the incoming missile — with a data-directive that captures the current trajectory flight plan. Then a second laser beam transmits a mirror opposite of that trajectory, reversing it one hundred and eighty degrees. The point is this, Senator, we can't — our nation can't — afford to let this technology get into the wrong hands."

Senator Hewbright glanced at his watch, nodded, and then gave a quick, "Good luck to you, sir." Then he excused himself.

Now it was Senator Straworth's turn. And he stared straight into Joshua's eyes.

TWELVE

"Mr. Jordan," Senator Straworth smiled as he began grilling Joshua, "you just said you have a concern about your RTS technology getting into the wrong hands. Correct?"

"Yes, sir."

"And *who* exactly do you think of as the 'wrong hands'?"

"I think the wrong hands are anyone outside of the United States."

"By 'outside the United States' do you mean our allies too?"

"Yes, sir," Joshua answered forcefully.

"So you would deny our allies the same defense measures as we have?"

"No, sir." Joshua's lawyer leaned in to whisper something urgently to Joshua, but Joshua just shrugged him off. "I believe we should share our technology with our most trusted allies, but we shouldn't just hand it over to them."

"Hand it over to them?" Straworth feigned ignorance.

"This isn't just another weapons system we can sell to the highest bidder. This system — my system — can alter the nuclear balance for the better of our country, for the better of the world, but only if we maintain strict control over it. Imagine if every missile, any missile, fired at us could be turned back on itself. With my Return-to-Sender system, there is a probable certainty that any missile attack by a rogue nation would result in their own self-destruction. So the threat of a nuclear missile attack on our country or our allies drops to almost nothing."

"*If* your system works the way you say it does," injected Straworth.

"I think we proved that two weeks ago, don't you?" Joshua shot back. "Just as when we put nuclear weapons into Western Europe to deter the Soviet menace in the 1980s, we did not turn over our nuclear arsenal to the Europeans, even though they were our allies. That way we could assure the world the weapons wouldn't fall into the wrong hands."

"And I am here to assure you, Mr. Jordan," said Senator Straworth, "that we have the same concern today."

"That's good to know." Joshua relaxed. This was easier than he thought.

"But I think you have things turned around, Mr. Jordan."

"Oh?"

"Yes," the senator said, his voice now building in intensity. "You see, protecting military secrets, with all due respect, is not the province of some private businessman like yourself. It is the province of the United States government. That's our job. Not yours."

"I think you're forgetting something," Joshua said.

"And what's that?"

"I'm part of the United States government. Not because I work for the Pentagon, but because I'm an American citizen. I'm part of 'we the people' in the Preamble to the Constitution. In that respect, Senator, I guess you could say that you work for me ... and for all of us."

Straworth could now see that the gloves had come off.

"That's right, Mr. Jordan, that's right. I do work for you. I was elected by Americans just like you and put into a position of authority to make the tough decisions that affect my country's security. That is the job I've been given by the people of this country. That's not the job you have been given, sir."

The senator's face was turning crimson, and he was just getting started. His voice boomed out. "There's a certain hubris, sir, in your refusal to produce your documents on this project, an arrogance in your taking it upon yourself to decide when and how military secrets ought to be shared with the United States Congress. An attitude that, quite honestly, I find shocking, and dare I say it — unpatriotic — "

Harry Smythe leaped forward to his microphone before Joshua could get to his. "Sir, there's no need to impugn the patriotism of my client." The lawyer held his hand over Joshua's mic to make sure his client didn't start cursing.

Straworth continued, "It is precisely because of your previous record of patriotism and service to this country that I find it particularly puzzling why you won't comply with a simple request from your government — "

Joshua had heard enough. He ripped his lawyer's hand off his mic. "Because I don't want to give a single piece of technology that could save our country to the very people who are trying to destroy it!"

Senator Straworth sat back, like a spider watching his prey fly straight into his web. He smiled, then leaned forward again. "Do you mean the United Nations and the signers of the Six-Party Missile-Defense Treaty?" intoned Straworth.

"Exactly," blurted out Joshua.

"You mean our allies then?"

"Allies?"

"Yes," confirmed the senator.

"Allies like China and Russia?" sneered Joshua.

Harry Smythe knew he couldn't stop his client, so he simply sat back to watch these two men going at each other like heavyweights in the ring.

"They are our allies, Mr. Jordan," said Straworth, now clearly enjoying himself.

"That's right," said Joshua, "but only because we need oil from one and owe trillions of dollars to the other."

"So we should just throw out all our alliances because of an injured sense of pride?" the senator said, toying with him now. "So who can we trust in this world then?"

"That *is* the question, isn't it, Senator?" Now it was time for Joshua to fight back. "Who can we trust?" He turned to his lawyer. "I can trust Harry here because I know he's taken an oath; if he repeats anything I tell him in confidence, he could lose his law license, maybe even go to jail. I trust my wife because I know she loves me and would never betray me. I trust the Constitution because I know it has the greater good of our country at its heart."

He paused for a second, thinking carefully before going on. "But the question is, who can I trust in this room? ... Truth is, I just can't come up with a satisfactory answer to that question."

The room exploded in an uproar, all the senators and representatives on their feet talking and yelling at once. Senator Straworth pounded his gavel hard and brought the chamber back to order.

"Mr. Smythe," Senator Straworth's eyes were steely as he glared at the attorney, "please inform your client of just how close he is to a contempt citation."

"I'm right here, Senator," Joshua shot back, "so you can talk to me directly. And I'm well aware of the implications of contempt."

"I don't think so, sir. Otherwise you wouldn't have insulted these honorable members the way you have. It is outrageous the way you have come in here today, thinking you could bully this committee with your self-centered assertions about duty and honor. I say to you, sir, it is your duty to turn over your work on the RTS project. It is your duty, sir, for the good of your country. And I warn you, if you or your lawyer tries to stall us on this, we will subpoena you with the full weight of both houses of Congress and the United States government, and it is your duty to honor any such subpoena as a citizen of this great country you profess to love. Anything less, Mr. Jordan, would be an affront to this committee and the honorable men and women who serve on it and to everyone in America, as well as an outrage and a crime. If necessary, we will put you in jail, sir, if you persist in your refusal to cooperate."

The senator let that sink in for emphasis. "And I'm sure my feelings are shared by all my colleagues on this committee." The senator sat back in his high-backed chair, feigning disgust.

"I'll tell you what I find to be an outrage and a crime," Jordan spoke calmly. "But, Senator, it has nothing to do with this committee. What it has to do with is the fact that out there, right now, in terrorist cells, in dark rooms, in rogue nations, and in the palaces of dictators and international drug lords, there are men who are willing to do absolutely *anything* to get their hands on my technology."

Joshua had one more word on the subject. He spit it out like a bit of rotten apple.

"*Anything* ..."

THIRTEEN

Bucharest, Romania

Atta Zimler, also known as the Algerian, swung open the stylish French doors, causing the first abrupt rays of dawn to invade the sixth-floor suite of the elegant Athenee Palace Hotel. As he peered from the narrow balcony, which overlooked the famous Piata Revolutiei below, he couldn't help but notice the long, oddly shaped shadow created by the Iuliu Maniu statue, which sat in the center of the historic square. Wrapped in a luxuriant hotel robe, Zimler sipped his Turkish espresso and contemplated the upcoming day's events. He wiped his mouth with his napkin as he ran through the checklist in his head.

He'd always been a careful man, organized, some might even say obsessively meticulous. He knew the outcome of each of his actions in advance, along with the potential reactions of those around him, and he planned for every possible scenario. He credited this preparation for his ongoing success in his chosen line of work — preparation, and a total lack of emotion. Had anyone else been in the room, they would not have been able to discern from his calm demeanor that he was in the process of formulating the minute details of the murder he would soon carry out.

Turning back to the room, he set his cup on the dining room table, removed his robe, and folded it neatly over the chair. Clad only in his undergarments, he lowered himself onto the Oriental rug and began his daily rapid-fire routine of fifty push-ups, fifty sit-ups, and as many leg raises as he felt were needed. By the end of the workout he was breathing heavily, though not exhausted in the least.

For years he had trained his body far beyond the capacity of most human beings. He had mastered karate, judo, and aikido. His strength was not obvious, not like those American bodybuilders and football players. But that was what served him. He was stronger than most athletes, yet on the street, he looked like everyone else. He had accepted that most people were either too stupid or too self-involved even to notice him.

After a shower Zimler extracted some clothes from his Louis Vuitton suitcase. Today would be casual — an imported silk shirt from Italy, nicely tailored linen pants, leather shoes from Spain. As he dressed, it occurred to him, albeit briefly, that it would be the last time he could wear these particular items.

The phone rang. A male voice on the other end was direct and emotionless.

"Is this the Algerian?"

"Who is calling?" Zimler countered while simultaneously fastening the last button on his shirt.

"I am calling on behalf of someone who has a serious problem."

"Oh?"

"His mail keeps getting returned ..."

"Sounds like he has a bad mailman."

"Yes," the voice responded. "A very bad mailman. The mailman needs to be eliminated."

"Is that what you are really after?" Zimler asked. "The mailman?"

"Well ... the bigger problem lies in the delivery system."

"I would have to concur. I assume you are calling because you have agreed to the price?"

"Yes."

"And the other terms as well?"

"Yes, yes," the voice on the other end replied.

"Then we have an understanding," Zimler concluded. "However, if at any point in the future you fail to make the correct deposits in the designated accounts at the proper times, I will immediately discontinue our relationship."

"Yes. We understand that. When will you begin your work? My superior would like to have the technology in his hands as soon as possible."

"Certain events have already been put in motion," the Algerian assured.

"You know," the man on the line offered, "we have chosen you because of your ... well ... your reputation."

"Of course."

"Please, don't fail us."

"You needn't concern yourself about that," Zimler stated confidently. "I'm not about to compromise my reputation."

With that, Zimler ended the conversation.

Twenty five minutes later, the Algerian rode the hotel's mirrored elevator down two flights to the fourth floor. He waited until the hallways were clear before making his way to room 417, which he knew was unoccupied. From his right pants pocket he pulled out a pair of latex gloves and put them on. From his left pocket he took out a magnetic programming device, similar in size to a standard deck of playing cards. Zimler then extracted a blank hotel room card key from the magnetic box and inserted it into the room's door lock.

Nothing.

He then slid the electronic card key back into the device and punched in a new code using the numeric pad on top of the box. He tried the key again.

The door opened.

Zimler smiled, entered the empty room, and closed the door securely behind him.

And waited.

ㅁㅁㅁ

Yergi Banica was clearly nervous — and it wasn't simply because he was running a few minutes late. Having already parked his car on the north side of the Piata Revolutiei as instructed, he quickly made his way across the square toward the hotel. His mind was on euros — ten thousand of them to be exact. His job, teaching political science at the Romanian University of Craiova, paid little, barely enough for him to get by in his small apartment with his much younger new wife. Personally, he didn't mind the close quarters, but he knew Elena aspired to better things.

Yergi was of average size and, although not unattractive, had added those few extra pounds that come with age. He knew he was lucky to have found his beautiful Elena, lucky that she found him interesting, lucky that she had agreed to marry him. He knew about her unsavory background, but he didn't care and never talked about it with her. And he was well aware that his luck could end if his financial situation remained unchanged. But as luck would have it, his finances were about to improve.

A year earlier, Yergi had been approached by a Russian student in one of his political science classes. The student was friendly, bright, and engaged in his studies, but that was just a ruse. In reality, the young man wanted to know if the professor would be interested in earning a little extra money. All Yergi would have to do is slip him some details about the political persuasions of some of the more radical professors and wealthy students on campus. Yergi was old enough to have lived through the KGB and their successor, the secret Russian Federal Security Bureau. So he knew what they were asking of him; to be their informant. He really wouldn't be hurting anyone, he rationalized, just passing along little innocent bits of information. Besides, the extra money would come in handy.

As an unintentional side effect, this new arrangement actually brought Yergi a newfound sense of confidence. Always trying to impress his wife's younger friends, he'd let it slip a few times after several drinks that he was a man who knew things, a man with connections. He might have even jokingly referred to himself as a spy. Yes, he even privately entertained the idea he was an Eastern block equivalent of James Bond.

But then, three weeks ago, Yergi received a strange phone call. A man who claimed to be an Algerian had learned of him through an associate and asked if he might be able to provide information about a certain American defense contractor. At first, Yergi was suspicious. Why would this man think he could get this information? Did he know about Yergi's connections with the FSB? And who was this "associate" who had recommended him?

Then he became more practical. The Algerian was offering twenty thousand euros for the information, half now, half upon delivery. It was more than enough money for him and Elena to move away and start a new life together somewhere else. So he turned to the young FSB agent he'd been working with and offered him a deal — to exchange half of his upfront payment for any information that could be found pertaining to the American, Joshua Jordan. But did the young FSB agent have access to that? He said he would see what he could turn up.

A week later Yergi received a copy of the FSB's comprehensive dossier, which included pictures, biographies, personal data, and all manner of classified details on the American in question. This should make the Algerian happy, he thought. Yergi allowed his imagination to drift about freely once again. Perhaps he and Elena could move near the sea. She loved the sea. And she would love him.

As he turned the corner and the Athenee Palace Hotel entrance came into view, Yergi's dreams of his future abruptly morphed into nervousness. Shaken, he concluded it was the promise of wealth that had his nerves jangling, and not any potential danger. Certainly he could trust the Algerian. After all, the man had already paid ten thousand euros in advance, half of which was secure in Yergi's small apartment near the university. And he was moments away from being handed another ten thousand. Yes, the transaction would go smoothly. He had exactly what the Algerian wanted.

FOURTEEN

At 9:35 a.m. there was a knock at the door of room 417. Zimler opened it to reveal the slightly rotund, bespectacled Romanian with the small satchel under his arm.

"I am Yergi. You are ... the Algerian?"

Zimler nodded and ushered him in. Pointing to a coffee table in the living room area, he persuaded the currier to set his package down.

The professor was clearly nervous. His eyes scanned the room, then his host.

"Funny, y-you don't really look Algerian ...," he stammered.

Zimler smiled, then walked over to the balcony's French doors and swung them open to let in some fresh air.

He began with a question. "The information you have in the package," he began, pointing to the satchel, "is it up-to-date?"

"Yes, very much so. The Russian agent whom I obtained it from vouched for its authenticity. I have quite a bit of information here for you, including the basic research and development agreement between Mr. Jordan and the Pentagon in reference to his work on the Return-to-Sender technology. Of course, no one has the actual schematics for the system ... but this should provide you with an excellent starting point ..." Yergi was hoping this would all be over soon. "So, in regards to my payment —"

"Did you bring your passport, as I requested?" Zimler responded.

Despite the cool morning Bucharest breeze flowing into the room, the Romanian was nevertheless starting to feel the first signs of sweat beading on his forehead.

"I need to verify you are who you say you are," Zimler continued.

"Of course." Yergi fumbled a little and then removed his passport from his coat pocket and offered it to Zimler, who proceeded to flip through it.

"You haven't been to America then?"

The already uncomfortable professor now added confusion to his growing list of anxieties.

"No, why?"

"I was hoping you could tell me a little something about any experiences you might have had there. I plan on going there myself someday." Zimler smiled, handed the passport back, and turned toward the balcony.

"A good view of the Piata Revolutiei, wouldn't you say, Yergi?" He motioned the professor over toward the open French doors.

Yergi, of course, was already familiar with the view. In fact, he had taken Elena to the restaurant located on the same floor of this very hotel on their first date. He'd wanted to impress her, and it had obviously done the trick. What she didn't know was that Yergi had a student who worked at the restaurant who had offered up a free meal in exchange for a passing grade.

Still, the view was spectacular, and it was indeed turning out to be a beautiful day.

Then Zimler added something unexpected: "Oh, look over there, is that your car ... being towed?"

Yergi scurried toward the open doors and glanced in the direction of the street on the north side of the square.

"No, I don't think ... I'm afraid I don't see what you are talking about —"

Before Yergi could turn around, Zimler, now behind him, looped a garrote over the man's head and around his neck — like a noose.

Yergi's first reaction was to grab at the steel cord constricting his throat and try to dislodge it. Panic set in instantaneously. He desperately wanted to breathe, but couldn't. He then reached back and seized the arm of the Algerian. It was like steel. He was beginning to lose consciousness in the grip of his assassin.

Zimler knew from years of experience that the process of extracting life from a body in this manner would take less than two minutes.

Vainly the Romanian attempted to cry out to the people below who were within earshot of the room's open balcony doors, but he could only manage a few faint gurgles. He continued to grab futilely at his neck and the Algerian's arm.

Zimler pulled harder.

Yergi's knees buckled.

The waves rolled gently toward the shore under the Adriatic sun. The day was very still. Yergi could smell the sea air; feel the warmth on his skin. And there she was, Elena, with her American baseball cap, waving at him and smiling. It would be the last image to cross his mind.

A moment later, the struggling stopped … along with his breathing. Yergi's lifeless body slumped to the ground.

The assassin calmly rose to his feet, brushed off his wrinkled linen pants, straightened his silk shirt, wound the cord in a loop, and placed it back in his pocket. He then plucked the passport from the Romanian's hand and grabbed the satchel from the table.

Again, making sure the hallways were clear, Zimler hooked the Do Not Disturb sign around the doorknob before closing the door firmly behind him with his latex-protected hand.

Quickly returning to his own room, Zimler stripped off his shirt, pants, and shoes and shoved them into a plastic bag, which he then stuffed into his Louis Vuitton suitcase. He dressed in another set of clothes and headed downstairs to the lobby to check out.

"Pleasant visit?" the hotel clerk inquired in a thick Romanian accent.

"Very," Zimler responded, smiling broadly.

The assassin calmly walked out of the hotel and down the street. In an alley three blocks away, behind the Calea Grivitei, he slipped the plastic bag from his suitcase and placed it in a trash dumpster just as a garbage truck turned onto the street for its weekly pickup.

Minutes later, in the back of a cab heading south on the Blvd. Dimitrie Cantemir, the Algerian opened the satchel and removed a portion of its contents. The photo resumé of Joshua Jordan was the first item to catch his attention.

Zimler's eyes narrowed into laser-sharp focus as he studied the target.

He then put the resumé and other papers back into the satchel and closed it up.

"Please hurry," Zimler remarked to the cab driver, "I have a rather busy day ahead of me."

FIFTEEN

Washington, D.C.

Inside the White House, the violent images flashing across the panel of Internet television screens deeply troubled President Virgil Corland. He shook his head and wondered exactly how much PR damage was going to result from the coverage of heavily equipped riot police overpowering unarmed truckers in the heart of the nation's capital.

Corland fidgeted uncomfortably in his swivel chair like a man with a bad back problem.

"I don't like what I'm seeing here, Hank. You'd think this was Somalia, not Washington."

Chief of Staff Henry Strand was seated near the president on a white leather sofa, nodding in agreement. He too was concerned with the fiasco taking place down the street and over the airwaves, but he wasn't about to let it show.

The president's eye was then drawn to the third screen from the left where a young female reporter, standing with a mic along Constitution Avenue, was about to go live. With his remote, Corland selected that particular screen's volume and pumped it up.

"The protesting truckers," the reporter announced, "are angry with the administration's recent decision to allow the four-month-old federal gas-rationing initiative to remain in place for the trucking industry. Last month, President Corland sent special envoys to OPEC and Russia

83

to try and resolve the oil crisis that has been escalating since August of last year. The administration's resolution to lift the rationing order for some industries and not others has been controversial, particularly with our continuing financial crisis. Most Americans realize that a crippled trucking industry will lead to even higher prices for goods. And with the president's approval rating dwindling in recent weeks due to ..."

Corland huffed as he squeezed the mute button quite a bit harder than necessary. "Who is this woman? I don't recognize her. She must be new."

"A recent hire," Strand responded. "I'll have Finley talk to her boss this afternoon. As you know, Mr. President, it's sometimes difficult to control these kinds of media events when they're happening live. I wouldn't get worked up too much over this. By seven p.m., after all the network anchors have signed off from their nightly newscasts, the majority of the American people will believe that you are the hero and that these foul-mouthed truckers are the bad guys. Because that's what they'll have been told to believe."

Corland glanced over at Strand, who simply smiled. Both men recognized that to make such a statement was the height of arrogance and elitism. Yet both men also knew it was true.

Strand continued. "I don't know how heated this thing is going to get, but we'll make sure our PR people get us booked on the Sunday shows just in case. We can send our assistant secretary of commerce, Bud Meyerling, over to handle the TV stuff. He's great on the talking-head shows. Two weeks from now, no one will remember any of this. The streets will be clear."

"Hank, I hope you're right. But you and I both know nobody watches those Sunday shows," Corland replied with a slight laugh. "Heck, they're not even watching the nightly news anymore. Who knows? Maybe the conservatives are on to us."

Strand paused for a moment before reacting, unsure whether or not Corland was trying to be funny. "I'm sure some of them are, Mr. President."

"So what's the latest timetable for keeping this inflation business going?" Corland asked. "Remember, I'm the one who's taking the brunt of the blame for it."

"Sir, as you know, this economic crisis is actually helpful in moving our global agenda forward. We can get a lot more things pushed through when the American people are sidetracked with concerns over their finances. Obama's guys proved that a few years ago. The conservatives out there would want our hides if they knew what we were doing, just like they wanted to with Barack. But it's to everybody's benefit that we go global, even if the pick-up truck crowd in the Bible Belt does't recognize it."

"Hank, you're stalling. How long?"

"Till the end of next year."

"What? That's cutting it awful close!" Corland retorted.

"It still gives us ten months before the November elections to get the economy back on track, which, of course, will be a direct result of your policies. You'll easily win reelection. In fact, I predict a landslide," Strand reassured.

"And what if the economy doesn't respond in time?"

"Sir, I like being in the White House. I want to be here for another term just as much as you do. We won't let that happen."

"Okay, keep me posted." Satisfied, Corland paused, then turned his attention to another challenge. "Now, let's talk about national defense for a moment. Is the secretary of state going to be at the briefing?"

"I believe so, Mr. President."

"And the fellow from the Joint Chiefs?"

"Yes, sir. The Pentagon is sending over the vice chairman."

"What's his position on the North Korean incident?"

"The Joint Chiefs have been informed of the secretary's suggestion that we share our Return-to-Sender weapons technology with several other nations. However, several people at the Pentagon are opposed to the idea," Strand reported. "Hopefully we can get around them."

"Well, the Return-to-Sender technology would be a great leveraging tool. It'd be nice to get some more oil flowing in our direction. And more credit. We can never have too much of that. So what's their objection?" Corland asked.

"They still have national-security concerns about other nations having the technology. You know, the risk of it being leaked to rogue nations or terrorists. Unfortunately, these Pentagon guys are really dug-in on this. They're even arguing that the congressional committee ought to ease off a bit on Joshua Jordan. They don't want him pressured into giving up his documents."

Just then Hank Strand's digital memopad buzzed.

"Excuse me, Mr. President. Madam Vice President is here."

"Okay. Let's get her take on all this."

The door to the Oval Office swung open, and Vice President Jessica Tulrude confidently strode in. The forty-six-year-old brunette ex-senator had helped Corland take the swing states in the last election — aided by the media's palpable love for this outspoken feminist.

"Mr. President ... Henry," she began, smiling politely.

"Jessica, let's talk about this briefing."

"Thank you, Mr. President," Tulrude responded, charging ahead without waiting for a wider opening. "It's critical that we back up Secretary Danburg. He wants to begin immediate negotiations with the EU, Russia, India, and, of course, China, who, after all, remains our biggest financial creditor, to try to do something in terms of a swap — their economic chips to us in return for the RTS technology."

"How do you suggest we broach the subject?" the president inquired.

"Well," Tulrude offered, "the peace conference in Davos, Switzerland, is coming up soon. We haven't responded to their invitation yet. We have a lot of nations outraged at us over this North Korean incident. The president of the European Union has called us 'warlords' because of our use of the RTS system."

"Is he still asking for proof that we didn't provoke the North Korean navy into firing their nukes?"

"Yes, as a matter of fact," Tulrude responded with eyebrows raised. "So this conference would provide an excellent platform for the administration to address the issue."

"Would you say this would be a good opportunity for me to start laying out some of our global agenda?" Corland asked.

"Actually," Tulrude replied, "I would counsel against that, Mr. President. This peace conclave is not a high-profile-enough venue for a personal appearance by the president of the United States. I feel, frankly, that Vance Danburg should be there. Let's have our secretary of state make a short speech. Drop the hint that we might be willing to share our weapons technology. Open up some dialogue … that sort of thing."

"All right." Corland paused to think it over. "Any other suggestions, Jessica?"

"Yes, Mr. President … about the congressional hearings."

"Yes?"

"It is an international embarrassment that this Joshua Jordan, a private defense contractor, is creating the impression that he's holding the president and the U.S. Congress hostage by refusing to release information on his weapons technology."

"That's valid," Corland agreed. "One single private citizen can't be allowed to direct our national defense policy."

"Send a message to Congress," Tulrude continued, "that they had better do their job. Don't tolerate this man's defiance. You must pin Joshua Jordan to the ground."

Tulrude then turned to the flickering TV screens, which were filled with images of truck drivers with zip-tied wrists being hauled off by riot cops.

"Pin him to the ground like you would any other criminal," she added.

SIXTEEN

Joshua Jordan relaxed in his grey sweatpants and one of his old Air Force Academy T-shirts and stretched out on a comfortable chaise lounge. This was one of his favorite escapes. Private. Secluded. Even though it was in the middle of New York City. Out on his lavishly landscaped penthouse terrace, he could see for miles along the skyline and farther, out toward the harbor. Surrounded by a few small potted trees, manicured greenery, and various plants in bloom, up where the birds soared, with the city stretched out below him, he felt insulated … and simultaneously free. But he knew this moment wouldn't last much longer.

Such a euphoric sense of peace was becoming increasingly elusive. Joshua was glad to have slipped away from the political and legal flack that was exploding all around him back in Washington.

But on that Sunday morning, at least for a few precious minutes, he had found refuge. Only one other place on the planet could give him more peace — his massive log-house retreat in the mountains of Colorado. He and Abby would be there soon. But not soon enough for his taste. Now he was simply trying to forget about Senator Straworth and his theatrical strutting and arrogant threats to have Joshua cited for contempt of Congress.

As he took a sip of his morning coffee, he heard Abby's steps on the tiled terrace. She was wearing a bright peach-colored dress and was fidgeting with a simple gold chain necklace.

"Honey, would you hook this for me?"

She sat down next to him and pulled her hair aside to reveal the back of her neck.

His thick fingers fumbled for a while until he finally got the clasp closed on the thin wisp of a chain.

"There, got it. Man, that's a tough one." Then he leaned forward and kissed the back of her neck.

"Do you remember how I got this?" she asked with the flash of a big smile.

Joshua thought for a moment, then shook his head.

"It was the first thing you ever gave me, when we started dating," she said.

"Not very flashy," he replied with a grin. "I'm surprised you stuck with me!"

"I don't need flash," she said, patting his cheek. "I just need you."

"Oh, two points for that one," he shot back with a laugh. *Beauty and brains. I am one lucky guy*, he thought.

Abigail sort of scrunched up her nose, subtly and quickly. Hardly discernable. But Joshua recognized it. That is when he knew that something was up.

"You used to do that when you went into court to try a case," he said.

"Do what?"

"That little thing with your nose," he teased. "It's a dead giveaway. I'm surprised the opposing attorneys didn't catch on. Something's on your mind. I can tell."

"So, you tell me," she proposed, rising to his challenge. "What's on my mind?"

"Hey, I couldn't even begin to figure that out."

"Well, then neither could those other lawyers," she said with a sly grin.

"See, I ought to know better than to try and out-argue my wife, the attorney ..."

Abigail then breathed deeply and became silent.

Now he really knew something was bugging her.

"All right, out with it. What's up?"

"It's about Cal," she offered. The smile was gone. It had been re-placed by a gentle, motherly kind of expression.

"Has something happened to him?"

"He's okay. But something did happen recently. I thought you should know about it."

"What?"

"It was the day of the missile crisis."

Joshua waited. Abigail continued. "Cal was in New York when it all happened ..."

"No, he couldn't have been. He was already on his way back to college," Joshua said correcting her.

"That's what he told us, Josh. But he was actually caught right in the middle of it. He'd just arrived at the train station. He was right next to a woman who ... Josh, the poor woman got trampled to death. Right in front of our son."

"Wait ... why was he still in New York? I thought he'd left early and gotten safely out of the city."

"Well, he hadn't. He wanted to spend the day at an art lecture with Karen. Then he tried to leave that evening, which is when everything happened — "

"So Cal lied to us?" Joshua was shaking his head with a look as if his son had dared to slap him across the face. He could never tolerate lying from his kids. Never. And he let them know it. Why would Cal disrespect him like that?

"Josh, dear, you're missing the real story here."

"No, I'll tell you the real story. The day before the North Korean attack, he wasn't here with us. I assumed he'd already taken the train back to Liberty. So where was he? Did he spend the night with that girl?"

"He just wanted to spend the day in New York before he went back to college. He was trying to make sense of his life." Abigail's voice was strained and pleading. She was holding her hands out to her husband, cupping them, as if she were caressing something fragile, like a delicate piece of china.

Both of them fell silent for a moment. Joshua's face was tightening. Abigail could see it. That hardness, the stern, unshakable resolve that always served him well in battle, and in business, but was so often his undoing when it came to his own son.

"Let me finish before you judge, Josh," she finally stated. "The whole point is that he was here in New York when the attack was launched. He was alone, trapped. He saw a women killed by a rioting mob. He was almost trampled to death himself in that train station! And he was scared to death."

She paused to let that sink in. Joshua's eyes were fixed on her, but it was as if he were trying to look through her, to someone or something else, off in the distance.

"Your son," Abigail continued, "was paralyzed with fear. But he couldn't admit that to you. Ever. Because you're the war hero. The guy who flew into war zones without blinking. You're the man who saved New York City. How could he ever tell you that he was afraid? You haven't exactly made it easy for Cal to bare his soul."

Joshua tilted his head back and forth just slightly, as if rattling the idea from one side of his brain to the other could make it fall into the right hole. But it didn't fit.

"So he lies, and *I'm* the bad guy — is that it?"

"I didn't say that," she said, "but I do think you're part of the problem. And you're going to have to be part of the solution."

It was quiet again between the two of them.

Finally Abigail stood up. "I'm on my way to church. I'd love you to come with me, but … it's up to you."

Joshua didn't budge

"So you're staying here," she said with a note of finality.

Again, only silence.

"Okay." She then turned and was gone.

Joshua was left alone in his own private place of turmoil. His thoughts turned to two of the most important people in his life.

His son had lied to his face. But there was more to it than that. Joshua remembered his feelings about his son when he had decided not to pursue military school. Then his decision to leave engineering and go into art. At every step, at every crossroad, Cal had ignored Joshua's advice. Even Joshua's cautions about his son's girlfriend fell on deaf ears.

Now Cal was dealing with a lot of baggage, having lived through the panic at Grand Central Station. Joshua understood how seeing someone die in front of you, even for a military veteran, could shake you up like nothing else in life. And Cal was ashamed to talk to his father about it.

Then there was Abby. He loved her like crazy. But there was a kind of uncertainty between them ever since she'd started this spiritual journey of hers. Not that he resented her recent pursuit of a higher purpose. Not really. He tried to respect her choice to disappear into this new world of Bible reading, church going, and God talk. She seemed happy enough. But he had his own goals. And especially now that he'd been drawn into this national crisis over the North Korean attack and his RTS design. His plate had become full to the point of overflowing.

He was a mission-specific guy. And God was not part of his mission. He had nothing against religion. In fact, in the quiet moments he often wondered about what Abby had found that had worked so well in her life. He even questioned what his real motives were in keeping God at a safe distance. Was it a perfectionistic pilot's need for absolute control over his own life, his own "flight pattern"? Maybe too much need for control ... So, was that the problem between him and Cal too? Trying to exert too much control over his son?

Just like my own dad? Déjà vu?

Joshua's dad was a career airman, a chief master sergeant in the Air Force. In his home nothing was out of place. Not a bed sheet. Not a dirty dish. Not a bicycle left on the lawn. Nothing. God was given a kind of hat-tip. But ultimately, in his house, you figured things out on your own. You took responsibility on your own. Your problems were your own, and you fixed them.

Of course, that kind of order and discipline later served Joshua well in his own career. Mental toughness was a must. Like when he flew five secret reconnaissance flights over Iran, taking pictures of their nuclear sites. On his fifth flyover he got a scrambled code from his air support that he'd "just been made." Iranian radar had apparently picked him up. The sky was about to get jammed with ground-to-air missiles — all aimed at him. But he wasn't done. Joshua patiently kept his recon camera whirling so every last-minute detail of the nuclear plants could be documented, knowing he could be blasted from the air at any minute.

But the missiles didn't come. Only months later did he learn why. An Israeli plant within the Iranian air defense sabotaged their radar at the last minute. The Israeli Mossad agent was found out and brutally executed by the Iranians. But Joshua and his mission were saved.

So from Joshua's perspective, the world was a rough, dangerous place.

But there was still the lingering questions Joshua had, not about the world outside, but about his own family.

Up there on his terrace "crow's nest," as he called it, Joshua had no answers for the loose ends that seemed incapable of being tied neatly together. Personal things that seemed to defy a schematically engineered resolution. He was a decision maker. A problem solver. Lack of resolve was not something he was comfortable with. Least of all with his own son.

Sitting up there alone he knew he needed to find something more tangible to focus on.

He grabbed his small digital newsreader off the garden table and clicked on the InstantNews function. After scrolling through some sections, one headline grabbed his attention.

JORDAN DEFIES CONGRESS IN MISSILE PROBE

"That was a closed hearing!" Joshua yelled out into the air. "Who leaked it?"

As he read the electronic article from the *New York Examiner* he realized someone had given the press a blow-by-blow of the secret session. What was even worse was the way Joshua had been *spun* in the article: "Warmonger ... Profiteer."

The report concluded with a scorching personal indictment:

Sources hint that Joshua Jordan may be attempting to drive up the price of his RTS system while haggling with Congress over his design documents.

Joshua grabbed his Allfone and dialed Harry Smythe's private cell number. After several rings, his lawyer picked up.

"Harry, this is Joshua — "

"I know, I know," the attorney interjected quickly. "I just read it — "

"One question," Joshua demanded.

"Ask away."

"How fast can we start fighting back?"

SEVENTEEN

Agent John Gallagher was alone, patiently waiting inside the media conference room of the FBI's New York office, slouched in one of a half dozen black padded chairs that surrounded a large glass table. An imageless HD flat-screen filled one of the room's walls, where agents would routinely gather to watch and dissect recorded witness interviews and review surveillance footage. Gallagher's video interview with New York's favorite shock-jock radio host, "Ivan the Terrible," was cued up and ready to go. But Regional Director Miles Zadernack was running late. Gallagher tried to pass the time by going over in his mind what Zadernack's response to the interview would be, although he already had a pretty good idea of what to expect.

Zadernack was a rule-book fanatic. Straitlaced to the hilt. Gallagher's investigative techniques, though effective, were admittedly eccentric at times. And if there was one thing that his boss, Miles Zadernack, couldn't stomach, it was anything that strayed outside the pages.

Gallagher took a couple of gulps from the carton of milk he'd brought with him. It was the only thing that could stop the crushing, burning sensation in his chest. The doctor called it gastric reflux. Job-related stress ... but that was for the yuppie-types on Wall Street, not for him. Gallagher had his own personal diagnosis and figured the stuff he'd inhaled on 9/11 had finally caught up to him. So he didn't bother filling the prescription. Downing some milk seemed to help. That was good enough.

"Come on," he muttered as he shot a look at his watch. "It's show-time; let's go."

Then he heard Zadernack's footsteps in the hallway. Even paced. Not too fast or too slow. His boss stepped into the room, wearing a dark navy suit and solid nonpatterned tie as usual. And unlike Gallagher's, Zadernack's ties never had any hint of stains from his last chili-dog.

"Morning, John," Miles began in his monotone. "Let's see what you have for us today."

"Teretsky, the talk-radio guy, better known as Ivan the Terrible," Gallagher began. "I videoed my interview with him. Couldn't believe he agreed without a fight. And no lawyer with him either. That was a shocker."

"I see the man enjoys litigation," Miles replied, glancing through Teretsky's investigation file. "They must know him pretty well down at the clerk of the court's office."

"Yeah, I hear they had to build a new wing just to store all the files from his lawsuits," Gallagher quipped.

Miles gave a courteous smile and said, "Says here he sued the NYPD — twice." Then, in an attempt at a colorful exchange, Miles added, "Looks like he'll sue any guy who wears pants."

"Yeah, and some who don't." He didn't want Miles, the poster-child for the humorless, to have the last word on anything, especially one-liners.

Miles closed the file and nodded toward the remote control. Gallagher clicked it and took another gulp of milk.

On the screen, Ivan was sitting in his studio chair. Just before speaking he reached up and pushed the boom microphone out of the way so he could look straight into the eyes of his FBI interrogator.

Ivan was bald-headed with a full black beard and a slightly wild, roaming look in his eyes. Ivan adjusted his dark-rimmed glasses.

"Okay, Mr. FBI man," Ivan began. "You called for this party. So let's p-a-r-t-e-e ..."

Gallagher started with the usual drill. He declared for the record that Ivan was giving his permission for the recording. He gave the date, time, and place of the interview, and that Ivan was speaking with him voluntarily and under no coercion or duress and had the right to have an attorney present but had waived that right.

Gallagher chose not to give him his Miranda rights for two reasons. Technically he was simply a witness and not a suspect. But more importantly, he didn't want to light Ivan's fire. At least not yet. Not before they'd even started.

The FBI agent identified the scope of the interview for his interviewee. He told Ivan that they were investigating the North Korean missile crisis and the information Ivan had received regarding the nukes coming toward New York City.

Then Gallagher started into the details of that day. The time Ivan got to the studio that afternoon. The time he first learned about the missiles. And more importantly, *how* he found out about them.

"A telephone call," Ivan said. "It was from some woman."

"Who?"

"She said her first name ... like I was supposed to know her or something, which I didn't. Can't recall her name now. I think I blanked it out of my head 'cuz of what she said next."

"Which was?"

"She started talking really intense at me, but not loud, sort of whispering like she didn't want anyone else to hear, and she said, 'Get out of New York now' ... or if I couldn't do that then I was supposed to head for the basement. That there were two North Korean missiles heading for Manhattan. Then she hung up."

"You went on the air with the fact that New York was under nuclear attack based on a phone call from some woman you didn't know?"

"'Course not. What, do I look stupid to you? Naw, we then put a call in to a Pentagon contact. He sounded a tad nervous and refused to comment. We made one more phone call, to the woman at the local emergency preparedness office. I posed as an NYPD officer and acted like I knew what was going on … she spilled the beans in two seconds flat."

"Which phone were you at when you got the original call about incoming missiles?"

"The call came directly into the studio line," Ivan said pointing to the phone on his desk.

"Is that the same telephone number the public uses to call into your program?"

"Naw. The public line's a different number. We use this one in the studio for internal stuff. We have our program guests call this number. Also, our tech guys call on that line."

"Do you have any kind of electronic log or caller-ID on that line?"

"Nope. Only on the public line."

"But your tech staff, and any special guests on your show, someone you're going to interview on-air, they would have this studio number?"

"Yeah."

"I'd like to see a list of all your guests for the last twelve months," Gallagher requested from the other side of the camera. "And all your tech people. Anybody with access to that number. Let's start there."

"Are you nuts?" Ivan blurted out. He was now sitting perfectly erect in his chair, as if he'd just received a low-voltage electrical charge.

"That's confidential information," Ivan said. "We got rights. My lawyer says we got a journalist's privilege not to disclose information to people like you."

"Tell your lawyer to go back to law school, Ivan," Gallagher fired back. "The guest list is public information because you've already aired it. And probably put it up on your website. Besides, I could get it from the FCC or from your public file. Do you really want to play the legal game with me? I can have you served with a subpoena to appear before a grand jury. Then you can be forced to testify. Unless you want to claim your Fifth Amendment right, that is. So, do you want to claim your right to remain silent because you might incriminate yourself, Ivan? You feeling guilty about the deaths of those New Yorkers who were killed in the melee that happened because you opened your big mouth on the air without talking to us first?"

Ivan exploded. "I don't believe this! You saying I'm a murderer?" The shock jock was now on his feet swearing and screaming at his interrogator and putting his fists to the side of his head like he was doing some kind of bizarre ritual dance.

But Gallagher kept rolling. "Now you don't have to answer my questions. Call your lawyer. We can stop right now. You have that right, Ivan. In the meantime, I'll talk to my lawyers. Only difference is that my federal attorneys have the power to put people in prison. Your attorney, on the other hand, only has the power to send you and your radio station a bill in an amount close to the budget of a small country. So, you wanna rumble? Bring it on ..."

Ivan kept on sputtering. What the video was not catching was the look on Gallagher's face off-camera, grinning at the out-of-control talk-show host. Finally, Ivan started to collect himself. Then he pointed to the camera and shouted, "Turn that thing off!"

The picture went dark.

"What happened next?" Miles asked. Gallagher knew his boss and recognized in his voice that strained attempt to keep cool.

Gallagher reached into his briefcase, took out a substantial pile of papers, and tossed them onto the table.

"All the names and addresses of each guest on Ivan's talk show for the past year. Plus the contact information for the station's tech staff."

"Your approach is not protocol," Miles said matter-of-factly, but his eyes were closing nervously as he spoke. "You know the standard procedure. You go to the U.S. attorney's office. They go to the DOJ and get permission for a subpoena to the telephone company for a listing of the telephone calls to Mr. Teretsky's studio. Set a court date. The telephone company responds — "

"My way's quicker."

Miles pointed at the video screen. "I don't like what I just saw," he warned. "I'll have to decide whether I write you up because of this."

"Miles, think about it. We can still get a subpoena if you want. As this investigation continues — "

"*If* this investigation continues," Miles threatened with a little less monotone than usual. Then he stood up. "Please secure that videotape in the evidence room," he demanded and turned to leave.

Gallagher was stunned. He had to chew on that for a minute while he remained in his chair. Finally he reached over and snatched up the papers off the table. He couldn't believe what his boss was suggesting. That the FBI would actually drop an investigation into leaked information which compromised national security.

Come on, Miles, what's going on here?

EIGHTEEN

Davos, Switzerland

Two entire floors of the Hotel Belvedere had been rented by Caesar Demas to accommodate the large staff that operated his private foundation. For his own comfort, though, the billionaire had secured a sprawling villa in the nearby mountains. He was a man who loved quiet whenever possible. And on the day before the start of his organization's fifth annual World Peace Summit, he had a lot of thinking to do.

Demas, with his neatly trimmed beard and carefully managed salt-and-pepper hair, stood on the massive veranda with a cup of mint tea in his hand. The view of the Alps was stunning, to be sure, but that particular moment, he wasn't contemplating the scenery.

That afternoon Demas was expecting a visitor who might be able to help move him, maybe, just a little closer to his ultimate goal.

He had not yet finished his tea when Alexi, Demas's longtime administrative chief, entered the security foyer of the villa's private quarters, along with the visitor from the U.S. State Department, and pressed the buzzer signaling their arrival.

Using a remote, Demas unlocked the door. He gave a warm welcome to his guest, while Alexi simultaneously vanished from the room.

Strolling out onto the veranda, Demas made small talk with Mr.

Burke until he sensed that it was time for business. Then he jumped right to the point.

"I was very happy to hear that Secretary of State Danburg will be addressing our peace conference. Has he arrived?"

"He has. We traveled together. The accommodations are greatly appreciated. Secretary Danburg should be settled into his suite shortly after our security people complete their sweep."

"I was hoping to be able to get a sense of his remarks."

"We knew you would," Burke replied with a smile and handed Demas an envelope. "Here's a draft of his speech. I had the privilege of working on it with him. We're asking that it remain embargoed until thirty minutes prior to his remarks tomorrow afternoon."

"Of course," Demas said courteously. He understood the rules. He opened the envelope and began to scan the draft. After a minute, Demas looked up.

"There is a strong implication here," Demas responded tapping the printed speech with his finger, "that the United States might be willing to initiate a unilateral offer to share some of its weapons technology, in the hopes of obtaining what you refer to as 'the hope of universal deterrence.'"

"Yes, in the interests of peace," Burke replied. "Mr. Demas, the administration also wants you to know that we recognize the fact that you've been a good friend to the Corland administration. When the rest of the world was denouncing our use of the RTS weapon system, I know you consulted with U.N. Secretary General Beragund on our behalf. The secretary general's conciliatory remarks regarding the United States were deeply appreciated by President Corland. I am certain you played a primary role in making that happen."

"America is a key player in our hopes for global peace. Anything I can do to help, just ask. And yet ..."

The envoy from the State Department listened carefully for Demas to finish his thought.

"And yet," Demas continued, "if the United States is willing to seriously consider sharing its weapon technology with other nations, then the question remains ..."

"Yes?"

"Which weapons systems are we specifically referring to?"

"Of course, that's a key question," Burke replied, eyeing his host closely.

"For instance, would the United States be willing to share its RTS technology?"

For the next few moments there was dead silence. Burke's expression showed a lack of surprise. He knew where this was going. But he had to avoid jumping in too quickly. He was certainly not about to reveal any details about President Corland's willingness to negotiate an international credit-for-weapons trade.

Caesar Demas was a master at getting to the core of an issue, while maintaining a perfect poker-face demeanor. There wasn't an ounce of emotion on his face. Nothing to reveal just how important the RTS weapons system was to Demas's ultimate mission.

Finally Mr. Burke responded. "There may be the potential for dialogue on that subject, yes. Which is why we are bringing this subject up with you first. Rather than using the usual official diplomatic avenues of exploration, we thought we'd approach you directly. Here at the conference. As you can imagine, this is a tremendously sensitive issue."

"Yes, of course," Demas agreed. "Using the formal diplomatic methods between nations can be clumsy. And so very public. And if things don't work out ... it could be an embarrassment to your administration. With me, on the other hand, I can act as an unofficial envoy for your position. I can do some investigation regarding the sharing of the RTS system with those nations that could provide economic and trade assistance to the United States. I could test the waters ... find out its net value. I can work a lot of that through the U.N. And if my efforts fail, and the press gets a hold of it, … you can just denounce me to the media as some kind of nosey busybody!"

Burke and Demas shared a polite laugh. Finally the State Department official extended his hand to the billionaire. "I think we have an understanding," Burke said.

"At the same time," Demas added with a note of hesitation, "I am aware that the designer of the RTS system, a former Air Force pilot, is engaged in a dispute with Congress. A brazen act, if you ask me … refusing to divulge his design to his own government. Are you sure that the specifications for his weapon system will be available to share with other nations at some point?"

"That's just a minor issue. Joshua Jordan will be forced to comply. You needn't worry about that."

"Just one final suggestion," Demas stated as he walked his guest through the cavernous living room to the front door of the villa's private quarters. "I hope you don't consider me arrogant in saying this, but you may want to modify Secretary of State Danburg's speech slightly."

"Oh? How?"

"I would make your intentions at sharing weapons technology even more ambiguous. Not quite so obvious. That might give me more leverage in my private negotiations, behind the scenes. Just a thought."

Mr. Burke acknowledged the request with a nod of his head.

As soon as Burke was gone, Demas immediately placed a call to an ocean shipping office in the industrial harbor of Rotterdam.

□□□

A phone rang in the small import-export office tucked among the miles of shipping docks and mammoth industrial loading cranes that stretched along the Dutch coast.

Petri Feditzch, the office manager, answered the phone.

"It's me," Caesar Demas began.

Feditzch was a good soldier in Demas's small army. He knew better than to interrupt. He waited for his boss to continue.

"You need to inform the messenger that our project has to be delayed temporarily."

"Should I give him a timeline? How long does he wait?"

"You will tell the messenger," Demas elaborated, "a few days, at least. Perhaps longer. Maybe permanently. Tell him to hold until he hears further. Is that clear?"

Petri Feditzch hung up the phone and wiped his mouth. He lit a cigarette. He would delay the call until he had finished his smoke. Feditzch's background as a former member of the Soviet KGB made him a tough customer.

But even with that, he was not looking forward to the phone call he now had to make.

NINETEEN

"So, you told him ... Dad, I mean?"

"I did. Cal, he's your father. He has a right to know. You confided in me as your mother, and I'm glad you did. But your dad and I don't keep secrets from each other."

"So, whatever I tell you, you're gonna turn right around and tell Dad. Is that it?"

"Honey, God looks at your father and I as one. And you should too. That's just the way it is."

"Still, I don't understand why this has turned into such a big deal."

Cal Jordan was leaving the Demoss Learning Center at Liberty University with his backpack slung over one shoulder and with his Allfone plugged into his ear. In the distance he noticed Karen Hester with her friend Julie, crossing the campus. Karen spotted him and waved.

"Because you're in pain," Abigail Jordan replied firmly on the other end of the line. "That's always a big deal. If it hadn't been for the missile attack, we still wouldn't know you'd stayed in New York, would we? Besides, if it was such a minor thing, why'd you tell me?"

"I couldn't keep it in anymore. Missiles were flying. People were getting trampled. New York City was on every channel. And my father was the one right in the middle of the whole thing. *My father.* Not somebody else's. Mine! He's the big hero, but I couldn't even help a woman three feet away. I was frozen, scared to death. That's what I have to deal with."

"I know that had to be devastating —"

"It was ..."

"But just put yourself in your dad's shoes. He thinks you're safely out of the city during a horrible disaster, and then he finds out that you weren't, because you'd lied to us about where you were and what you were doing."

"So this whole thing is just because I didn't give you guys the straight scoop? That instead of leaving the night before for school like I told you, I went up to New York City to be with Karen instead. Okay, so I didn't tell you the truth. Look, I know Dad doesn't like Karen. And I knew he'd blow a gasket about the two of us spending an overnight in New York — even if we weren't sleeping in the same room. I just can't believe how this is becoming such a big deal —"

"Cal, you know I expect you to be truthful. Because you're my son —"

"Sure, yeah, okay —"

"But even more important than that. You're a Christian. You made the same decision to put your faith in Jesus Christ that I have."

"Of course —"

"And because you're a Christian, then truth ought to be a priority —"

"Fine ..."

"Isn't that right?"

"Yeah ..."

"And in the same way truth is a priority to me."

"Right, Mom. Fine."

By this time, Karen was just a few feet away. Cal put his finger to his lips to keep her from saying anything. Her response was to put one hand on her hip and flash a pretend display of anger, almost making Cal laugh.

"And your dad considers telling the truth a big deal," his mother continued.

"No kidding," Cal shot back.

"So, then your lying to your parents *was* a big deal after all."

Cal mouthed the words *my mom* to Karen.

"Yes or no?" Abigail repeated a little more forcefully than before. "Yes or no, Cal, your lying to us was a big deal after all ..."

"Mom, don't do the lawyer thing with me. It drives me crazy —"

"It's not a lawyer thing. It's a mom thing. Two very different things, Cal."

"Okay. So it was a big deal. I was wrong. Dad is ticked at me. Wow, there's something new ..."

"Cal, I want you to listen carefully to me. He loves you. Your dad loves you so much."

Abigail's voice caught a little. Cal could hear that. He could hear the tenderness. It was the thing he loved most about his mom. And yet he hated it when it happened. When her love and passion got to the breaking point and the tears would start filling her eyes. Now he was starting to get teary-eyed himself. Cal quickly turned away from Karen so she couldn't see.

"You are *so* important to him," Abigail said. She was pacing her words, forming them in her mouth with an exquisite kind of care. Her voice was slow and soft. "He'd lay down his *life* for you ..."

Cal didn't speak for a few seconds. Neither did his mother.

"It's just that ..." Cal was trying to sound sure of himself. After a few more seconds he continued. "It's just that he's always on my back — about everything, all day, every day, twenty-four-seven —"

"Cal, you're going to have to love him the way he is," Abigail added. "I do. He's a wonderful man. He wants nothing less than the absolute best for you. That makes him demanding, I know. But cut him some grace, Cal. That's something you ought to know about ..."

Karen had moved around Cal so she was facing him again. But this time no comic routine, no attempts to make him laugh. She could see what was in his eyes.

"Gotta go, Mom."

"Okay. Love you, Cal. So does Dad. Keep in touch. *Call* us ..."

Cal clicked off his Allfone, then looked at Karen.

"Sorry about that ..."

"Your mom?"

"Yeah."

"Sounded serious."

"Same song. Different melody."

"Oooh," she said breaking into a bright smile. "Nice metaphor. I thought *I* was supposed to be the music major and you were the art major."

He smiled and shrugged, then asked her if she wanted to catch a cup of coffee before the next class. Karen agreed and tugged at his arm as they walked together.

"So, anything you want to share?"

"Not really. Constant issues with my father."

"About New York?"

"Right."

"You in trouble?"

"Nothing I can't handle."

"Now you *do* sound like your father."

"How do you know? You only met him once — "

"Twice. Remember the football game? Up in the stands? We all sat together."

"The point is — ," Cal started to say.

"The point is," she said finishing the thought, "that maybe you are more like your father than you'd like to admit."

"So what, now you've switched from being a music major to a psych major?" he joked. Then he added, "Hey, I hope they've still got some

109

of those sugar donuts left. I'd love to have a couple of those with my coffee."

"Nice move, Mr. Jordan. Trying to blow me off. Changing the subject."

As they walked together to the student café, Karen could see Cal was thinking hard.

Finally he let it out. "So, I've got a question for you. A serious one."

"Okay," she said. "What?"

He paused for a moment and stopped. She stopped with him and tilted her head a little, studying him closely. Then Cal asked her.

"Exactly who would *you* be willing to die for?"

TWENTY

The reporter was having a hard time keeping up with her interviewee. The subject of her focus, an impeccably dressed middle-aged man who hailed from Pakistan, was walking at a fast clip toward the diplomats-only elevator inside the Davos Conference Center. The reporter was trying her best to get as many questions in as possible before Hamad Katchi disappeared into the elevator's sanctuary — beyond the reach of the press.

Twenty feet ahead, Katchi's executive assistant was holding the elevator door open for him.

"Mr. Katchi," the reporter continued, "you were at one time one the world's most notorious arms dealers. Supplying advanced weapons systems to a wide variety of countries, rogue nations, and terror groups — "

"Correction. I have never done business with terrorists," Katchi retorted with a smile. Now at the elevator's entrance, he paused, then turned. "Besides, I am now out of the weapons business completely — "

"I understand," she replied. "Still, there are many who believe your decision to align yourself with the Society for Global Change, the organization you cofounded with Caesar Demas, was to camouflage your past — "

"I am now fully committed to building peace, rather than expanding war," Katchi stated. "You may have heard the story already. How the death of my own brother was caused by one of the very same weapons systems that I had sold. Therefore, several years ago I chose to redirect my energies into humanitarian causes. Now, please, I am sorry, I have another commitment ..."

Katchi turned again and, along with his aide, stepped into the empty elevator.

Both of them were quiet until the elevator slowed to a stop and the doors hissed open.

Waiting for them in the small hallway was Caesar Demas, flanked by two plainclothes security guards. Katchi and his aide stepped out to greet him.

"Let's take a walk alone," Demas insisted and motioned to Katchi to follow him down the hall while the aide stayed behind by the elevator. Demas waved a finger toward the door of a restroom. Then he blew through the door with Katchi close behind. The two bodyguards quickly took a position to block the entrance to the men's room.

Demas and Katchi began perusing the bathroom, flinging open every stall door to make sure they were alone.

Then Demas walked over to the two hand dryers on the wall and punched them both on until the sound of their roaring filled the room.

He leaned over to Katchi and spoke directly into his ear.

"I have given the order for the messenger to stand down. At least temporarily."

"Really? I would have waited. I know your reason. You are banking on the U.S. caving in. Well, maybe they will. And maybe not. I think you should have put the messenger securely in place first before delaying his mission —"

"Why? So he could be poised to grab the RTS information first? Then bypass us and sell the data directly to someone else? Hamad, I thought you were smarter than that."

"Even if the United States decides not to share the RTS specifications, then, per our plan, our man will still be able to get his hands on the designs anyway."

"Yes," Demas replied, "but by that time I will have my own people in place around him to make sure he doesn't go rogue on us ..."

□□□

At that same moment, on the other side of the Atlantic, cars were stacked up in a long line at the Canadian-U.S. border. Those wishing to cross from Lacolle, Quebec, to Champlain, New York, could expect delays of up to forty-five minutes. The U.S. customs officers were carefully checking passports of all incoming drivers.

Behind the steering wheel of his rental car, the Algerian took a few moments to examine himself in his rearview mirror. He had Yergi Banica's passport open on the seat next to him. He glanced down at the passport photo and then up at his own face in the mirror.

It was a good match.

Zimler had grown a mustache to match Banica's. He had accomplished that even before he had murdered him. Funny, Zimler thought, that Yergi never even noticed the similarity before the zip cord was looped around his neck. Despite his academic prowess, Banica had failed to realize that his executioner had actually taken great pains to create a close resemblance. To complete his transformation into the middle-aged Romanian professor, Zimler had obtained a pair of spectacles and had tinted portions of his hair just slightly.

Now, all that was left was to slip through the border station without incident. And if that went well, then one of the world's deadliest assassins would be roaming free within the continental United States.

Zimler's Allfone started ringing.

He glanced down and saw the word "Restricted," but he didn't answer it. He had more important business right now. No suspicious movements. He was in plain view of the border guards with only two cars between his and the checkpoint.

No message was left on his Allfone. He muted the ringer.

Now just one car remained between Zimler and the border stop.

Zimler tuned the car radio to a French station playing classical music. He listened for a few moments, keeping the level down to a soothing volume. Had he heard this piece before? He thought it might be Debussy, one of his favorite composers. Perhaps it was the *Estampes* for piano. It was a pity, he thought, that the business of his "professional life" had frequently kept him from enjoying the truly finer things in life. Like the beauty and complexity of music.

But the music was not merely for pleasure. It would also help him focus. Lower his heart rate. Help loosen the facial muscles, creating a relaxed expression. Everything had to look normal.

His car was next. He pulled up to the window.

"Good afternoon," Zimler announced, confidently holding out the stolen passport to the U.S. border official.

The official smiled. Then studied the passport. Then he looked hard at Zimler. "What brings you to the United States?"

"I have always wanted to visit America," Zimler said in a polished Romanian accent. "Now is my chance. Business mostly. I will be studying some documents at Library of Congress for my research."

The border guard smiled but didn't take his eyes off Zimler. "May I ask why you didn't fly directly into the United States from Romania, Mr. Banica?"

"Well," Zimler said with a slight laugh, "the flight into Quebec was cheaper, of course, than direct flight to Washington. But if you want to know secret ... I have always wanted to see New England. I can catch a little of it coming in from northern part of state of New York while I drive. I just hope now I'm able to find gas station that has petrol ... you know, with your president's rationing plan ..."

The border guard smiled back and then handed the passport back to Zimler. "Have a good trip, Mr. Banica."

Zimler pulled ahead, through the U.S. border crossing station, leaving Quebec behind. He turned up the music on the radio.

I'm in.

A few miles down the highway his Allfone vibrated. Again, it said, "Restricted."

He turned down the music and clicked on the cell.

"I would like to speak to the messenger," Petri announced from the other end of the line.

In his Europoort office in Rotterdam, Petri Feditzch was flicking the end of another cigarette he'd just lit. He was looking out of the grease-streaked window toward the junction of the Rhine and Meuse rivers. He had decided to wait awhile before connecting with Zimler. Just in case Petri's superiors changed their minds and decided not to delay the project after all. Such an occurrence would have required making multiple contacts with Zimler rather than one. And that was something Petri wanted to avoid. His days with the KGB had taught him a few things about the more perverse side of human nature. Dangerous, unpredictable people must be managed in a simple manner. Unnecessary complexity, well, that was not a good thing — especially when negotiating with a sociopath like Zimler. Keep things straightforward. Predictable.

"Please, I must speak with the messenger," Petri repeated.

"Talk," Zimler responded.

"Is this the messenger?"

"If you are the exporter, then I am the messenger."

"Good," Petri said. "In that case I have a message for you."

There was silence.

"My superiors want you to delay the project."

There was more silence ... then an exhale of disgust.

"I don't like delays. I rarely tolerate them."

"I understand. But in this case, it is critical, I'm afraid."

"For how long?"

"I'm not sure."

There was another pause. The former KGB agent knew Zimler's seething anger was about to be directed at him.

"I am on a very strict timeline," Zimler snapped. "Cretans like you can't appreciate that."

Petri took another drag on his cigarette, then simply replied, "I was to deliver the message. I have done that. Your instructions are unequivocal. You must halt the project until you receive further instructions from me."

Zimler did not respond. Instead, he disconnected the call and turned the volume knob up on the radio.

As he drove, Zimler reached over to his briefcase and pulled out a file with one hand and laid it on the seat next to him. He flipped it open. Joshua Jordan's picture was there. Along with the other documents he had been given by the late Yergi Banica. There were also several new clippings about Joshua and the RTS controversy.

Zimler didn't need much time to ruminate on Petri's call. He would not delay his mission. He refused to be treated like a schoolboy waiting for the teacher to give him his next assignment. Who did they think they were dealing with?

He already knew exactly what he was going to do and how he would do it. Zimler glanced again at the picture of his target.

As he drove on, listening to the piano piece nearing its conclusion, a satisfied smile broke over his face.

Yes. He was right. It was Debussy after all.

TWENTY-ONE

Three blocks west of Market Street in San Francisco, not far from City Hall, two armed officers had just disembarked from their parked vehicle. Both were wearing dark blue jackets with the words *U.S. Marshal* emblazoned on the back in gold block letters. It was obvious that the senior officer, Deputy Marshal Jim Talbot, was less than enthusiastic about what he might end up having to do today.

This was the high-rent district of San Francisco's downtown area, and the building the two officers were standing in front of fit right in. Gazing up at the high-rise's smoked-glass-and-steel façade, they could guess that the interior was expensively furnished and filled with shiny chrome and polished marble, though neither officer had ever set foot inside. Talbot could only shake his head while thinking to himself, *What an absolute waste of taxpayer money.*

But it was the item centered directly over the building's exquisite glass entrance doors that had Talbot tied up in knots. Even though he'd seen the big globe-shaped blue symbol countless times before on the evening news, and once when he had passed by the world organization's well-known headquarters while visiting New York City, it still bothered him no end. The familiar olive branches, one on each side, embracing an outline of the world's continents in the center.

To Talbot, the whole thing seemed bizarre. To have this building with that logo right here in San Francisco. In his own city. How could this have happened?

The transformation of his home … his country … had occurred quietly … when no one was looking.

Just above the symbol were the words:

United Nations Monitor for Human Rights
California Division.

Talbot wanted to blurt out what was on his mind right then and there. *What was happening to America?* But he didn't. He was a man of honor. He loved the United States. And that meant he was duty-bound to enforce its laws. Including the unfortunate U.N. treaty that his beloved homeland had signed.

Talbot and his junior deputy strode in and introduced themselves to the woman seated at the receptionist desk. Above and behind her on the wall was a smaller replica of the same words and symbol that was featured prominently outside. She spoke with a distinctive but hard-to-place accent. The two marshals were there to see Chief U.N. Monitor Catalina Obreras, a lawyer from Spain. Her office, said the receptionist, was on the third floor.

Upon entering the U.N. chief's sanctuary, the walls of which were lined with photos of her posing with various heads of state from around the world, Talbot realized that Ms. Obreras was not the type of person he would ever associate with socially. Perhaps that had something to do with her job.

She had two copies of the report in question on her desk. After the obligatory introductions and pleasantries, she held one copy out to Talbot, who snatched it up.

"It's all here, Deputy Talbot," Obreras explained. "The original complaint against the Reverend Teddy Berne from three months ago. He was only issued a warning in the form of a written citation at that time and wasn't arrested. That was in accord with the U.S.-U.N. Compact of Protocol. As you know warnings are given for first-time offenses out of respect for your free-speech customs here in the United States. But despite being told to cease and desist, Reverend Berne has continued his illegal rantings and dangerous public displays. He is scheduled to hold a rally in about ten minutes here in the city. The location is on the front page of the report. In there you will also find the certification from the U.S. Department of Justice accepting the referral from us to prosecute Reverend Berne, which they have agreed to."

Talbot leafed through the papers until he came to the DOJ letter authorizing him to take the pastor into custody. The document stated Berne was the head of a group called the Foundation for a Christian America. It specified that Reverend Berne was being charged with a violation of the United Nations Covenant of Tolerance and Human Rights (UN-CTHR) as ratified by the U.S. Senate and signed by President Corland. The letter read:

> Reverend Theodore Obadiah Berne has repeatedly violated the UN-CTHR, section IV, subsection 6 (defamation of religion) as made a part of the laws of the United States by the act of the United States Senate, and as signed by the president of the United States. The said Rev. Berne has engaged in the unreasonable and offensive defamation of the religion of another in a manner subjecting such religion to contempt and tending to provoke, or threatening to provoke, the likelihood of a public disturbance; to wit, through public proclamations and communications that have denigrated the religion of Islam and its followers.

Deputy Talbot handed the paperwork to his partner and offered a rather unconvincing "have a nice day" to Ms. Obreras. He then turned on his heels and strode out of the U.N. monitor's office.

By the time the U.S. marshals pulled up at the Justin Herman

Plaza, Reverend Berne, who was standing on a small platform in front of the large fountain before a crowd of about two hundred, was in the middle of his speech.

And things were beginning to come unglued.

A small group of pro-Islamic protestors had just arrived on the scene, carrying signs that read "Stop the Christian Crusade against Muslims" and "Bye-Bye Bible Bigotry."

Talbot and his partner got out of their car.

At that same moment, one of the protesters decided to run over to the side of the stage and yank the plug on the PA. He then jumped onto the platform and charged directly at Reverend Berne. The reverend's assistant leaned in and blocked the assailant's path with his forearm, causing the attacker to fall. While down, the protester quickly removed one of his boots, then stood and smashed Reverend Berne's assistant in the forehead with its heel, causing him to reel backward slightly and fall to his knees.

Talbot watched as several San Francisco police officers, who were already on duty near the perimeter of the plaza, sprinted toward the stage with batons raised. Two of the officers jumped onto the platform and swung their batons down hard onto the shoulders and arms of Reverend Berne's assistant who was already down, while a third officer pulled the pro-Muslim attacker aside, scolded him, and simply ordered him to leave.

Berne began shouting to the officers to stop beating his friend. "You've got the wrong man!" he cried.

As Talbot and his partner neared the platform, it was all he could do to keep his angry thoughts to himself. *I ought to be out tracking down dangerous fugitives from justice. Not handcuffing some preacher and watching the local cops beat up innocent people.*

Talbot ordered the baton-wielding policemen to stop. "Stand down, officers. We'll take care of it from here." The two San Francisco cops reluctantly did as they were told.

"Are you Reverend Teddy Obadiah Bernes?" Talbot asked when he was in front of the preacher.

Berne wasn't surprised. He had expected it. He raised his head just a bit higher as he answered.

"I am."

"Sir, I am a United States marshal. Reverend Berne, you're under arrest for violating the Covenant of Tolerance and Human Rights."

Talbot's statement triggered an immediate chorus of boos from a small number of Berne supporters who were in the crowd, along with an equal number of cheers from the protestors. It was apparent, however, that this crowd was not about to become unruly. And for that Talbot breathed a sigh of relief. There was no need to alert the riot squad. The majority of those who had assembled to hear the preacher were merely curious and couldn't care less about the outcome. The show was winding down.

"God save the United States of America!" Berne bellowed to the largely disinterested crowd who were now starting to disperse. "May Jehovah save this country from the tyranny of the global lords and from the United Nations — and from the oppression of the San Francisco police force!"

Two hours later Berne was in custody after having been booked at the federal building. The reverend was allowed one phone call, but it wasn't to his lawyer. It was to a friend. And the friend called an associate who knew a retired Air Force general by the name of Rocky Bridger.

□□□

Within the hour General Bridger received a call on his Allfone. His fishing boat was just about to dock at Charleston Harbor along the coast of South Carolina. The man on the other end of the line explained what had happened to Reverend Berne.

The General listened intently as he waved to the marina master who was tying his boat off to the harbor slip. Bridger promised the caller he would look into it.

"I'm about to meet with some people who'll want to hear about this," he explained. "I know nothing about this Reverend Berne fellow other than what you just told me. I have no idea whether he's an honorable man or not. But let him know his case will not be forgotten."

After hanging up, General Bridger tapped in the number for his friend Joshua Jordan.

Joshua was mulling over some paperwork in his penthouse home office in New York when the phone rang.

"Josh, it's Rocky. I know we got a full agenda for the Roundtable, but I got something I'd like to throw into the pot."

"General, whatever it is, I'm sure it's worth discussing. How about sending out an encrypted email to all the members. Let them know what you've got."

"Okay."

"Abby and I are really looking forward to seeing you in Colorado. Maybe we can arrange to shoot eighteen holes at the club while we talk."

"Only if you give me a decent handicap. In fact, as ranking officer, I'll make that an order."

Joshua laughed. General Bridger was one of the finest men he'd ever known. Joshua had served under him when he was detached for a stint at the Pentagon, and he reported directly to him when he flew several secret U-2 missions over Iran, leap-frogging over military chain of command.

They said their good-byes, and Joshua pulled out his briefing book for the Roundtable. He flipped open to the cover page with the typed agenda. At the top he took his pen and handwrote, "Rocky Bridger's Concern."

Then he closed the notebook. Everything in him was indicating that the timing of his upcoming trip to Colorado and the subsequent secret meeting he would convene couldn't be better.

TWENTY-TWO

The White House,
Washington, D.C.
Mr. Joshua Hunter Jordan
1 Plaza Court Towers
New York City, New York 10004

Dear Mr. Jordan:

On behalf of the United States of America, I am extending my appreciation for the assistance you rendered during the North Korean missile crisis. Your cooperation during that dangerous time provided an important service to our country.

Sincerely,

Virgil S. Corland
President

Abigail was rereading the letter. It had been issued to her husband from the White House just days after the near-destruction of New York. She hadn't seen the document in a while, and she took the time to look closer at the gold-embossed seal at the top. It bore the familiar symbol of her country, the one with the eagle holding an olive branch in one claw and a host of arrows in the other — just like on the back of the one-dollar bill. Now, in light of the ferocious attack against her husband brewing in Congress, and the White House's recent lack of support, she was rereading the letter from a new angle.

"President Corland's thank you was really no thank you at all," she murmured to herself.

She leaned back in the seat next to her husband in their Citation X private jet. The sky was clear and cloudless as they winged their way from New York to Denver. As Abigail gazed out the window into the deep blue, she continued to contemplate everything that had transpired. Trying to fit it together.

"You say something?"

She turned and noticed that Joshua was studying her. She didn't realize she had spoken out loud. Joshua was now looking up from his thick file of work documents.

"Just thinking out loud, that's all."

Joshua dug deeper. "About what?"

"This ..."

She handed the White House letter to Joshua, who grinned. "So, you've been rifling through my file, I see."

"Just happened to see it among those papers you were working on."

"And?"

"I think Corland's thank you letter was pretty tepid. Overly cautious, especially considering that you had just saved the entire population of New York City from being incinerated."

"Yeah, well, not really," Joshua countered. "The real heroes were my tech team and the guys at the Pentagon and the crew of the USS *Tiger Shark* ..."

"All right, I understand. My husband, humble as ever. But my point is about the president's motives. Politics are all over this letter ..."

"Well, after all, he *is* a politician. Funny thing about politicians — you can always count on them to be political."

"But Josh, not like this," she argued, tapping a manicured nail on the letter that was now sitting on the top of his file. "Come on ... 'I am extending my appreciation for the assistance you rendered ...'? And what about the way they 'honored' you? A private little reception in the West Wing. Not the Oval Office. No press invited. Just the White House photographer. The president, the chief of staff, and, what, one or two reps from the Pentagon? That was it. They sent a little press release to the media late on a Friday afternoon. That's what they do in Washington when they want to bury a story. Which is exactly what happened. Josh, honey, you deserved better."

"I agree, Dad. You deserved *much* better."

Deborah was seated in the row behind them, listening.

"Wow, it seems I have a cheering section here," Joshua quipped.

His daughter reached over the seat and hugged his neck. "Forget the politicians, Dad. All the cadets at Point think you're great."

"Have them call Congress and tell them that, will you?" her father suggested with a half-smile.

"Deb, we're so happy you could come with us. I'm glad you had a break at the academy. Perfect timing. I bet you can't wait to ride your horse again," Abigail added.

"Yeah, it's been awhile. How is Sergeant Pepper?"

"Frank says he's doing fine," Abigail reassured. "So are the others. He just did the farrier work on their hooves. But I told him not to groom any of them. I knew you'd probably want to do that."

"Great. Hey, why don't we all go riding? All three of us?"

Joshua immediately gave Abigail "the look." She knew what it meant. He never liked being torn between family and professional commitments. But Joshua was a driven man, especially when he was at Hawk's Nest for one of his secret Roundtable meetings. Single-purposed. Focused like a laser beam on the agenda. This particular meeting was critical.

"We'll see," Joshua replied.

"Oh, I know that voice," Deborah responded, staring up at the ceiling of the jet. "It means 'Request denied. Stand down.'"

Abigail reached over and squeezed his arm. "Oh, Josh, let's try. It'd be wonderful. The three of us on the trail together again."

Joshua always found his two girls hard to resist. And they knew it. A smile beamed all over Abby's face as she stared at him. Joshua tried to keep it serious, but after a few seconds of absorbing his wife's radiance, he couldn't continue. And a smile started to form in the corner of his own mouth.

"All right. I'll make the time to do some trail riding with you. I promise."

"Great!" Deborah sat back in her seat and hooked her iPod to her ear but then stopped.

"Hey ... I heard the two of you talking about something in the airplane hangar before we took off ... something about security issues at Hawk's Nest?"

Joshua and Abigail gave each other a quick glance. Her father decided to address it.

"My lawyer, Harry Smythe, suggested we beef up security a little around the complex."

"Is there a problem?"

"Not really, Deb," Abigail cut in. "Just a precaution."

"A precaution about what?"

"Because of the leaked story about my testimony in Congress," Joshua added, "and all of the media coverage since then, most of it negative. He just thought it might be prudent. You know, just because there may be a few zanies out there that might want their fifteen minutes by showing up at our front door. That sort of thing."

"Hey, I've already taken combat fundamentals," Deborah exclaimed. "And I'll be studying security intelligence this semester. So as long as I'm around, you got no worries!"

There were chuckles all around. But then Deborah stopped laughing and got serious. "Dad, you didn't really say what you're going to do about security."

"Well, we've got Bill Lawrence," Joshua assured. "He's familiar with Hawk's Nest. Been there a couple years now."

Deborah wasn't impressed. "Yeah, but he's, well, he's getting pretty old. Isn't he retired?"

"Retired detective from the Denver police force," her Dad pointed out. "He's in great shape. Still got the steadiest hand on the rifle range I've ever seen. He puts me to shame."

"But, Dad, one guy?"

"And we've got our electronic surveillance. It's state-of-the-art. So, Deb, dear, I'm not worried about it. I think Harry Smythe was over-reacting. Lawyers are paid to be like that."

With that, Joshua looked over with a smirk at his wife. She smiled back and just shook her head.

Deborah gave up and went back to her music.

Joshua went back to his papers.

But a minute later, Abigail brought it up again. "Okay," she whispered, bending over toward her husband. "Just between us. What would be so terrible about increasing the security detail on the property?"

"Because it's not necessary."

"It's never necessary, until it's too late."

"You don't think between Bill and myself that we couldn't take care of things if a situation came up?"

"I'm not saying that."

"Well, what are you saying?"

"Just that, from the time Harry first brought it up . . . I don't know . . . a feeling I guess. Ever since the North Korean thing, you've become a kind of national target, that's all."

"Anybody who's unfortunate enough to make the national head-lines these days — for any reason — is eventually going to gain some enemies. That's life. Abby, listen to me . . ." He took her hands in his. "If I thought there was a risk, I'd do whatever I needed to do to protect my family. You know that. But I'm just not that concerned about what Harry said, that's all. Everything's under control. So, let's not worry about it, honey. Okay?"

Abigail felt the warmth and strength from the covering of his hands. There was security in his grasp. Abigail had always felt safe with Joshua. He was a man of immense courage in the face of danger. But this time it was different. She could feel it. A sense of dread she couldn't shake. As if, out there somewhere, unseen, clawing its way toward them, was some kind of unnamed threat. And because she couldn't put her finger on it, she hadn't shared it with Joshua.

In her own growing relationship with God, she had learned an important lesson whenever she was faced with the challenges of life that were breathtaking or scary. In those situations the options were pretty straightforward: either act with faith or be governed by fear.

Without knowing exactly when or why, she wondered whether she would have to face that choice.

TWENTY-THREE

"I have clearance to share this with you."

"Really?"

"Of course. You think I'm lying?"

FBI Special Agent John Gallagher wasn't taking any chances. So he asked again. "You sure?"

"Come on, John. What's going on?"

The look in Gallagher's eye clearly indicated that he wasn't kidding. CIA Intelligence Officer Ken Leary decided to probe a bit deeper. "Why so timid, John? It's not like you. Where's the bull-in-a-china-shop John Gallagher we all know and love?"

"Yeah, well, my supervisor's been breathing down my neck lately."

"You mean cardboard-cutout Miles Zadernack."

"Right. The guy who goes to bed every night wearing a starched white shirt and tie."

"What kind of trouble have you gotten yourself into?"

"Let's just say he doesn't approve of my interrogation techniques."

"Oh, man, I bet you didn't get the memo," Leary offered in mock seriousness. "Liberals are running the show now ... no more waterboarding the suspects."

That provoked a deep laugh from Gallagher. Leary was one of the guys in the intelligence community who shared Gallagher's cynical dark sense of humor. Somehow, laughter always helped to buffer some of the horrendous stuff they had to deal with on a regular basis. Occasionally, Gallagher would trek over to CIA headquarters in the New York Agency station to drop in on Leary. Gallagher exercised oversight on multiple investigations. But he also maintained a short list of a few special terrorism subjects that were his own primary targets. Some of whom he'd been tracking for years.

This time Leary had called him over to the Agency but hadn't said why.

"Okay, let's get down to business," Leary announced. "Seeing as you are still working counterterrorism, I thought you might be interested in this ..."

Leary laid a bulletin on the desk in front of Gallagher.

Top Secret Clearance Required

Bucharest, Romania: A body found in room 417 at the Athenee Palace Hotel in Bucharest has been identified as Dr. Yergi Banica. The Romanian professor of international studies at the University of Craiova has been a person of interest to the Agency. The cause of death was strangulation. Dr. Banica is reputed to have associated with persons also of interest to the Agency, including persons making inquiries into international weapons systems and designs. Banica was not an Agency asset.

"Okay. Mildly interesting," Gallagher reacted. "What else you have on this guy?"

"We've been tracking Dr. Banica's comings and goings. For the most part, just the usual stuff. Except there was one recent trip that was a bit odd. It seems our friend traveled from Bucharest to Glasgow. And from there to Iceland for a short stopover in Reykjavik. Then onto Quebec."

"And the reason for the journey?"

"None that we can determine."

"Okay, what am I missing?" Gallagher wondered. Had Leary called him across town just to go over the murder of a enemy informant?

"We've got a reliable autopsy protocol on Banica along with an estimated time of death. The ETD is important."

"Why?"

"Well, you know the old saying ... dead men don't fly," Leary quipped with a twisted smirk. "At least not in first class."

"You tracked his passport?" the FBI agent asked.

"According to immigration, customs, and the airlines, Dr. Yergi Banica was in the air sipping white wine and eating microwaved chicken fourteen hours after he was strangled to death."

"Any idea who's using his passport?"

"Not with any precision. We have some airport surveillance footage that shows a guy who was a pretty good Yergi Banica look-alike. Nothing close up."

"Why wasn't Banica's passport on a watch list?"

Leary gave an airy laugh, the kind you let out when something really isn't funny. "That's a long, complex, and very sad story. Needless to say, travel watch-list procedures are not foolproof. And just because the CIA thinks someone is suspicious doesn't guarantee that Homeland Security is going to agree. There are some rather intricate policy judgments involved."

Gallagher threw Leary a dubious look. So the CIA official made it simpler. "To put it bluntly, the Corland administration has dumped a truckload of politics on top of the intelligence and counterterrorism business."

"I get the picture," Gallagher remarked. "So, we've got someone, we don't know who, using Dr. Banica's passport — after he's been murdered. Your bulletin says the professor may have been consorting with some guys with an unhealthy interest in weapons. Okay, so maybe one of them was using his passport. Have anything else?"

"I can only give you this other thing on a verbal, no documents,"

Leary indicated. "This is Agency-only stuff, John. I'm treading on thin ice talking to you. So we're going to have to play a little Q&A. Now, I can't give you the answers. But nothing's stopping me from asking you the right questions."

"Always up for a challenge."

"Here we go. How many special terror subjects do you still have on your personal roster over there at the Bureau?"

"Okay, let's see." Gallagher took a few seconds. "Five. There used to be more, but the rest were either killed, apprehended, or are presumed to be dead."

"Five?"

"Right."

"And who's the number-one bad guy on your list?"

"They're all bad."

"Yeah, I know, but who's the baddest of the bad guys on your hit list?"

Gallagher looked at Leary. Leary looked back and smiled. Then Gallagher started to shake his head. He had to know.

"You mean Atta Zimler? Assassin-for-hire. Subcontract killer for Al-Qaeda, Hamas, Chechen rebels. Occasionally used by the old KGB, then flipped on a contract and turned around and killed some of them too. Did some murder projects for warring factions in Cyprus. Also skilled in intelligence theft, cyber crime, false identity. That Atta Zimler? Mother was Algerian, father was Austrian. Never caught. Never even close to being caught."

"Here's what we know. According to a single source of ours, one of Yergi Banica's contacts may have been Atta Zimler."

"So you think there's a connection between Banica's interest in weapons systems and his possible association with Zimler?"

"We don't know that."

Gallagher's eyes were starting to glaze over, and his brain was whirling. He leaned back in his chair with an agitated look. He stuck his finger in his ear, jiggled it around like he was trying to clear an air pocket, then brought his hands down to his lap.

"John, there's one more thing," Leary announced, breaking the silence.

Gallagher didn't talk. He didn't move.

"We have a trace of Banica's passport."

Gallagher still wasn't moving.

The last time it was scanned was at the Canada-U.S. border crossing at Lacolle, Quebec. Whoever's using it made entry at Champlain, New York."

Gallagher continued to process everything Leary was saying.

Leary tucked his head down a little bit so he could look Gallagher directly into the center of the pupils of his eyes and leaned forward.

"It means, John, that this guy, whoever he might be, is now inside the United States."

TWENTY-FOUR

Matt Christensen was trying hard to keep it together. With eighteen minutes of airtime still remaining, he knew he'd better get some control back. As the long-running host of *Crisis Point*, a talking-heads television/web simulcast, it was his job to help push the agenda forward while giving the impression that he was unbiased. And he was good at it. That's why he got paid the big bucks.

Last week's show had gone smoothly. The truckers had been marginalized exactly as the White House had wanted. Both of Matt's guests, a leftwing journalist and a liberal strategist, had, of course, been personally handpicked by Corland's press secretary. And the resulting program had served its purpose. But the ratings, along with the program itself, had been lackluster. There was no conflict. No reason to watch.

Today's show, however, was proving to be a different story altogether. Inside the Global News Network's New York studio, a verbal free-for-all had erupted. And while these types of scuffles could increase viewer numbers and ad revenue, if the agenda suffered, heads would roll. The same reliable guests from the previous week had already been booked. So the show's new exec, to spice things up a bit, decided to add a third guest to the mix. It would be his first and last mistake.

Matt had tried to discourage this young new producer from book-ing Patrick Forester because Patrick was … well, he was articulate. And he could hold his own under pressure. Despite a barrage of interruptions and constant ridicule from his opponents, the conservative strategist was able to fire off a couple of key points, even though he was outnumbered by a margin of two-to-one — three-to-one, if you counted Matt.

"Fifty-eight percent of the American people feel that Secretary of State Danburg's speech at the Davos peace conference went too far," Patrick announced. "They believe that America shouldn't be so quick to trade our RTS weapons technology with other countries. Fifty-eight percent! And that's using *your own* poll numbers! I imagine the numbers are in reality quite a bit higher."

Michael Kaufman, the journalist, shot back. "Whoa, hold on! So now you're claiming the polls are rigged?"

"The parent company that owns the very news service you work for, Mike, conducted the poll. And everybody knows you guys are nothing but a mouthpiece for the Corland administration. You guys wouldn't know how to conduct an unbiased poll if it snuck up behind you and bit you on — "

"All right, fellas. Let's try to calm down." Matt interjected. "Look, we don't yet know exactly what this weapons system can do. All we know is that we've had one test run during the New York City crisis, and it liquidated a North Korean ship."

"Yeah, and it created an international scandal," the liberal strategist added. "And a lot of unanswered questions. North Korea claims the ship was unarmed."

"Doesn't surprise me that you're gonna side with the Communists on this," Patrick quipped.

"Now wait a second. That was — "

But Patrick charged ahead like a bull pushing his way through the noise. "The Pentagon has confirmed that the North Koreans were the ones who launched two nuclear missiles. And it was good ol' American technology that was able to turn them around and send them back. The studio we're sitting in right now, along with many New Yorkers viewing this program, wouldn't even be here if it wasn't for the RTS system."

"That may be true," the journalist responded, "but the administration has released a statement to the Special Select Congressional Committee investigating this incident, stating that President Corland did *not* authorize the use of RTS during the crisis. His understanding was that our air-defense people at NORAD and NEADS would be taking those missiles down with conventional airborne intercepts."

But Patrick had an answer for that too. "If you recall, Mike, there wasn't enough time for that."

"Nevertheless, without notifying the White House and Congress, a defense contractor took the matter into his own hands. Now this same defense contractor is refusing to cooperate with Congress," Kaufman continued. "He's stonewalling. The American government has a right to know exactly how this system operates."

"The only reason this administration wants to know is so they can sell the technology to other countries, as Secretary Danburg so eloquently announced during his speech at Davos — "

"Hey, nobody said anything about selling anything, Patrick!" the liberal strategist shouted. "If anybody's trying to make money, it's your buddy Joshua Jordan, who's obviously holding out for the highest bidder — "

"Okay, guys, come on," the host interrupted. "Let's take a deep breath. This is a good time to take a break. When we come back, I want to talk about the real problem, in my opinion, the ethical repercussions of turning nuclear weapons back onto civilian populations. Because Joshua Jordan's RTS defense system will certainly lead to that. And I also want to discuss just who Mr. Jordan really is and why he's in the hot seat before Congress. Until he's more forthcoming, we're all going to remain in the dark. And in today's volatile world, that's never a safe place to be. We'll be right back."

ㅁㅁㅁ

The White House Press Secretary bolted out of the West Wing at a fast clip. He was heading directly toward the Oval Office.

Halfway there he was joined by the president's chief of staff, Hank Strand.

"Do you have a statement drafted yet?" Strand bulleted, a little out of breath as the two strode together like Olympic long-distance walkers.

The press secretary tapped his head and said, "I've got it all in here."

"Well you'd better get it down on paper for the president to read. And *stat*."

"I already know the basics of the line we're going to use. Secretary of State Danburg's speech was taken out of context. The administration has made no formal decision to trade RTS designs for international economic assistance. Then we quickly shift the focus off of the president and onto Congress. They need to exercise their congressional authority. You know, use the oversight committee's contempt powers to force Joshua Jordan to be forthcoming ... blah, blah, blah ..."

ㅁㅁㅁ

An hour later, Caesar Demas, who was back at his palatial, column-studded compound outside of Rome, received a phone call from the U.S. State Department. The message was cordial, but blunt ... and not surprising.

"Mr. Demas, we appreciate your offer to negotiate as a mediator between the United States and other key countries regarding the sharing of our RTS technology. But regrettably, we will have to decline your offer."

"I understand," Demas casually responded.

"As I'm sure you can appreciate, current political realities have rendered such a trade ... well, not feasible at this time."

"Yes. Too bad."

"Have a good day, Mr. Demas."

□□□

Five minutes later, Petri Feditzch got a call on his cell. He was just about to leave his industrial harbor office in the Netherlands and head into downtown Rotterdam for a late dinner.

Caesar Demas was on the line. "It's me."

"Yes, sir?"

"You know, Petri, I told the State Department to have that idiot Danburg avoid making it obvious in his speech about swapping the RTS for better international trade terms. But no, he wouldn't listen. So the poll numbers went south for the White House, and now they've got cold feet. It looks as if we'll have to get the RTS the hard way. We are returning to Plan A."

"And the messenger?"

"Tell him we are back on track."

"All right. I hope this is the last time we have to change course ..."

"Just deliver the message," Demas barked. "Considering your former KGB status, Petri, I am surprised at you. You are like a little girl. Are you afraid to talk to the messenger?"

Petri glanced into his rearview mirror to see if he was being followed.

"Not at all. My sole concern is for success of the mission."

"Fortunately, we didn't lose much time. Our man should be able to reach the target and retrieve the information without compromising the timeline."

"I would think so."

"Oh, and one more thing," Demas added.

"Yes, sir?"

"I would appreciate it if our messenger didn't leave a messy trail behind him."

"That may be a problem."

"And why is that?" Demas asked.

"Because creating a human mess is what he does best."

Demas couldn't argue with that.

"Fine. Just make sure he gets everything we need related to the RTS."

□□□

By the time Atta Zimler got the call from Petri Feditzch he was already driving a different vehicle and had left the highway. After heading down a deserted dirt road in a wooded area in northern New York State for a few miles, he pulled off and entered a fire lane that cut through the forest. He then drove a half mile into the woods before coming to the edge of a clearing where there was a peaty bog full of black mud. Before getting out, he stopped and looked at himself in the mirror.

Zimler had already shaved off his mustache, removed the spectacles, and dyed his hair red.

Then he climbed out of the car.

That is when his cell rang. He clicked on the cheap, untraceable InstaAllfone that he had picked up at a local gas station and answered the call while popping the trunk of the car.

It was Petri. "The boss says the mission is a go. Exactly as planned. You can start up again."

Zimler had to smile at that. He had only one thing to say. "I never stopped."

He clicked off the call and stuffed the Allfone in his pocket.

Then he lifted the trunk of the car and reached in. Grabbing a big, heavy burlap sack, Zimler lugged it out of the trunk and tossed it to the ground. The resulting thud would likely be considered sickening to most people, but it didn't bother Zimler in the least.

He then snatched a box of lime from the trunk.

The Algerian opened the burlap bag and looked in.

Inside, staring blankly up at him, was his latest victim, wearing the final grimace of death on his face. He was the owner of the car that Zimler was now driving. The assassin methodically poured the lime into the bag, added a few bricks, then tied it shut and dragged it over toward the edge of the bog.

He then hoisted the bag containing the body over his head like a weightlifter, took a few tottering steps forward, and tossed it out into the deepest part of the swamp.

The bag hit the watery bog and floated on top for just an instant. Then it quickly sank into the muddy black ooze, disappearing entirely from sight … hopefully forever.

TWENTY-FIVE

Abigail had had to ask herself whether some dark secret might be lying just under the surface. She knew her friend Darlene well enough to know that she seemed to be carrying some great weight on her heart that morning as they drove together. While their husbands prepared for the first day of meetings of the clandestine Roundtable group, the two women had driven to Aspen for lunch. The idea had been Darlene's.

Abigail was several years younger than the round-faced Darlene. The two had known each other for nearly a decade and had initially met through their husbands. Darlene was married to Judge Fortis Rice, a former Idaho State Supreme Court justice. He was a charter member of Joshua's Roundtable.

As a longtime resident of Colorado, Abigail had traveled through that fashionably rustic little village more than a few times. She privately didn't care for the celebrity-conscious, Beverly-Hills-of-the-Rockies atmosphere of the famous ski resort, which was home to a number of Hollywood stars and even a Saudi prince. But Darlene had never been there and wondered if they could go. Abigail said she would be happy to take her and agreed to do the driving. They would travel in the little yellow Jeep for the daytrip, the one that Darlene thought looked so cute, which the Jordans kept year-round at Hawk's Nest.

As they sat down together at the crowded outdoor café for lunch,

Abigail wondered if Darlene may have arranged their day together so she could open up about whatever it was that had her in its grasp. But Darlene wasn't ready just yet. Instead, she was busy cracking jokes about the Aspen society: the trendy Labradoodle mix of designer dogs being walked past their table by the locals, and the wealthy chic women wearing artfully ripped blue-jeans and eight-carat diamonds strolling by and swinging their Prada bags.

Darlene had Abigail laughing and enjoying herself. But as Abigail studied her friend, she saw it. A sadness just beneath the surface of Darlene's humor.

They continued to pick their way through their salads while chatting about nothing in particular. Darlene had ordered a huge chef salad while Abigail had fancied the lean "Aspen Forest Special," which consisted of a bowl of greens garnished with nuts and fruit.

Darlene finished a bite, glanced over at her friend, and shook her head. "Oh, you're still so good with calories. Look at me. I've loaded up with all this ham and cheese. And I forget to order the low-cal dressing ..."

"Darley, don't be so hard on yourself. Just chalk this up to a little celebration. Two chick-friends doing lunch. It's really been too long ..."

"Not since New Year's Eve."

"We've got to get together more often. I mean it, Darley ..."

Suddenly Darlene got very quiet. She looked at her salad and listlessly stirred the lettuce for a moment. She then sighed, put her fork down, and rested her chin on her folded hands.

"You know Abby, I used to think you were a friend ..."

Darlene paused. Abigail wondered what was coming next.

"But now I think of you as my *dearest* friend."

Abby blushed a little and reached across the table for Darlene's hand. She squeezed it while Darlene continued.

"We don't see each other but, what, maybe twice a year on average. And lots of phone calls in between, of course ..."

Abigail smiled at that.

"I feel I can really share anything with you ..."

Now Abigail was waiting.

But then Darlene suddenly darted off course. "You look so fit, Abby. You must still be jogging?"

"I try to. Our schedules have become impossible lately. It's hard to stick to the routine with everything that's going on ..."

"I know. Fort and I have been following how the media has been going after poor Josh over this missile crisis. What a mess this country's in."

Abigail nodded and smiled, but she knew Darlene was just dancing around the issue now, whatever it was.

"I bet there's been a lot of pressure on the two of you," Darlene continued.

"There has been. But funny enough, I feel so close to Josh lately, despite the tension and stress."

"Hmm, stress ..." Darlene repeated the word with almost a kind of whimper.

"But on the other hand, I know of so many other folks who have it much harder than we do," Abigail offered with a gentleness in her voice that unexpectedly caught her friend off guard. Darlene quickly covered her mouth with her hand as her eyes began to fill up. It took nearly a minute before she could collect herself and respond. When she did, her voice was noticeably trembling.

"I will never forget how you helped me through Jimmy's death. It's one of those things that a mother doesn't ever let go of. So many questions. How could my perfectly healthy twenty-five-year-old die like that from an aneurism? No warning. No symptoms. A call from his friend ... they were playing basketball at the Y. 'Jimmy collapsed,' he said. Your whole life changes in an instant. From one phone call."

"I'm just glad I could be there for you," Abigail reassured. "And I'm still here."

"I tried to talk with Fort about it. But you know him; he sort of retreats into himself. I don't blame him. It's just the way he is. I know he was devastated. I still wonder whether all of that contributed to his heart problems. And ever since he had to retire from the bench it's been ... well ... *interesting* at home, and not in a good way."

Darlene paused. She was getting closer. Abigail let her friend continue.

"So I've had to cope as best as I can. Find my own little methods to live with all of this. Funny how when you're younger you don't really fear much. Then you start losing things, losing people you love, and suddenly you're afraid of everything. So you do whatever it takes to put one foot in front of the other, maintain your balance."

As she stared off into space, her hands were now on the table, and her fingers were gracefully moving in a rhythm, as if she were strumming some tiny, invisible guitar.

Then, abruptly, she sat straight up and began looking around. "Where is it? Where's my purse?"

There was a look of panic on Darlene's face.

Abigail spotted it under her chair and reached down to pluck it up. Darlene thrust her hand over the table to grab the purse. As she did she inadvertently knocked her purse out of Abigail's hand and down onto the table where the contents spilled out.

Including a dozen prescription pill bottles.

Abigail picked up one of the bottles. Then another. And another. They all read *Diazepam.*

Abigail recognized what it was.

"These are all valium ..."

Darlene reached out to grab them and stuff them back in her purse. She was trying to look unruffled. But it wasn't working. Her hands were trembling, and she accidentally dropped several of the pill bottles on the floor once again. Abigail quietly helped her pick them up and placed them on the table.

Then she reached over and squeezed Darlene's hand. "Okay, friend. You're dealing with a lot, aren't you?"

Darlene was struggling to crack a joke about her moment of embarrassment with the pill bottles. She tried to smile and started to speak, but she couldn't, at least for a moment or two. She glanced around nervously at the other café guests while her chin trembled and the tears started rolling down her cheeks.

Finally she summoned the strength to speak. "Okay, Abby. Now you know. My nasty little secret. This is how I cope."

"That's a lot of valium, Darley ..."

Darlene nodded. "I have three different doctors. In three different cities. All of them prescribing. I don't think they know about each other. Although two of them know about Fort, and because of who he is, they don't ask a lot of questions. So I triple-dose. I'm using this to exist, Abigail."

"And?"

"And I find that I can't live without it. Literally. I can't give it up. God help me, I've tried to stop. But whenever I quit, fear and anxiety start to suffocate me. I can't breathe. Can't sleep. I can't even begin to tell you how terrible it is."

"Does Fort know?"

"I don't think so. He knew I was taking some medication right after Jimmy's death to relax but that's about it."

Abigail thought about the next question she wanted to ask her friend. She knew it might sound a little brusque. But it was necessary. So she decided to move ahead.

"I am asking this only because I care about you, Darley. But I was wondering, why did you decide to share this with me?"

Darlene shrugged and slightly shook her head.

For an instant Abigail feared that she had offended her friend. But then Darlene spoke up.

"I suppose, I don't know … maybe I thought you were one of the few people who wouldn't judge me but who would be honest with me."

"Honest about what?"

"My, uh … you know …"

"I'm listening …"

"Okay. My addiction. Fine, I said it. I'm totally dependant on my pills to survive. Please don't hate me for this …"

"Darley, of course not. I love you like a sister. But what are you going to do about it?"

"I don't know. Maybe you've got some advice. I've run out of answers. I'm just surviving from one minute to the next. Just barely."

"Look, I'm glad you confided in me. I'm no expert. But I know a little about addiction. Back when I was practicing law full-time I had a few clients dealing with similar issues. And I know enough to know that your willingness to admit you've got a problem is the first big step."

"That's good to hear …"

"The next step is to find a place that is discreet, where counselors can help you to kick this thing. I can help you look for a good rehab center."

Darlene was weeping gently.

Abigail continued, "You're also going to have to talk to Fort about this …"

"Abby, he's going to be devastated …"

"But he loves you, Darley. I'm sure he'll support you. But there's one more thing, an even more important step …"

Just then the waitress walked by. Darlene glanced at the last pill bottle on the table, snatched it, and quickly thrust it back into her purse.

She then looked up at Abigail through her tears and asked, "An even more important step? Like what?"

"You said it yourself."

"I did?"

"Yes. When you said the words *God help me* ... I believe He can and He will. If you let Him. God's in the business of fixing people."

Darlene's face relaxed into a mildly surprised look. As if she had just been told something she assumed she had known all along but now realized she had never really thought about.

PART TWO
When the Lion Tells the Story

In less than a generation, the five intertwined media corporations have enlarged their influence in the home, school, and work lives of every citizen. Their concentrated influence exercises political and cultural forces reminiscent of the royal decrees of monarchs rejected by the revolutionists of 1776.

Ben H. Bagdikian, Pulitzer Prize – winning journalist

The media can determine foreign policy, and it can help to win or lose wars. It can bring about recession, or it can bolster confidence in the economy. In short, we live in a dictatorship of the media. It controls what we know, what we think, and what we buy. It is not Big Brother we have to fear as much as it is Citizen Kane. And if we are to be really free, we must lift the veil that blinds us.

Tom Neumann, publisher,
The Journal of International Security Affairs

By contrast, in the case of the BBC and CNN, you are explicitly aware that rather than presenting the world as they find it, those channels are taking a distinct side — the left-liberal internationalist side — in an honest and fundamental debate over foreign policy.

Robert D. Kaplan, "Why I Love Al Jazeera,"
The Atlantic (October 2009)

TWENTY-SIX

Jerry Hendrickson was pacing back and forth like a hamster in a cage. It was one of those cold-sweat moments.

As desk manager for the Global News Network's Los Angeles studio, Jerry had just finished reading the thick transcript of congressional testimony. It was stunning. Now he was on the horns of a dilemma. He glanced at his watch. Bob Kosterman, the executive vice president of the network, should have left his private lunch in Washington with Vice President Tulrude at the Executive Mansion about five minutes ago. Jerry was scheduled to call Bob right about now, while Kosterman was alone inside the limo furnished by the administration and being driven back to the airport.

So he did. Three rings. Then Kosterman picked up. Jerry didn't waste any time.

"Mr. Kosterman, I've read through this transcript of Joshua Jordan's testimony in front of the congressional committee. I think we have an explosive issue here."

"Explosive. Yes, no pun intended." Kosterman was chuckling at the play on words.

"Right. Well, I think we've been casting this whole story in a slightly ... uh ... *misdirected* fashion. This Jordan guy is not squeezing the Pentagon for a better business deal. Not at all. It says right here the real reason he's reluctant to disclose all his research on the RTS design is —"

But Kosterman wouldn't let him finish. "Jerry, are you accusing your own network of creating a false story?"

"Uh, no, sir."

"Did GNN commit actionable defamation? Is that what you are saying?"

"No, sir, but — "

"You've read the transcript?"

"Yes, sir."

"And it was delivered to you anonymously?"

"Absolutely."

"A transcript from a closed congressional committee investigating high-level national security issues? You realize how much trouble we could be in if we publish that?"

"But Mr. Kosterman, we published that original leaked report from the committee about Jordan defying Congress. And it now appears that the slant of the story as we reported it was all wrong — "

"No, it wasn't. You said yourself we didn't create a false story."

"Well, not intentionally, no. But it appears now that the accuracy of — "

"Jerry. Do not — I repeat — do not put anything from that transcript on our web-news service. Anywhere. At anytime. Is that clear?"

"Yes, sir."

"And deliver that transcript immediately to my executive assistant. And don't make any copies."

After Jerry hung up, he had that rolling seasick feeling of regret again. It was happening more and more lately. He had been in the television industry for twenty-two years. Long enough to have seen how the media business had turned rotten, like spoiled bananas complete with fruit flies hovering around. And he knew why.

Jerry was there back during the 2009–10 transition when all of America's television stations, responding to the requirement of the federal government, had to convert from the old analogue signal system to a digital format. From a technical standpoint, that one made sense and seemed to work reasonably well for the consumers. So when several years later a second media "conversion" was ordered by the U.S. government, most Americans weren't too upset. They had seen it all before. Of course, at the time, some media watchers and pundits had warned about the potential for an ugly monopoly developing after that media transition. Jerry agreed.

Most of the politicians didn't see it — or didn't want to — so Congress failed to act. After all, the public had been assured that the conversion of all TV and radio broadcasts over to Internet delivery would result in spectacular, new entertainment options. Viewers would still have the convenience of watching on their big, flat-screen monitors, but once television and radio were switched over to the web, the average American would have a banquet of fantastic features. If John and Jane in Lansing, Michigan, were watching a TV movie about the Lincoln assassination, they could pause the program and do a Google search on their screen about Abe Lincoln's death — all from the comfort of their easy chairs. Or if the crowd at Casey's in Boston were watching the World Series on the television screen, they could mute the sound and pull up the audio of a favorite radio sportscaster from any station in the country — on that same television set and get his take on the game. Besides, the government said it needed to commandeer the old-fashioned "over the air" broadcast spectrum that TV and radio had used for decades so it could be used for other purposes, like emergency services and large transmissions of high-speed technical data to federal agencies, contractors, and industries.

Few people saw what Jerry and other media veterans saw coming. But most of the media insiders like Jerry found it easier to keep their mouths shut. After all, he had a family to feed and a job to keep.

By that time almost all of the nation's newspapers and magazines too had fled to the Internet. The print-publishing world had been facing financial ruin, so going electronic was a matter of survival.

Television and radio had converted to a single Internet-based system of transmission; all forms of national news and information had now been transferred over to a single platform: the web. It was as if every media company had booked a ticket for themselves onto the same ocean-going cruise ship. But few people had asked the right questions: like who were the pilots of that vessel, and where was it heading?

Jerry and some of his cronies in the industry could see how it could become a ship of fools. The news conversion to the Internet had created the open door for a monopoly over all news and information that could be exercised by a few huge telecommunications companies.

And he didn't miss, either, the effect of the international takeover. Foreign nations used cleverly disguised sovereign wealth funds to buy up a controlling interest in America's news networks and the telecoms during the national economic crisis. Jerry would overhear Bob Kosterman's secretary telling him that the big investors from Paris, Moscow, Beijing, or Bahrain were on the line. He knew it wasn't just about finance. How could it not seep into the decisions that were being made about what news and talk programs to pull and which ones to keep? The same scenario was happening in every other TV network. And the radio syndicates too.

And as for Bob Kosterman's edict about deep-sixing the truth about the Jordan testimony, well, he knew his boss would never go against the flow.

Jerry mouthed to himself the two words he knew were behind what had just happened.

Jessica Tulrude.

□□□

In the mountains of Colorado, the members of the Roundtable were taking a break, milling around in the massive meeting room of Joshua Jordan's Hawk's Nest Ranch, grabbing sandwiches and drinks off the twenty-foot-long split-log sideboard. The large wrap-around windows

gave a stunning view of the Rocky Mountains and a sweeping pan-
orama of valley down below, full of deep green sagebrush and juniper
trees, and a twisting river that ran down the middle.

Judge Fortis Rice, a tall, thin man in his fifties, was standing in
front of one of the large plate-glass windows with his hands in the
pockets of his Western-cut slacks, looking out.

"Josh, I never get tired of looking at that view of yours. Do you?"

Joshua Jordan shook his head and smiled. "Never."

People who visited his two-hundred-acre ranch often asked such
questions. Although he didn't show it, it actually made Joshua feel uncomfortable. It was almost as if they were asking if Joshua was content
when he was here. And, of course, he wasn't. He was restless. Despite
his splendid varnished-log mansion, where there was always a faint
smoky scent from its many fieldstone fireplaces and running jokes
about the big grizzly bearskin on the wall, about who really killed the
beast as it unexpectedly charged his hunting party, whether it was
Joshua or his buddy and ranch security chief, Bill Lawrence. They
had both fired simultaneously, and both were shooting identical Winchester Big Bore 94s, so the issue was never settled. Here was a place
that spoke to Joshua's soul more than any other place on the globe. A
place full of good memories of family and friends. A spot seemingly
away from the business decisions that forever badgered and consumed
him.

Yet he was never really at peace. Even when he was here.

"It truly is beautiful," Fort continued. "I've told you about the little
place Darley and I have on the lake in Idaho. Nothing like yours, mind
you. But I think I know a little about how you must feel when you're
here. I keep forgetting to bring pictures of our cabin ..."

"How's Darley doing, Fort? I know that Abby was looking forward
to spending the day with her."

"Well, she's never been to Aspen. It was nice of Abby to put up with
her insistence to see the place. Though for the life of me I don't know

why she wanted to go. Maybe to get as far away from the Roundtable as possible. I wonder if she thinks we're just way too serious at these meetings, you know, all-business ..."

Then Judge Rice turned away from the window abruptly, like he had just remembered something. "But no, Darley is doing fine. Just fine."

Halfway through lunch, Joshua brought the meeting back to order, and everyone sat down back at the long oval table, which was large enough to seat all fourteen members of the Roundtable.

As founder, Joshua was the permanent chairman. The Roundtable was comprised of five subgroups each with a separate focus and chairperson. Each subgroup had one or two additional associate members.

Judge Rice was the chairman of the law group. General Rocky Bridger headed up the national defense unit. The chairman of the media group was silver-haired Phil Rankowitz, a former television network president, current chairman of a satellite network, and founder of several experimental "new media" companies.

Beverly Rose Cortez, was in charge of the free-market business subgroup. Hers was a Cinderella story. At only twenty, she had developed her own clothing and jewelry line for a small single store in New Mexico. She then branched out with several high-end stores throughout the state a few years later. When her company finally went public, her controlling interest skyrocketed to nearly half a billion dollars. She was now on the boards of several Fortune 500 companies.

The political unit of the group was headed up by former U.S. Senator Alvin Leander, a short, fiery man who often spoke with a brutal kind of bluntness, who was familiar with the inner workings of the Washington beltway like few others.

The men and women of the Roundtable met regularly, at least quarterly and sometimes more often, usually at Joshua's Rocky Mountain ranch but occasionally at a few select, conveniently centralized hotels.

They were all accomplished in their respective fields. But there was another more important thread that bound them tightly together.

After opening the afternoon session, Joshua turned things over to General Rocky Bridger, who said, "You all have the email I sent to you regarding the arrest of the preacher in San Francisco. There have been numerous incidents like this involving the enforcement of the international treaty of tolerance that America has been roped into. It's sickening, frankly. Judge Rice, I know you can update us on the legal side of things. But from my standpoint, it's another in a continuing series of attacks on our national sovereignty. The mere thought of U.N. officials with offices right here in America singling out citizens of a particular religious persuasion and reporting them to the federal authorities so they can be arrested. This is not the America I fought for. I know nothing about this preacher. But we have got to do something. Isn't this why we started this group in the first place? To try to take back the United States of America from those who are auctioning off our freedoms for international trading terms that lets us buy more cars from China while our own workers are out of jobs here at home."

Judge Rice weighed in. He was by nature a calm man. His excitement over such matters wasn't reflected in his demeanor but in the intensity of his ideas. "I've been in touch with a few legal organizations fighting these tolerance-related treaty cases. Unfortunately, there isn't any good news. In one case, a federal district court presided over by Judge Anne Plymouth ruled that the First Amendment takes precedence over the treaty. Sad to say, her decision was overturned by the U.S. Court of Appeals. That terrible precedent was then cited by another trial judge in Boston where a radio commentator was arrested for criticizing a local Muslim caliph and cited for violating that treaty. So, ladies and gentlemen, as the saying goes, I'm afraid we're on thin ice, and there's an early thaw coming. This all started with a resolution from the U.N. Human Rights Council back in March of 2009. It picked up steam over the years. Nation after nation signed on. And finally our Senate, urged on by our good president, signed it too."

Alvin Leander was ready to explode. "When is the Supreme Court going to resolve this travesty? If I was still in the Senate, I'd vote to move their chambers outside onto the sidewalk until they took one of these cases up for review—"

"The Supreme Court is not going to help us," Judge Rice replied calmly. "The two most recent appointments made by President Corland both favor international law. The globalists now hold a majority in the high court. They would likely affirm the treaty and adjust the meaning of the First Amendment accordingly. At least when it comes to the treaty's defamation of religion section. The court has already stated that crimes allegedly involving intimidation, even if it's just a matter of verbal or written expression with no violence, don't have protection under Freedom of Speech and Free Exercise of Religion. The language is already there from previous court decisions. I've been watching this happen for a while …"

Beverly Rose Cortez likewise had had enough. "This is simply outrageous. That a person cannot speak out about his own private religious beliefs … no matter what they are. And since when can't we as Americans speak our minds about the religious beliefs of others? So I suggest we consider fighting these cases. I will personally pledge a million dollars for the legal defense of this preacher fellow, whoever he is …"

Several other members began chiming in. Then…

"We're missing the forest for the trees, people."

It was Phil Rankowitz. He had been listening intently. Always the pragmatist, he had a scalpel-like ability to cut through to the heart of the matter. He took off his reading glasses and tapped them on the table to quiet the group. "We're missing it. Sure this is outrageous. And I could name a dozen other disgraceful crimes against common sense that are being committed by our government right now. Major infringements to our liberties as Americans. The slow, steady devolution of our nation into a socialist country that is becoming just an amalgam of one big global state. Every one of us could name similar atrocities. Things that would have burned into the hearts of our founding fathers and mothers and incited them to action just as surely as the revolution that actually occurred. But all of that is still missing the point."

"So what is the point, Rankowitz?" Alvin Leander's face was turning red.

"It's the old African proverb," he replied quietly.

"The what?" General Bridger asked.

"The proverb. It goes like this: 'When the lion tells the story, the lion always wins.'"

"More wisdom from the high lama of media," Leander muttered under his breath. The group broke into polite laughter.

"Well, laugh if you like," Rankowitz said, "but the fact is, whoever controls the vehicles of communication controls the message. And in a country where we still have a few remaining vestiges of a republic left, an informed electorate is a powerful tool of liberty. On the other hand, a misinformed public is a pretty dangerous commodity."

"So Phil," Ms. Cortez asked. "What do you suggest?"

"I move that we put our entire focus on one thing right now: our long-awaited media project. We've got to break the monopoly of silence that the big media conglomerates have enjoyed ever since all the news went digital. As a news guy, I can tell you this: the damage that is done by media's sins of commission, such as the wrong facts, skewed information, and biased reporting, can be devastating. But as bad as that is, it doesn't hold a candle to the real threat: journalistic sins of omission. Leaving the truly important stuff on the editing room floor because you simply don't want the people out there to find out about it."

"Is the timing right?" Judge Rice inquired.

"It couldn't be better," Rankowitz announced. "Josh, the media has tied you to a whipping post over this RTS situation in Congress. Twisting the facts. Making you look like a weapons huckster going after the fast buck rather than the patriot we know you are. Okay, that's their sin of commission. But will they allow your side of the story? No. So that's also their sin of omission. And that's where our revolutionary AmeriNews idea comes in. Our media group has the pieces in place. The tech guys have the kinks worked out. We're ready to load our news service onto every Allfone in America. We've got the investment capital. We've got the satellite service. World Teleco is willing to sign the contract. All we need is the green light from you folks here at the Roundtable."

"Josh, you've been pretty quiet on this discussion," General Bridger remarked.

"I was just thinking," Joshua replied. "I told my lawyer I wanted to go to court to do something about this attack against me. He told me that we had almost no legal avenues to retaliate against the leaking of this disinformation. At least none that would be successful. And he was sure that a lawsuit against the media for defamation simply wouldn't fly."

Joshua stopped for a moment and collected his thoughts. Then he concluded.

"On the other hand, just think about the importance of communication to the cause of freedom and national security in American history. The committees of correspondence leading up to the Revolution. The pony express during the westward expansion. The telegraph during World War I. Folks, I think it's time for us to join the ranks of those who came before us. It's time for our own revolution!"

TWENTY-SEVEN

In the north wing of the twelve-bedroom ranch lodge, Joshua and Abigail had their own private quarters and master bedroom. There was a terrace off their bedroom that opened out to a vista of the valley during the day and a canopy of stars embedded in a black sky at night.

After a long day they sat, side by side, rocking ever so gently on their matching rocking chairs. Joshua was taking gulps from a bottle of water while Abigail sipped a cup of herbal tea. She broke the silence in a soft, almost reverent voice.

"Is that the Milky Way?"

"Yeah. It looks like a trail of diamond dust across the sky."

"Could you navigate using only the stars? I mean, if you had to?"

"We were taught to do that in flight school. I'd like to think I still could."

Then Joshua turned toward his wife with a funny look on his face. "After all the years we've spent sitting on this porch looking up at the stars, why is this the first time you've ever asked me that?"

Abigail had to think for a moment. Then she answered with a smile. "I don't know. Just occurred to me, that's all."

Then after a beat she added another thought. "Astrologers say our lives are wrapped up in the stars. Which I think is a bunch of malarkey. But I do think that God set the stars in the sky for a reason. Don't you?"

"And that reason would be ...?"

She took a second before she answered. "Well, the Bible says the heavens declare the glory of God ..."

"Sounds reasonable."

"So, then you agree with the Bible?"

"No, I'm not saying that. Not exactly."

"Then what?" she asked, probing a little further.

"Just that when you say it, it always sounds reasonable. And I know better than to debate with a lawyer!"

She had to chuckle at his dodge. Then she continued. "Anyway, you'd be surprised at the number of grown people I run into who still read their horoscopes every day. Darley said she does."

"How are things with her?"

"She's having a harder time than I thought."

Abigail was struggling over how much to tell her husband, but she needed to share this with her soul mate. "Something came up today when we had lunch."

"From Darley?"

"Yeah. Some personal stuff."

"Like what?"

"She's still grieving over Jimmy."

"I think about Fort and Darley losing their son like that. Bam, out of nowhere. Just when Jimmy was beginning his life as a man. I don't think a parent ever gets over something like that."

Then Joshua screwed the cap back onto his water bottle and prodded a little. "You said it was related ..."

Abigail decided just to lay it all out. Her husband needed to hear it. Not only because Darley and Fort were friends, but because Joshua and Fort worked so closely together with the Roundtable.

"Darley really struggled with guilt after Jimmy's death. She couldn't let go of the idea that there was something she should have done to protect him. Her doctor prescribed an anti-anxiety medication because she was having such a hard time sleeping. First it was just one pill; then that wasn't enough and she would take another. Then she decided she needed more. So she went doctor shopping. To three separate doctors. Now she's constantly dosing on valium. This has been going on since her son's death. Josh, she came right out and admitted she's addicted to prescription drugs. She says she can't get through the day without taking something."

"Oh, boy. Poor Darley. Does Fort know?"

"Not exactly. Although it may be what the law calls deliberate indifference."

"You make it sound like he doesn't care."

"No, just the opposite. Maybe he cares too much."

"I don't follow ..."

"I think people who deeply love another person are naturally going to think the best of them, not the worst. Fort may be seeing a lot of clues but unconsciously turning a blind eye. He really doesn't want to picture his wife as an addict. Who would?"

"So, what did you tell her?"

"I offered to help. Get her into a rehab place maybe. And I told her to tell her husband. He has a right to know, and she needs his support."

Joshua looked intently at his wife. He took her hands, both of them, and kissed them. "Thank goodness she's got you for a friend. You're outstanding, Abby. Really."

She leaned over and put a long, lingering kiss on his lips. "And you're an incredible man."

Then Joshua added, "If there's anything I can do to help, let me know."

"Thanks, Josh."

Then she brightened up and focused on her husband's project. "So, you finish up the Roundtable tomorrow?"

"Yep. We're going to focus on our media project. This is really going to be big. We're pulling out all the stops. Abby, this country will be shaken to its core."

"I'll be praying for your new venture. This is the AmeriNews project, right?"

"Exactly."

"So, after you wrap up tomorrow, then maybe you and I and Deborah can do some trail riding the next day?"

"Right ... uh, oh ..."

"Uh, oh what, dear?" Abigail was already translating the unspoken part of her husband's reply.

"I just remembered I am supposed to shoot eighteen holes with Rocky Bridger."

"Well, you could get up early, be the first to tee off, and still be back here in time for at least a half-day of riding with us. Right?"

He smirked. "Yeah. That's doable. I can take orders. I was a good Air Force officer. Flight plan modified by cencom."

"You are sooo overly dramatic." She grinned with a twinkle in her eye.

Then there were a few moments of stillness, where the only thing that could be heard was the faraway rushing of the river down in the valley. Abigail was the first to break the silence.

"So, any plans in the evening while we're staying here?"

"Nothing, except enjoying the lack of plans. One of these nights I need to review some acquisition and investment data. See how we're doing."

Then he caught on.

"You've got something in mind, don't you?"

"Actually, I do."

"What is it?"

"When we get back to New York, Pastor Paul Campbell is doing a special series of evening talks over at Eternity Church."

Joshua's face didn't flinch, but Abigail could hear the gears moving in his head.

"I know what you're thinking," she said.

Joshua laughed. "You sure?"

"When you have that look on your face, yeah. You're thinking, 'Wife, this is the two hundredth time you've invited me to church. And I've gone with you a couple times. Just two months ago. But I will have so much that I need to follow up on after the Roundtable when we get back to New York.'"

"Pretty close."

"But this is different. I think this series of messages are more for you than for me. The topic is right up your alley. Really."

"Well-played, madam lawyer. So I'm the one who'll regret it if I don't go ..."

"Absolutely. And if you do go, I think you'll be surprised. Actually, I think it fits into what you are doing with the Roundtable ..."

She had his attention.

"You've got my curiosity aroused. At least tell me what this is all about."

"Better than that, I'll let you read the brochure I got from Paul. It tells all about it."

"Okay, I'll read it. But no promises ..."

TWENTY-EIGHT

Moscow

Hamad Katchi threaded his way down a back alley littered with broken bottles and scraps of trash. It was right around midnight. For most people, in that particular neighborhood and at that particular time of night, it would be a hair-raising experience.

But not for Katchi. He wasn't afraid of the Russian mobsters who controlled that part of town. Many of them had done business with Katchi in the illegal arms trade. And for those who hadn't, they had certainly heard of him.

Over the years, Katchi had risen to the level of an international celebrity in the underworld. Who would have thought a "conversion" to global peace would give him the ability to continue to secretly negotiate with national leaders behind the cloak of legitimacy. This was a man no one wanted to cross.

The Pakistani weapons master turned a corner and walked another fifty feet toward a rustic shop with the word *Кофейня* on the sign out front: "espresso café." The storefront was dark, and a sign hanging in the window said "Closed." Katchi knew he was at the right place.

Cautiously he looked up and down the street, assuring himself that it was empty; then he opened the door and walked in. The café was empty, the chairs had been stacked up for the day, and the lights in the main dining area were out. But a soft light from the back room cast a glow through the darkened shop. Katchi walked into a small office and closed the door.

A burley man in a sloppy-looking suit and smoking a Cuban cigar sat in the corner next to a small wooden table. He slowly tapped the end of his cigar with his ring finger, causing ashes to carelessly fall to the ground, all the while eyeing Katchi as he entered the room.

"Good to see you again, Vlad," Katchi began.

The other man, Vlad Levko, was a former KGB agent and now an aging member of the Russian Federation's newest spy agency, the FSB. He smiled and motioned toward a bottle of vodka flanked by two shot glasses. Katchi shook his head no. Levko helped himself anyway, filled up a shot, and then tossed it down.

Levko didn't waste time on preliminaries. "What are we going to do, you and I, about our deal?"

"I was hopeful that we could negotiate a price," Katchi responded.

"And I assume you have authority to speak on behalf of Mr. Demas?"

"I didn't come all the way to Moscow for your vodka."

"Okay, but there is a slight adjustment since we talked last."

Katchi was prepared for some last-minute treachery from the Russians. What he was not prepared for was a deal breaker.

Levko took another draw on his cigar before proceeding. "We want the exclusive rights to the RTS. We don't want the system being sold to our competitors."

"That's not an adjustment, Levko — that's a complete overhaul. You should have informed me before I wasted a trip."

"And you should have anticipated that we would want to be the sole proprietors of this technology. Any advantage the RTS system would bring us diminishes the moment the technology is shared with any other government."

Katchi wasn't surprised, not really. As a result of the breakup of the Soviet empire decades ago, Russia's military domination had weakened. So in recent years the Russians were making a mad dash to rebuild to superpower status but still had a long way to go. They were being threatened from all sides, and if they were to have any hope of being able to fund their military build-up, they needed to protect their most prized possession — the vast oil fields that were their major source of revenue.

Katchi replied, "What you are asking is going to be a very hard sell to Demas."

"We are, of course, prepared to compensate you for exclusivity. You are, however, going to have to guarantee that you will be able to deliver all the necessary information regarding the details of the RTS laser-reversal protocol to make it worth our while."

Hamad Katchi casually responded without blinking an eye. "That won't be a problem."

"And we don't want to wait until next year for delivery. You can understand that."

"We expect to be in possession of the RTS any day now."

"One more thing. We cannot under any circumstance be traced back to your efforts to obtain the RTS design. Are we clear about that? We are not looking for a world war with the United States. At least not yet. Can you guarantee that you will keep us out of the spotlight?"

"That won't be a problem. In the meantime, I suggest you increase the U.S. allotment of oil above what you are currently offering, to make it look like you're helping to prop them up economically. You will continue to appear like a friend, and the U.S. does not become suspicious."

Levko was interested now in hearing the rest of the story. He poured himself another shot, tossed it back, and motioned for Katchi to proceed.

Katchi continued eagerly, "We have someone getting the RTS for us who is world-class. The best there is. Maybe the best there ever was. I am certain he will keep all of us out of the spotlight."

But then Katchi caught himself. Had he said too much? He did not want the Russian spy-masters to know whom they had hired for this project. The Russians had long memories. Atta Zimler's execution of three of their top agents had left a festering sore.

"This man you are using, is it anybody I would know?" Levko asked nonchalantly.

"A gentleman from South America. Well, maybe *gentleman* isn't the right word. He's been operating under radar for many years. He's excellent for this sort of thing."

After Katchi's lie, he studied Levko to see if he bought it. Vlad was simply smiling back at him and pouring himself yet another shot.

Katchi concluded as he rose to leave, "You are never going to reach retirement, my friend, if you keep up your drinking..."

"In our business, retirement is never guaranteed. Isn't that right, Hamad?"

Just before exiting the café's back room, Katchi added almost off-handedly, "For exclusive possession of the RTS design, you will have to pay double."

Levko didn't flinch. Russia's oil reserves were at an all-time high. And the Federation had successfully taken control of all private oil production. Another billion dollars was no big deal.

"Be safe, my friend," Vlad Levko muttered to Katchi as he made his way through the dim café and out onto the street. "The world can be a dangerous place."

TWENTY-NINE

Telling the truth had become a risky business.

For years, America's digital-based news belonged to the white-knuckled grip of a handful of corporate moguls, and they were not going to let go easily. Everyone in the Roundtable knew that. All the more reason, they figured, for their revolution to be launched immediately.

On the last day of the Roundtable, the pace picked up considerably. The big coffeepot in the window-lined conference room had already been filled up once, and now it had been drained down to empty again. The group was trying to fine-tune the AmeriNews project, but as much as they thought the concept was turnkey ready, more and more final details kept arising. Phil Rankowitz had spent the better part of the day going back and forth on the phone with the lawyers, ironing out last contract terms with the World Teleco, the huge telecommunications company whose satellite would carry the news service.

Funding the whole thing was not the biggest problem. Phil had been working with Beverly Rose Cortez to secure the financing. In addition to outside investors, several of the Roundtable members had either personally committed capital to the venture or backed loans from institutions with their own guarantees. The project would be structured through a shell corporation called Mountain News Enterprise, MNE Inc., which had already been set up for that purpose.

The challenge was to avoid tipping off the telecom company that this news network would be radically different. After all, World Teleco was a Corland administration supporter and was in tight with the existing news services. By contrast, AmeriNews would be a new breed of reporting, one that was willing to stand toe-to-toe with the existing news giants and would challenge the current political status quo. AmeriNews would cover hard-hitting issues that the mainstream Internet-driven TV and radio networks refused to cover. And it would be delivered right to the Allfone cell phones used by half of America's citizens. If all went well, within ten months the plan would expand and provide AmeriNews to nearly every American with a cell phone.

But Senator Leander was still hammering the group. He had serious doubts whether the news delivery concept was sound, and he also wondered if a successful deal could really be struck with the telecom company at all. So Rankowitz had to run through the basics again.

"The idea isn't complicated," Rankowitz explained to the group. "We cover the national news with no holds barred. I've got unemployed news directors and reporters laid off their jobs from failed print newspapers and magazines lined up to do the investigative reporting and to write national news copy. At the same time, local newspapers in key geographical areas are given free space for their local news. When someone with an Allfone equipped with our AmeriNews service comes within fifty miles of a city or county covered by a local digital newspaper that has signed up with us, then *bang*, that local news automatically shows up on their Allfone. Along with local advertisers. We do that through existing social-location systems that are already embedded in every Allfone. No hardware adjustments necessary. Each cell phone has an integrated GPS sensor and an electronic compass so it can figure out where it is. Now we just use that data to connect an Allfone user to the closest member of our local newspaper alliance. But remember that the biggest advantage of all of this is that every Allfone user ultimately gets not just the local news where they are at that moment, but our own coverage of national issues right at their fingertips. Readership via Allfone gives us entrée to the whole country from the ground up. We break through the media monopoly of silence on *our* issues. For the first time in years, the American people will start getting the real facts."

But Leander was still worried about leaks. "What if the Allfone telecom company, World Teleco, suddenly gets cold feet? Finds out that your news is going to challenge the big mainstream media that they already have as customers? That you're planning to bust up the news monopoly? I'm old enough to remember how the Fox network shook up the media establishment for a while and how the folks in the Senate with me had to be looking over their shoulders. It was healthy. Back when controversial radio talk-show hosts could actually challenge the White House. Then, finally, even the other news networks seemed to be getting off the dime too, started getting a little more edgy, more honest, more independent. But all that's over now. Phil, we're about to poke these almighty telecoms right in the eye."

Rankowitz wasn't fazed. "I'm okay with that, aren't you? Besides, we also want to give the news organizations in this country a black eye. They've sold out to the telecoms who control their access to the Internet. But now we're about to break the logjam."

Leander kept after the media chairman. "You're not hearing me. What if World Teleco gets wise on this? That they are about to invite a Trojan Horse into their wireless system. Maybe they'll pull out before signing the contract."

Judge Rice raised a finger. All the eyes went to him. "I've looked over Phil's contract structure," Rice said. "I don't think there is any way that World Teleco is going to know that this group or any of you people are involved. They'll think this is just one more news service. Phil very smartly has hired former general-market newspeople to be the front men in the contracts. What World Teleco doesn't know is that these people are media folks who quietly believe the way we do. Folks, I think we're okay."

Joshua had been pensive. Now he decided to put a capstone on the discussion. "People, this gets down to trust. Several of you are backing this with your own money and your own credit. But everybody here agrees on one thing: until we get the truth to the American people, this country will continue to unravel."

Phil Rankowitz was tapping his pen on the table with nervous energy, and his face was lit up with the kind of grin that a boy takes with him to the circus. Gesturing toward Joshua he said with an electricity to his voice, "We want to launch this new cell-phone-based news network with a headline series on your RTS story. Get the true facts out on why you won't turn your design over to Congress. And how Congress and the news media has been falsely painting you as some kind of traitor. Also, one more thing on that subject. We want to expose the White House's cover-up about what really happened inside the Oval Office the day those North Korean missiles were heading our way. Something stinks to high heaven about the president's explanation. The Pentagon brass that Rocky Bridger has been talking to privately have given a different story. They say that the White House knew full well that our military was going to use the RTS system to turn those missiles around and never objected. The Corland administration saying otherwise is just plain bull ..."

For a few seconds there was a hushed silence. As if it had finally dawned on them how big this really was. In one bold stroke they would be challenging Congress, the White House, and the American news monopoly.

Rocky Bridger called for a vote. "We need to formally approve this so we can start implementation. Now. The waiting is over. Remember, this one needs to be unanimous."

It was immediately seconded. The AmeriNews project was put to a vote.

"All in favor?" Joshua said.

Everyone except Senator Leander raised a hand in favor. He was sitting back with a stone-cold look on his face.

Then, after a moment's hesitation, his hand slowly went up too. Joshua announced what was now apparent to everyone.

"It's finished. AmeriNews is a go. How long, Phil?"

"I'm pushing this as fast as I can. We expect to go live in a week or two. Maybe a little longer."

After some final matters, including setting follow-up dates for the members, the group disbanded. That was when Rocky Bridger strolled over to Joshua.

"So, we're on the first tee time tomorrow?"

Joshua rolled his eyes and chuckled a little when he said, "Yeah, six-thirty in the a.m. But that way I'll still have time to go horseback riding with Abby and Deb."

"Got any plans after that?"

Joshua bowed his head with a patient smile and added, "We're flying back to New York the following day. With enough time for me to join Abby for a lecture at the church she attends. How about you?"

"Oh, I think I'll take an early flight out after our golf outing. I've got to attend a retired officers meeting out in San Diego. I'll be there for a couple days. Then I'm off to Pennsylvania. I'm really looking forward to that. See my daughter, Peg, and my son-in-law, Roger."

Joshua was trying to place the name. "Roger ... Roger French?"

"That's it. He's a commercial insurance broker in Philly. A good man. Ever since Dolly died and I've been on my own, family has really become precious to me. Can't wait to see them both — and my granddaughter as well."

Joshua told him he'd see Rocky for an early breakfast in the lodge at 5:30 the next morning; then he'd drive the two of them over to the golf club.

After General Bridger left, Joshua looked over at the judge. Rice, ordinarily an emotionless man, looked pensive, troubled.

He patted Rice on the shoulder and said, "You look like something's on your mind. You're okay with the media project, right?"

"Sure. I've been with you on this from the beginning."

"Great. Just checking..."

"Something *is* on my mind."

"Anything you want to talk about?"

Fortis Rice gave a little grunt and nodded in a way that struck Joshua as particularly unguarded and open, especially for the judge.

Rice said, "Darley told me last night that she had something she needed to talk with me about. But said it could wait until after our meeting. Just got me thinking..."

Fortis Rice's voice trailed off. But then Rice quickly changed the subject. He said, "Also, I was thinking about that lawyer, Allen Fulsin, that I was going to recommend bringing into the Roundtable to replace Fred Myster, to work in the legal subgroup. Fred's cancer treatments are progressing well, by the way. I'm hoping they got it in time. But the point is that I need to follow up with Allen Fulsin. I've already broached the subject with him personally, about our group. I tried to be as discreet as I could, of course."

"Tell me something about him."

"Super competent. Clerked for a Supreme Court justice. Did a stint in the solicitor general's office before he went into the private sector. That's not the issue. It's more the things I don't know personally about him. Like his character and his political philosophy. I've just had secondhand information. Though it all sounds good. And then I had that one conversation with him..."

Joshua keyed into Rice's concern, so he asked him pointblank: "Did you say anything to him that you regret? About the Roundtable I mean?"

"No. I didn't give him anything specific. I didn't give him the name or the particulars of our members. Just a little about what we do. You know, to feel him out. I think I may have mentioned that we were working on a media project. I did mention World Teleco to see if he had ever represented them. He said he hadn't."

"You think he's shooting straight?"

"I got that impression."

"And his politics?"

"Very gung-ho about our position on things. Says he's been wanting to do something for the future of America."

"So, any concerns?"

"Not really. Though last night I glanced over the CV he'd given me. I noticed that he had omitted something. Maybe just an innocent oversight. But he didn't list his work for a D.C. law firm the year before he joined Cobrin, Cabrezze & Lincoln, where he is working now."

"What was the other law firm?"

"Morgan & Whitaker."

"I don't follow. Why's that important?"

"Morgan, the senior partner in Allen's prior firm, was White House legal counsel to President Corland during the first year of his administration. We're using the Roundtable to attack the reckless policies of the Corland administration head-on. So I'm wondering if Fulsin deliberately omitted from his biography the fact that he'd worked with a pro-Corland law firm. Just need to make sure Allen doesn't have divided loyalties."

Joshua thought about the remote connection between Allen Fulsin working for a Washington lobby firm and that firm's lead partner having worked for President Corland. It sounded like Judge Rice was being nitpicky, but then, that's what lawyers and judges do.

Rice said unprompted, "Anyway, Josh, I'll do some more digging. Just to make sure that Allen's past association with Corland's lawyers won't color his judgment in his work with us."

Joshua thanked him for his diligence. Then Joshua added, "And I hope everything works out with Darley's conversation with you."

Rice smiled with a look that said he appreciated Joshua's kindness. But typical of him, he didn't put any words to that thought. Instead he snatched up his briefcase and turned and left the room.

THIRTY

The phone was ringing in the office of Consolidated Insurance Brokers in the downtown section of Philadelphia. It was bad timing. Everyone had left except for Roger French. He was now hesitating, torn between the guilt of leaving early and the benefit of avoiding rush hour traffic. He'd already been visualizing the route — over to JFK Boulevard and then from there onto the expressway. That would be the fastest way to make it to his daughter's basketball game on time.

Roger's hand reached down, hovering over the network panel button for the office phone system. Murphy's Law told him he ought to let it go to voicemail. But a strong work ethic urged him to pick it up.

As he reached for his briefcase he punched the button on the panel that read Roger — Earpiece.

The man on the other end spoke in a crisp British accent. "Oh, so glad to hear someone is still there. I urgently need to acquire commercial insurance for an international company I represent."

I knew I shouldn't have answered the call. Roger tried to put off the pushy client. "I'd be glad to meet tomorrow. As early as you'd like. But I have a commitment tonight ..."

"Yes. I'm sorry. But you see I only have limited time in the U.S. to set this up. My travel plans have been moved up, you see. I have to return to London tomorrow morning, so I have to discuss this with an insurance broker tonight."

Roger's voice was polite as he explained, "Actually, I am supposed to be at a my daughter's basketball game in a little over an hour — "

"No problem, really," the man said in a voice that had the smooth tone of accommodation to it. "I am just minutes from your office right now. I'm sure we can handle the preliminaries in thirty, forty minutes. I can pay you the fee for the initial binder. Then we can finish the details over the phone. That way you can still make your daughter's basketball event. Would that suffice? It really is very important that I get this started before I leave the country tomorrow."

Roger took a few moments to mull it over. "Sure ... as long as it doesn't take any longer than that ... Mr., uh ... I'm afraid I didn't get your name."

"Toby Arthur. I have a London-based business. And getting a certificate of insurance is the last hair on the dog so to speak, the one detail we still need for our financing so we can wrap up our expansion into the American market."

"Okay. Then, five minutes?"

"Brilliant. I'll be there."

Roger hung up and hit his wife's speed dial. After three or four rings, he was directed to her voicemail.

"Peg, this is Roger. I may be about ten or fifteen minutes late for the game. But don't worry, I'll be there. I promised Terri I'd make it this time. Love you."

□□□

Atta Zimler, hair dyed red, wearing an expensive pinstriped suit, and carrying a briefcase, walked toward the offices of Consolidated Insurance Brokers five minutes after finishing his call to Roger. Zimler considered this an irritating side trip. But necessary. The dossier that Dr. Banica had furnished him was superficial at best. The Russian agents who had compiled it had only skimmed the surface of the RTS system. And there was zero personal information about Joshua Jordan that would enable Zimler to track him down to his most vulnerable point. Not that he couldn't do it. He would. And Roger the insurance man was going to help him.

After Zimler entered the building's main lobby, skillfully moving his face away from the video surveillance cameras, he went up to the fifth floor. He rang the buzzer for Consolidated Insurance. Roger opened the door, looking a little distracted, but flashed a quick smile to his customer. Zimler took his hand and shook it firmly. While he greeted Roger, he sized him up.

When Roger turned his back to gather a large manila file, Zimler swung his arm around with lightning speed and delivered a karate blow to the back of Roger's neck.

Roger crumpled, hitting a small table in the lobby and scattering magazines as he collapsed to the floor.

When he regained consciousness, he was in a nightmare.

Disoriented, he tried to remember what had happened. Something covered the bottom of his face. Duct tape. But he couldn't reach over to pull it off. He was tied to one of the office desk chairs, his arms pulled tight behind him and fastened at the wrists — more duct tape.

But there was something else. Wires had been taped to several places on his body including his chest, thighs, and ear lobes. Roger's eyes followed the wires, trying to trace them. They led from his body down to the floor and over to some kind of box that had been plugged into a wall socket.

Atta Zimler waved a document in front of his victim. A copy of Roger's email that he had posted to an antinuclear blog.

"So nice of you, Roger, to defend Joshua Jordan in this web posting; let's see, how did you say it? — oh yes — 'a personal friend of my father-in-law, who is a former Pentagon general.' So, I have some questions for you, Roger French. Questions about Joshua Jordan. He is a difficult man to reach, and it is very clear from this email that your father-in-law, General Bridger, may have confided certain information about

Jordan to you. So you will tell me everything you know about him and his business, his family, everything."

Zimler came down close to Roger's face so he could deliver his sadistic warning in a quiet, calm voice. Zimler would make his victim understand that his body and his life, and everything about him was now in Zimler's control. No use to struggle. No making plans of escape. Help would not come.

Zimler said, "So, now I am removing the tape. There, it's off. You can breathe better now. Right? Okay. Now I will ask you the questions. And if I think that you are not telling me everything, then I will have to punish you with electricity. So, please tell me everything; don't hold back as you answer my questions. Let's begin with Jordan's family."

THIRTY-ONE

"Hanz, this is disastrous. Give me your take on this, will you? I'm looking at my screen right now, and the American dollar is sinking like a stone ..."

Sean, a currency trader in a large brokerage house on Oxford Street in the heart of London was sitting in front of his computer. He was on the phone with the manager of the Munich branch of the same company.

"I was looking over my open positions at the close of the day. The dollar versus the Swiss franc. The dollar versus the yen. The dollar against the pound ..."

From his office on Goethestrasse in Munich, Germany, Hanz blurted out, "Yah, we see it too. The dollar trend slipping. Every day. But this is bad ... there's still time for trades today. We'll dump our positions in the dollar. We're not waiting ..."

The money traders in the Amsterdam office of the same trading house were also watching the debacle with the American currency, and the order went out to sell the U.S. dollar and sell fast. In recent days they had all been making a dizzying number of dollar-carry-trades because U.S. currency had been so cheap to obtain. But that was coming to a screeching halt. The dollar was now just too risky to carry.

□□□

It was early morning in Washington, D.C. The sun had not yet hit the top of the Washington monument. An irate federal official was making another call to the White House. This time the president's chief of staff took the call personally.

"Sorry for the delays. I'm very familiar with the treasury secretary's urgent matter. But with the president's schedule, it's been virtually impossible to arrange this earlier ..."

The treasury official wasn't going to be sandbagged this time. "Hank, the secretary has to see the president. Today. No more excuses. If we don't do something quick, you're going to see our nation experience a financial Chernobyl. And I'll personally see to it that the whole world knows that Hank Strand, the president's chief of staff, is the one responsible. You'll make Bernie Madoff look like a Boy Scout."

"I don't like threats — "

"And I don't like incompetence. Do your job. Make this happen — today."

The assistant secretary of the treasury had called twice in the last two days to schedule a meeting between the treasury secretary and President Corland. But Strand had given orders for the meeting to be delayed. He knew Corland had been unable to make a decision on the issue. It was clear that once America headed down this road, there would be no turning back.

But time was running out. Today's reports from the monetary markets showed the dollar was no longer treading water — it was drowning. Pretty soon it would be unable to compete even with the Mexican peso. American currency showed signs of a catastrophic failure, and everyone in the Corland administration knew it.

Whether it was because of the unpredictable devastation of U.S. agriculture, the oil crisis, spiraling unemployment, crippling federal taxes, or the gigantic debt that America owed to China and Russia — all of that seemed irrelevant now.

Hank Strand cut the telephone conversation short and told the second-in-command at treasury that he would personally deliver the message to the president.

Thirty minutes later, Strand was in the Oval Office with President Corland, who was on his feet and was pacing like a caged animal. The chairman of his board of economic advisors, who had been seated on the couch, made a gesture of rising to match the president's position. But after a few seconds, Corland impulsively dumped himself back down into an upholstered chair. The chairman thought the president's behavior had been increasingly odd of late. He looked over at Corland's chief of staff, hoping to glean something from his expression. But he should have known better.

Hank Strand was a master of the blank poker face. He continued to sit, his hands open and relaxed on the arms of his chair. He had seen this all before. Corland was a smooth, steady communicator on television, but in moments of crisis, he was a man who couldn't sit still. And then, as Strand knew full well, there was that *other* issue with the president.

Fewer than a handful of people knew anything about President Corland's strange medical situation. Strand was one of them. He thought if he remained calm, paced and confident, around Corland, that one of the president's "incidents" would be avoided.

The economic chairman finally spoke up.

"Mr. President, this is simply the next inevitable step. Another stage in America's financial evolution."

The president was trying to control his emotions. His face was frozen into a tight-faced grin — trying to look pleasant, but the resulting expression was almost ghoulish.

"I don't want to be the one who goes down in history for ... you know ... killing the U.S. dollar. Washington's face is still on the one dollar bill, remember? The American public is not going to like this — "

The chairman blurted out, "I think that what the American public wants is an economy that doesn't look like Germany at the end of World War I."

Corland turned to look at his chief of staff.

Hank Strand wanted to interject an attitude of calm. But he knew that the handwriting was on the wall, and so he added soothingly, "Mr. President, the secretary of the treasury wants you to give him the go-ahead for the U.S. to begin the monetary conversion process. It can be gradual, of course."

"But not too gradual," the chairman added. "We don't want a melt-down of our markets, Mr. President."

Corland was trying somehow to tie a rhetorical bow on the whole thing. Then his face lit up. He had it. "We can describe this as historic. An end of an epoch, perhaps, and yet the beginning of a new age of financial freedom ..."

The chairman relaxed back in his chair when he saw the president coming around. "We've been in global markets since the end of the twentieth century, for heaven's sake. Is it really so radical that we now become part of a unified global currency?"

"And the precedent you talked about?" Corland asked.

"Yes, the International Monetary Fund. Right. It's a little known fact that the IMF's had the authority for years to issue a financial form of paper called Special Drawing Rights — SDRs — as a global form of money."

"And these SDRs — "

"They're just like an international currency, Mr. President. So this move for the United States to join the rest of the major nations in adopting the new international currency — the Currency Regulation Drawing Order — the CReDO — as part of our national currency, well, that's not that new after all. Besides, the CReDO is already a dual-purpose form of money. It's being used in the paper version, yes, but it also is available as an electronic form. Like an international debit card. A major plus since the entire world will be going the way of cashless currency very shortly. Besides, Americans are primed for this. They've been making more purchases with cards than they have with cash since 2007. So we are way overdue for this worldwide system of money."

Corland looked at Hank Strand to help him through the politics of this one.

Strand smiled and said, "The Congress is with you on this. You've got them behind you, sir."

"And the vice president?"

"Oh, Vice President Tulrude hasn't ever wavered. She believes that the United States needs to become a more evolved international entity. More integrated in the world community. Yes, she is very excited about this."

"Okay," the president said, "get our press secretary working on this. A series of short announcements about a 'monetary enhancement.' Something vague. That we'll still permit Americans to use the dollar. That sort of thing. But pretty soon, the American people will see their dollars are worthless but that they can use the CReDO, and suddenly they'll be saying, hey, you know, I can buy more with the CReDO than with the old currency. Right?"

There were nods all the way around.

The secretary of the treasury was scheduled for a 3:30 meeting in the Oval Office. President Corland would give him the good news then. America was soon going to join the new form of global currency.

By 4:30, however, someone in the White House, no one ever found out who, leaked the information to an underground blogger who ran a website called the Barn Door.

At 4:48, the Barn Door reported that the president had approved the U.S. disbanding the dollar and changing America over to the CReDO.

Seventeen minutes later, the big telecom Internet server that hosted the Barn Door blogsite, fearing reprisals from the White House, without warning shut it down permanently. So the webmaster for the Barn Door blog immediately called all the major news networks to complain about it.

None of them reported it.

THIRTY-TWO

The suffocating stench of death permeated the room.

After years of investigating crimes of violence for the FBI, John Gallagher had developed the knack of picking up the pungent smell of decaying human flesh. He was known to have a nose like a corpse-sniffing police dog.

But John Gallagher never really got used to the odor.

Ever.

Even with the organic vapor-filtering mask he was wearing, Gallagher cringed as the county medical examiner from Northern New York State used a heavy duty pair of scissors to cut away the soggy bag that contained the corpse. But the body wasn't in one of those plastic contractor bags like an amateur criminal might use.

That was the first thing Gallagher noticed, after the smell, of course. The person who had dumped the body had used a burlap bag.

"The killer knew what he was doing," Gallagher said, standing next to the body on the stainless-steel table in the coroner's office. "Wrapped this poor guy in burlap, so the elements could start the decaying process sooner rather than later. Then added lime to the mix."

The coroner opened the mouth of the cadaver to examine it. But he wasn't prepared for what he saw there. Gallagher saw it too.

Then the coroner closed the victim's mouth and said, "But the murderer made one mistake."

"What's that?"

"Dumped his victim into a swamp."

"Go on ..."

"Bogs like the one where they found this victim are high in tannic acid. Acts like a preservative. Sort of like a natural form of formaldehyde."

Gallagher thought about that. *So the killer wasn't local and didn't know much about peat bogs or swamps. Otherwise he would have known that.*

Now the coroner was inspecting the neck of the victim.

"How'd they find him?"

"Talk to Red Yankley, the county deputy. He's out there in the lobby grabbing a cup of coffee. He'd be able to tell you."

After a minute or so of closer examination of the larynx, the coroner looked up at Gallagher with a strange smile that reflected some professional pride.

"I think he was strangled. I'll be able to give you a definite by tomorrow after I do the full deal, lungs and all. But I will bet my bottom dollar that the ligature marks here on the neck were from a thin metal cable."

Gallagher was trying to keep himself calm. Zimler particularly liked to polish off his victims close up, and usually with a garrote. And he was known to be in the States.

Gallagher excused himself and stepped out into the lobby. He stripped off his mask and then hunted down the deputy who was standing next to the coffee machine with a Styrofoam cup in his hand. "Deputy Yankley, I'm Special Agent Gallagher from the FBI."

"What can I do for you? Is this some kind of federal matter?"

"Possibly. Wondering how the body was discovered."

"A hunter. Had his bird dog out there in the bog. No rain for a couple days and things dried up. Dog found it right off."

"Motive?"

"Well, we found tire tracks leading to and from the site. We think they were from the victim's car. So right there you've got car theft."

But Gallagher had the feeling in the center of his gut this was no simple stolen-auto case. He was trying not to get ahead of himself. *Take it easy, John. Don't jump to conclusions.*

"So, Deputy, anything else of interest?"

"Let's see ... oh yeah. All of the victim's ID was taken from his body. He was picked clean. I mean *really*. If you know what I mean. Maybe the killer was a dentist or something ..."

"Yeah, I noticed," Gallagher remarked. He'd seen that the murderer had broken all the teeth of the victim and removed them in order to prevent dental identification.

"Yeah, but not that smart. The killer left the victim with his fingers still on ... finger prints."

"We just got lucky," said Gallagher. "If that dog hadn't come across the body when he did, the prints would have pretty well dissolved with all the lime that he'd been packed in."

"Well," the deputy continued, "anyway, you've got to wonder. Yanking teeth from a dead man. What was going on with that?"

Gallagher didn't need to wonder. The FBI veteran had figured that the killer couldn't afford to leave any direct connection to the victim. So he wanted to make sure that the victim wouldn't be immediately identified. This was one sadistic, calculating killer.

The deputy slurped down the last bit of coffee and laid the hunting magazine down; then he eased his hands down on both sides of his leather gun belt. "You got some thoughts on all this, Agent Gallagher?"

Gallagher smiled. "Yes," he said. "I do." But he made a point not to tell him what that was and instead turned and strolled back to the swinging doors leading back to the tile-floored autopsy room.

He swung the doors open. The coroner was still bending over the body and looked up.

"You have an ETD?" Gallagher asked.

"I think so …," the medical examiner began.

But Gallagher raised a finger to stop him before he answered.

"No, let me guess. Six to ten hours."

The coroner's eyes widened and he wagged his head a little.

"Other than being maybe an hour or two off, you're right on the money, Agent Gallagher. How'd you do that?"

"It's a theory I'm working on," Gallagher said with a sly smile. He turned and exited the autopsy room, cut through the lobby, and threw a quick wave to Deputy Yankley as he headed to the parking lot and toward the exquisite pleasure of fresh air.

John Gallagher had more than a theory. His instincts told him that the same man who killed the Yergi Banica in Bucharest was the same one who used the dead man's passport to gain entrance into the United States at the Canada-New York State border. Also, it followed that the killer would need to exchange cars quickly once he entered the United States. The FBI special agent was betting that this assassin was a consummate professional. So he picked the car owner at random, killed him, and dumped the body in a way that was designed to leave almost no trace. All because the killer needed to use the car for a day or two without being tracked, and then he would soon rid himself of that vehicle and steal another.

So Gallagher used the date and time that the man with the passport entered New York as the starting point, figured it was the same guy who killed this poor car owner. Presto. Time of death all figured out.

Now that the coroner agreed with his estimate, that meant that the odds were increasing that the killer of Dr. Banica was the user of the Romanian professor's passport, and he was also the murderer of the owner of the car.

Now all he had to do was to determine whether his suspect, Atta Zimler, was the guy who strangled the professor in Romania. Back there is where the dominoes had started falling. Down deep, Gallagher just knew that Zimler was the man behind all of it, even though he couldn't explain it in any terms that you could find inside an FBI investigation handbook.

Which led him to the much more frantic question. What was Zimler doing inside the United States?

Gallagher's heart was pounding. His chest was tightening with the familiar burning, crushing sensation. He needed to find a quickie-stop gas station and pick up a carton of milk to soothe the pain. He thought that he had spotted one when he first drove into the sleepy little town after exiting Interstate 87.

Gallagher climbed into his car. He was hoping that there wouldn't be more victims for a while and that maybe the stench of death was behind him. On the other hand, if he was right about Atta Zimler being in the States on *business*, well, that would put the chances of that at around zero to the tenth degree.

PART THREE
The Global Tower of Babel

Some even believe we are part of a secret cabal working against the best interests of the United States, characterizing my family and me as "internationalists" and of conspiring with others around the world to build a more integrated global political and economic structure — one world, if you will. If that's the charge, I stand guilty, and I am proud of it.

David Rockefeller, *Memoirs*

To stabilize and regulate a truly global economy, we need some global system of political decision making. In short, we need a global society to support our global economy.

George Soros, socialist billionaire

If we can learn from our experience of turning unity of purpose into unity of action, we can together seize this moment of change in our world to create a truly global society.

Gordon Brown, British Prime Minister

THIRTY-THREE

"Chaos. Death. Destruction. Is that what you're thinking?"

He paused. No one was moving.

"Is that what floods your mind when you think about the end of the world? Armageddon. The Four Horsemen of the Apocalypse. Whatever phrase you might want to use.

"When people imagine it, they visualize the horror. But let me challenge that idea. The God who controls the future is a merciful God. In the midst of catastrophe, He will still give us all the choice to be saved through His grace. In fact, I believe that the end of the world will in reality be the first chapter in a radical new kind of life. It isn't just about the ravages of destruction. The future world that God has for us after the birth pains are finished here on planet Earth will really be all about life — and life abundantly. And life with Him for eternity."

Pastor Paul Campbell was addressing a packed church from his position in the ornate pulpit of the Eternity Church in downtown Manhattan.

Sandwiched between his wife and daughter in the pew, Joshua Jordan was waiting for the minister to get to the point. He knew a little about Campbell's background. He had checked out his credentials on the Internet. Ph.D. in philosophy, Th.D. in theology. Campbell had written two books, both of them about the Bible and end-times prophecy. And yes, Joshua had to agree, Campbell was a dynamic communicator. He had heard him a few times before at his wife's urging.

But now Joshua was waiting for the punch line. Campbell's message had been publicized — "Globalism — Three Signs of the End Times." Frankly, Joshua had expected something else. He was getting antsy and regretted coming. Maybe he should have pushed back a little when Abby encouraged him to leave Colorado early just to attend the service.

When are we going to get to the dangers of globalism? That's why I'm here.

Joshua's mind started drifting. Back to their log mansion in Colorado. They had left their ranch in the Rockies at the crack of dawn that same day by private jet. Joshua was now smiling as he was thinking about the trail ride on horseback that he, Abby, and Debbie had taken the day before. Joshua had been scheduled to shoot some early golf with Rocky Bridger first, just after sunrise, but he found out from their housekeeper, Ronda, that Rocky had already left the ranch with his bags in hand while it was still dark. She said that Rocky had a concerned look on his face and said something about an "urgent family matter."

Joshua had tried Rocky's cell phone, but his friend wasn't picking up. So he left a message. He wanted to know if everything was okay and whether there was anything he could do.

By late morning, Joshua still hadn't heard from him. So he and Abby and Debbie mounted their horses and took the familiar trail that broke into a large meadow full of wild flowers. That's when Joshua, without warning, decided to throw down the gauntlet. He playfully heeled the sides of his quarter horse, General Billy Mitchell, gave him a loud kiss, and lunged ahead, daring his wife to race him to the other side of the clearing. He beat his wife to the other side, but only by a nose. She playfully called him a cheater. Joshua smiled a little thinking back to that. *Okay. So maybe I didn't give her a fair shake. Come on Josh, admit it. She's a better rider than you any day . . .*

But then something brought Joshua's mind back from the towering vistas of the Rocky Mountains. What was it? He was back again in the crowded sanctuary of the church. It was another comment by Campbell that had caught Joshua's attention. A little like someone gently tapping him on the shoulder in a crowded room.

"To clearly understand what God intended for our future, we need to recognize that He has laid it all out for us in the Bible. The Bible contains God's agenda for the future of planet Earth, and everybody who dwells here. All right, so how do we know that the Bible is true?"

Joshua clicked with that. *Okay, let's hear it. I've respected Abby's "new relationship with Christ" that she talks about all the time. But the Bible as a predictor of the future? That's a stretch ...*

Campbell said, "Besides being the inspired word of God, the Bible has proven itself over the centuries. Let's focus first on just one major prophecy. It is, perhaps, the most astounding evidence of the fact that we are seeing the approach of the end times of the planet Earth and the coming of Jesus Christ to establish His new kingdom. And that proof comes in a single word. *Israel.*"

Campbell's argument was simple. When Israel was recognized as being a sovereign state on May 14, 1948, by the United Nations, it was nothing less than a modern-day miracle. "That one fact — the rise of modern Israel as a nation — was a startlingly accurate fulfillment of the 2,500-year-old prophecy recorded in the Old Testament book of Ezekiel, chapter thirty-seven. A prophecy that says:

> "Behold I will take the sons of Israel from among the nations where they have gone, and I will gather them from every side and bring them into their own land; and I will make them one nation in the land, on the mountains of Israel.

"Prophecy is defined," Campbell continued, "as 'history written in advance.' Now anyone can 'predict' history once it's already written. But only God can predict it *before* it happens and have it come to pass exactly as He says it's going to occur. That's how we know that the Bible comes from a divine origin. That it's not just a bunch of writings that came from the minds of men. Most people are unaware that at least twenty-eight percent of the entire Bible was prophetic at the time it was first written down."

With that Campbell clicked his remote, and screens on each side of the sanctuary lit up with a huge image of a black Bible. Emblazoned across the bottom of the Bible was a red arrow pointing to the word "prophecy." He zoomed in on the arrow. Suddenly, the cover of the Bible disappeared and a parade of prophetic Scripture verses started appearing one after another, scrolling down the screen. Old Testament predictions of the terrible curse that would befall the man who would rebuild the city of Jericho, in the ninth century B.C. Prophetic warnings delivered to King David that as a result of his sin, "the sword would never depart from your house," a fact later established beyond question. Verses containing precise predictions about the manner of death that would befall the evil king Ahab and his equally corrupt wife, Jezebel, all fulfilled down to minute detail. Six separate prophecies regarding the fate that would befall the ancient city of Tyre, each having occurred just as foretold.

"Over half of those events prophesied in the Bible," Campbell said, his voice growing more intense, "were later fulfilled. The other half relate to what we call 'end time events.' But listen carefully ... many of those events are being fulfilled in *our* very lifetime ... which is why many of us believe we are living in the 'time of the end' that the disciples asked Jesus about in Matthew 24. Now speaking of fulfilled prophecy, God Himself used those many fulfillments to prove His very existence. Eight hundred years before Jesus Christ was born, in Isaiah 46:9–10, God used one of the greatest prophets of the Old Testament to rebuke His chosen nation for worshiping idols. And then, speaking for God, the prophet Isaiah said, 'I am God, declaring the end from the beginning ... I have spoken it: I will also bring it to pass.'

What God is saying here is that one of the great proofs that He exists is the astonishingly precise fulfillment of His prophecies. Only God is able to do that.

"Dr. John Walvoord was one of the greatest prophecy scholars of the twentieth century — a prolific writer and president of Dallas Theological Seminary. He once described over a thousand prophecies in the Bible, more than half of which have already been fulfilled. Only God can write history in advance and have it come to pass. Those fulfilled prophecies prove to us beyond a shadow of a doubt that the end time prophecies of the Bible will also be fulfilled literally, just as over five hundred of God's predictions have already occurred throughout the past ages. Some of those end time prophecies are unfolding even now, in our own generation."

But then the pastor took a turn that caught Joshua by surprise. Campbell began to zero in on a single person in the Bible. Seconds later Joshua realized that he should have seen it coming.

Campbell was forging an argument about who Jesus was, based on His fulfillment of multiple prophecies.

"I'm convinced that fulfilled prophecy confirms that Jesus was truly the one and only Messiah who came to 'seek and to save the lost.' Just think about it for a minute — He fulfilled all 109 Old Testament prophecies regarding the Messiah when He came to this earth. No other human being even comes close, yet Jesus fulfills them all. From being born of a virgin in Bethlehem — predicted seven hundred years before — to being spirited away to Egypt as a young child, to healing every kind of disease, particularly restoring sight to the eyes of blind men ... to being betrayed by 'a familiar friend' for thirty pieces of silver ... to being hung on a cross between two thieves, to being resurrected on the third day after His crucifixion, as He predicted six times in the Gospels ... and finally announced miraculously when the angels who rolled away the stone first told the women. Remember that? They came to the tomb on the first day of the week and were told, 'He is not here. He is risen as *He said.*' Obviously this Jesus of the Bible was one-of-a-kind. Unique in all of history. And here we are, two thousand years later, still talking about Him. Why? Because He rose from the dead, signaling that God Himself was satisfied with His sacrifice for our sin on the Cross. Christianity is the only religious faith in the world that is based on the resurrection of the founder. And the best evidence for the resurrection is not just the unanimous testimony of the twelve apostles, and not just the five hundred witnesses of Jesus who saw Him in the flesh after He rose, but it is also proven by the very existence of Christianity today. And remember, Christianity was birthed in the first century in the midst of a furnace of unimaginable persecution, yet people still believed in Jesus, the Messiah, the Savior. Such is His supernatural impact on those who receive Him. If Jesus' resurrection were a fraud, do you think anyone would be here worshipping Him today? He and His followers have influenced this world more than anyone who ever lived. Friends, listen, today Christianity is the largest religious faith in the world. Why? Because Jesus is exactly who the Bible says He is."

Joshua found Campbell's comments interesting enough, but his mind was starting to wander. What about the title of the sermon? What about the rise of "globalism?" That was the threat that he and his fellow members of the Roundtable had recognized. An increasing loss of American sovereignty to a world order. That's why he came to the church that night.

But Campbell seemed to beat him to the punch.

"So, now let's look at prophecies about the future, the end times. While there are many important signs of the return of Jesus Christ and end of this age, signs that the disciples asked Jesus about, one of the most prominent in our current world is one we call 'globalism.' Previous government officials had called it a 'one-world government.'

In fact, the world planners, whoever they might be, came up with the idea after World War I. So they called it the League of Nations. The Senate of the United States rejected the idea, and the notion wasn't revived until 1945. That is when it was called the United Nations.

"Now you can look at the idea of a unified world system, what the Bible refers to as the future 'Babylon,' like a three-legged stool. Global Government, Global Economy, and Global Religion. In the Bible, each of those are prophesied to be world powers at the end of the age. And by the way, each of them will be destroyed by God according to biblical prophecy. You can read it for yourself in last book in the Bible, Revelation, chapters seventeen and eighteen.

"Ever since the seventeenth century there have been those who dreamed of a global government and used the slogan 'global peace' as the supposed goal. But what was behind it? Ultimately a craving for control over the lives of people through the iron grip of ever-expanding government. In recent times you can find countless leaders in media, education, and the government who have tirelessly supported the goal of a global economy. George Soros, one of the most influential and richest men in the world, has gone one step further, openly declaring that you can't have a world economy unless you also have a world government."

Campbell stepped away from the pulpit and put his hands behind his back. He stared silently at the audience for nearly thirty seconds. Then he continued.

"The rise of this kind of political Babylon, a global system of government, will be an integral element of the end times as predicted in the Word of God ... and as I stand here today ... and listen carefully to what I say next ... this very day I believe we are seeing the stage-setting for the eventual rise of this new Babylon. For there must be, the Bible says, a global unification among the nations gathered around its grand capital. A political and legal coalition. It's right there in chapters seventeen and eighteen of the last book of the Bible."

Then Campbell put a capstone on it in a voice that cracked a bit and grew raspy with emotion. His words rose up, almost pleading, as he said, "Be honest with yourself … as you look around, don't you see the beginning movement among the nations of this planet to work together to create a new world order?"

THIRTY-FOUR

Paul Campbell had captured Joshua's attention. He was beginning to see the connecting points between the Bible prophecies that the pastor was describing and the issues that were consuming his Roundtable. The erosion of American sovereignty. The movement to force United States courts to embrace the international laws of the nations of the world. The mantra calling for a single global government.

For Joshua it was a little like being at Hawk's Nest Ranch in the fall when the fog rolled in with a cold snap early in the morning. But when the sun broke through, the white blanket of fog would clear, and the imposing mountain peaks rising up all around would suddenly show themselves. Joshua wondered for just an instant whether his mission statement in founding the Roundtable might have been too small. *So, I wanted to save America ... but was that enough? What if all of this is bigger than just the United States?*

Campbell moved to his second main point.

"So there will be a *political* Babylon, certainly. A unification of the powers of the nations of the planet. But there will also be a *religious* Babylon in the end times. Another leg of our three-legged stool. A merging of the religions of the world into one massive conglomerate of false spirituality. When will that happen? Ultimately not until the Church ... and by that I mean the sum total of all true believers in Jesus Christ ... until the Church is 'raptured' ... taken up instantaneously to God ... and when that happens, with the restraining power of the Church gone from the earth, there will be nothing to stop this massive global merger of the world's religions. And that is when there will be the hideous appearing ... a false prophet will come and set in motion the blasphemous idol worship of the Antichrist exactly as predicted in the thirteenth chapter of Revelation.

"But in addition to the political and religious aspects, there will also be an *economic* Babylon. The apostle John, in Revelation, describes this future global financial center: '... the merchants of the earth have become rich by the wealth of her sensuality.'

"When God finally vanquishes Babylon, as we are told that He will, who is going to mourn her great fall? We are told that 'the merchants of the earth weep and mourn over her, because no one buys their cargoes anymore ...' What are the signs of this coming global economic Babylon? We are warned in the Bible that there will be a future international system of buying, selling, trading, and investing. Revelation chapter thirteen tells us that the Antichrist, the 'beast,' will eventually establish a world financial and monetary system that will have the entire planet within its deadly grip:

> And he causes all, the small and the great, and the rich and the poor, and the free men and the slaves, to be given a mark on their right hand or on their forehead, and he provides that no one will be able to buy or to sell, except the one who has the mark, either the name of the beast or the number of his name.

Campbell pulled a piece of paper out of his Bible. He said it was something he happened to stumble across on the Internet. A recent piece from a small web log called the Barn Door.

"I am holding up a short article that mentions a decision that apparently was made by lawmakers in Washington. A decision to convert American currency to the new international form of money being used widely among nations along with the euro, a new currency called the CReDO. Strangely, when I went back to follow up on this blogsite, it had disappeared. Why, I don't know. But I will keep looking. And I would advise you to do the same. Jesus rebuked the Pharisees of His day for failing to recognize the signs of the times. Of course, some people will say that the Bible assures us that we can't know the specific time that Christ will return to the earth. And that's true. On the other hand, why would Jesus, as we are told in the gospels of Matthew and Mark, have given us an exhaustive list of the events that will precede His return if He didn't want us to use that information? If He didn't want us to watch the times and to discern them so we could recognize the signs of His coming soon? One of the great questions that has plagued philosophers over thousands of years is this one: how can I truly know that what I know is true? I have a suggestion for you. You can know for sure what you know by basing your knowledge on those things that God has chosen to reveal. And the only way you can do that is by relying on His Word, the Bible. His Word says that the world is heading toward a global, unified economic system. And that, my friends, is something you can definitely bank on ..."

□□□

It just so happened that matters of banking and finance were on the agenda in the Senate offices of Washington, D.C., that night.

The congressional staffers were working late again. That was one of the things that came with the territory. Low pay and long, grueling hours — at least while Congress was in session. But there was always the hope that soon they could move up the political ladder. Perhaps a job as chief legal counsel on one of the influential committees some day. Or maybe the possibility of moving into the private sector, with a six-figure job in a D.C. law firm or lobbying shop.

A young female legislative assistant, who was part of the political night crew, ripped an urgent note off the top of the message pad in the lobby of Senator Wendell Straworth's office. In her panic she tore the corner of the note. So she riffled through the receptionist's desk, found some tape, and slapped it on the torn note, piecing it together.

Then she scurried across the lobby, down the adjoining hall, and up to the closed door at the end, leading to the senator's office. The LA paused in front of the door. She knew he was in there with the Senate Majority Leader Russell Beyers. They were not to be disturbed unless it was something absolutely critical.

The LA took a deep breath and then knocked twice on the door, still gripping the taped note in her hand.

The door was opened by Senator Straworth's chief of staff. The LA thrust the note into the COS's hand. In the background she glimpsed Straworth and Beyers sitting across from each other in leather chairs.

The chief of staff closed the door and handed the note to Senator Straworth.

He read it and then looked up at Beyers.

"The vice president wants a decision. She's demanding a call. Immediately."

"We asked for a call directly with the president," Beyers mumbled to himself. "Why are they cloistering him like this? What's going on? Does he have cancer or something? Has he suffered a nervous breakdown? I get the feeling that Tulrude is now running the Oval Office."

Straworth just shook his head but suggested they make the call. They had no choice.

When the vice president was finally on the line, they put her on the speaker phone. She was typically blunt. "Are we going to get the vote on this new monetary currency or not?"

Beyers bristled a little. As majority leader he didn't like being treated like a schoolboy who was turning in his homework late. But then again, that was the style of Jessica Tulrude.

"Madam Vice President, we have everything under control," Beyers said. His voice was confident, polished. Calm.

"Which means what?"

"A vote tomorrow to begin converting the entire U.S. currency system over to the CReDO."

"What's your plan to deal with public opinion?" Tulrude shot back.

"Well, the CReDO issue is buried in a huge omnibus spending bill. The thing's as thick as the New York phone book. Frankly, most of the senators haven't read the whole bill. I doubt if the press will. But our people in the Senate generally understand that this is a *must do* because of the dollar being devastated in the currency exchanges."

"Have you counted noses?"

Beyers tensed his jaw a little but forced a smile as he spoke. "Of course we've counted votes. It shouldn't be a problem. We've got a solid majority."

Then Beyers paused and added another thought. He moved closer to the speaker phone and said, "Madam Vice President, I assume that when we give you the vote on the currency issue, as I know we will, the administration will back me on the three bills I described in my message to the president the other day."

Jessica Tulrude cleared her throat and said, "Russ, you know I'm as good as my word."

That's all that Russell Beyers needed to hear. He said his good-byes to Tulrude and strode out of the office to a caucus meeting while Straworth quickly offered his apologies and said he couldn't attend.

On a signal from Senator Straworth, his chief of staff left the room closing the door behind him.

Straworth took the call off speaker and began talking on the tiny voice-activated phonecell clipped to his lapel.

"So, as you can see," Straworth tried to explain to the vice president, "I've kept my part of the bargain. I've got the majority leader and the Senate behind the currency conversion."

"And?"

"Are you going to make me spell it out?"

"No need."

"Good."

"But you still have one more assignment ..."

"Yes, I know, the RTS business. But I just want you to know that this morning I secured the approval of the sub-committee to authorize subpoenas to be served on Joshua Jordan. He will have no choice now but to appear and produce his RTS documents — or risk going to jail. And if he thinks he can weather a jail sentence, he will be sadly mistaken. It will take his professional career and his business reputation and reduce them both to an oil stain on the sidewalk. Checkmate. So, Madam Vice President, I've done everything I've promised."

"And the position that you're interested in, that's still the same?"

"I think I'd make an excellent Supreme Court justice."

"Well, the inside rumor is that Justice Manweiller is going to last through the present term and will probably be announcing his retirement after the presidential election next November. If all goes well, I'll be the person in the Oval Office making that appointment. Wendell, with the support of your fellow senators, your confirmation to the Supreme Court should be a shoo-in."

Wendell Straworth smiled. He had waited a long time for this. The pieces were falling into place.

"And has the President definitely agreed to step away after only one term and give you his full support during the primaries? That rarely ever happens ..."

"We've never had a president in this situation before," Tulrude snapped back. "Just remember, I'm in control over here ..."

"I wouldn't think of questioning that," Straworth said. His voice was dripping with apology.

"Fine," the vice president said. Her voice was condescending, but there was also an air of satisfaction now that the big-dog-versus-little-dog situation with Senator Straworth had been cleared up.

After the vice president said good-bye, Straworth exhaled a long breath and leaned back in his chair. He was poised to set in motion a series of events that would be certain to cinch his professional future. He reached over to his work table and grabbed his copy of the subpoena. The original was being couriered over to the U.S. Marshals Service first thing in the morning.

Straworth relished the words at the top of the document:

By the authority of the Senate of the Congress of the United States of America

To: Mr. Joshua Jordan

You are hereby commanded to appear before the below-named committee of the U.S. Senate, at the time and place below designated, and then and there to produce all documents, records, and papers relating to the design, conception, engineering specifications, production, and operating principles of the weapons system commonly known as "Return-to-Sender" (RTS), including the use of lasers to reverse the direction or trajectory of offensive missiles.

Fail not or you will face the full penalty of law.

TH1RTY-F1VE

The crowds were spilling out of Eternity Church now that the evening service had ended. Deborah Jordan was busy chattering with some friends in the vestibule, making use of her time off from West Point and quickly catching up before she had to return the next day. At the front of the sanctuary by the pulpit, Abigail was holding one of Joshua's hands with both of hers as they approached the pastor, but she let go so her husband could shake hands with Paul Campbell.

"Pastor Campbell, this is my husband, Joshua. I think you've met before ..."

"Yes, once or twice awhile back," Campbell said with a relaxed grin. "It's a pleasure. And a privilege. I consider you an American hero."

Joshua always flinched a little with that one. Not that he was embarrassed. But he could never see himself that way. He was a mission-and-duty guy. How could he accept the "hero" label for just doing his best at what had to be done?

"Some folks might disagree with you on that."

"That doesn't change my opinion."

"Thanks for your message tonight," Joshua said. "Very interesting."

Joshua was minimizing the impact that the sermon had on him. He was holding back and he knew it. But he didn't see any reason to spill his guts all over the floor of the church. Campbell had given him some food for thought.

Campbell said simply, "Glad to hear it. You folks back in the city for a while?"

"Just got back from Colorado," Abigail said.

Then Campbell looked over at Joshua and studied him for a minute. "This may be a shot in the dark. But here goes. Are you a golfer by any chance?"

Abigail giggled. She was struggling to keep quiet.

Joshua quickly threw his wife an amused glance before he answered. "Yes, I've been known to hit a few golf balls."

She couldn't hold back any longer and blurted out, "He's understating it, pastor. He's practically a pro. You ought to see his handicap."

"Oh," Campbell said with a chuckle. "Maybe I'd better rethink my invitation then. You're liable to humiliate the rest of us ..."

Joshua's curiosity was piqued and he asked, "What do you have in mind?"

"Well, tomorrow is my day off. It's a dark secret among the clergy. We really do like to go out and play rather than work all the time. Anyway, we had a foursome scheduled for eighteen holes tomorrow. But one of our group had to bail out. So we need a fourth. Would you be interested?"

For an instant Joshua knew exactly what his answer was going to be. He had a ton of work waiting for him at the office. He had financial reports from his multiple companies that needed review. He had an R&D meeting with his engineers on refinements for the RTS system. And he also planned to have an extended phone call with his lawyer, Harry Smythe, to find out what else he knew about his congressional situation.

Then Joshua caught his wife out of the corner of his eye. She was looking right at him, straight as an arrow, with a glowing smile on her face.

Wow, he thought, *there is a beauty about her right now that I can't really describe. Different.* He was caught off guard for a second.

"So," Campbell prodded, "are you going to join us and show us how the game is played?"

"Sounds like your kind of fun," Abby added.

That is when Joshua surprised himself. "Sure. All right. Why not? I'll make the time. I was supposed to shoot some golf in Colorado with a buddy of mine yesterday, but it didn't work out. This will make up for it."

"Great. How about we all meet out at the Hanover Golf Club? Do you know where it is?"

"I do. What time?"

"Tee-off is nine thirty a.m. Let's get together in the clubhouse at nine fifteen."

"I'll be there."

As Joshua was driving home through the New York City traffic, he noticed that Abigail wasn't talking, but she had her head back against the headrest and a smile on her face. There was a special aura of peace about her.

"You're noticeably quiet."

"Contented, that's all."

Joshua almost chuckled at that. During the sermon that night he had felt like he had a freeway rush-hour running through his brain. Contentment?

"I wish I was," he shot back. "You'll have to share your secret with me."

Deborah suddenly laughed in the back seat.

"What's so funny?" Joshua asked.

"Okay, Mom, share your secret of contentment with Dad ..."

Abigail threw her daughter a look that without any words seemed to contain all the wisdom and experience of womanhood in it.

Deborah got the silent message and muttered, "Fine." She quit talking and sat back in her seat.

Then Abigail turned to her husband and said, "I'm glad you're golf-ing. I think it will be a nice change for you."

"You know how seriously I take my golf game. Your pastor won't be preaching to me out on the links will he?"

After a long dramatic pause, Abigail took a deep breath. "Probably will."

Both she and Deborah burst into laughter.

Joshua shook his head and groaned, "Wonderful ..."

Despite his misgivings about being a captive audience to a sermon lasting eighteen holes, Joshua was looking forward to playing golf. The Hanover Course was an excellent one, and he'd had the chance to play it only twice over the years.

Standing on the high plateau at the first hole, Joshua took a few seconds to gaze over the forest tree tops, out to the cityscape at the end of the horizon. He had forgotten what an impressive view there was of the New York City skyline from the first tee. *What if the RTS hadn't worked perfectly ... just think. Abby and I would both be gone. Cal and Deb too. Manhattan out there would be nuked. So many dead. Come on, Josh, it wasn't really you who saved the city. No way. You've always known that ...*

"Okay, you're the leader of the foursome."

Paul Campbell was taking a few swings with his driver as he ap-proached. He was flanked by the other two golfers, Bob and Carl, busi-nessmen from his church board.

Then the pastor added with a mock grimace, "Now let the pain and suffering for us duffers begin ..."

Joshua walked over to the tee. He set his ball. After his customary stretching exercise while holding the shank of the driver over his head with both hands, he stepped back and took two practice swings.

"You guys may want to keep a safe distance," Joshua cracked. "I'm about to commence firing ..."

The other three laughed.

But when Joshua swung through, it was with the velocity of a pitching machine. There was that sound of the solid crack as his round, little white-coated Bridgestone B330 lifted up into the air and continued arching and then finally disappeared down onto the fairway past the two-hundred-yard marker. The laughing had stopped.

"Beautiful shot," Campbell said with admiration.

The pastor was second.

Joshua noticed that Paul Campbell had a strong athletic build and an easy swing. He didn't tee off with the power that Joshua had. But he was controlled. He put his ball about sixty feet behind Joshua's.

Joshua was on the green in two strokes. Campbell was there in three. But Joshua had a long, tough putt, and it just rimmed the cup. They both ended up tying the first hole with a par.

By the seventh hole Joshua was feeling at ease with Campbell as his playing partner and had sized him up as a decent golfer. He was ahead of the pastor by two strokes. The other two were playing back, lagging behind.

"You like the course?" Campbell asked.

"It's well laid out. Beautiful, really. But you can't let your guard down on this course."

"No, you're right. Hazards popping up everywhere. Shifting elevations. I've been out here a half dozen times with Bob and Carl. They're both members. But I never got the feeling I've completely mastered a single hole."

"That view from the tee-off by the clubhouse is spectacular. You can see all the way to the skyline."

"You can, when the air's clean and the sky's right. Like today."

There was a pause while Joshua took a second to dunk his ball in the ball washer and wipe it clean.

Campbell went on to say, "Golf always reminds me of something."

"What's that?"

"It reminds me of life. Similar in some ways. But also dissimilar."

Joshua thought to himself, *Here it comes. I wonder if he's got his Bible hidden in his golf bag.*

Campbell had posed an intriguing question. But Joshua didn't want to bite. What he wanted to do was lengthen his lead on this par four coming up. But he engaged him anyway.

"Let me guess," Joshua said with a slight air of amusement. "Golf is like life because it's full of unexpected hazards. Water hazard over here. Sand trap over there. Deep woods that will put your ball down onto a tree root. Am I close?"

"Right on target," Campbell said with a chuckle. "You've landed on the green ..."

"So, how is golf *dissimilar* then?"

Campbell didn't respond. Instead he looked Joshua Jordan in the eye with a look that had nothing to do with swinging a club.

The pastor finally said, "I think I'm going to let you figure that one out on your own." Then he added, pointing to the tee, "Okay, leader, swing away ..."

TH1RTY-51X

Agent John Gallagher was now looking at another dead man. *Oh well. All in a day's work.*

The FBI agent was in a dark, sardonic mood as he hunched over the corpse. The victim was still strapped to a chair in his inner office in the insurance company. The police had to get a locksmith to open the door, which had been locked from the outside.

"What's his name?"

One of the two Philadelphia police detectives on the scene flipped open his little day book where he had written it down.

"Roger French. Insurance broker. Commercial insurance."

"So, any thoughts on all this?"

"Remind me again," the detective said. "Why's the FBI interested in this?"

"I am investigating a federal crime."

"And what *federal* crime would that be?"

"One that is currently under investigation." Gallagher said with a half-smile. "Look, fellas, I caught the report on my laptop while I was out doing fieldwork on a case a couple states away. I had put a crime profiler submission out over interagency-net. Crimes within driving distance from upper state New York ... crimes of a certain nature. Yours popped up. Here I am. Don't mean to be pushy, but you know we feds have superior jurisdiction. So, what's your theory?"

The detective wasn't pleased. But he knew for the time being he had to humor this federal intrusion.

"Maybe a drug deal gone bad," he suggested. When Gallagher tossed him a skeptical look, the detective added, "This part of town has developed some illegal drug traffic."

The FBI agent had to ask the obvious, "So, is our guy here, Mr. French, a known drug dealer or user? Or maybe a frequenter at coke or heroin parties?"

The detective looked over at his partner who shook his head no.

"Any hint of drugs found here in this office?"

"Just some Tylenol in his desk."

Gallagher had to restrain himself at that one. But he kept it professional.

"Any prior criminal record?"

Both detectives shook their heads.

"Any prior arrests? Outstanding warrants against Mr. French? Any judicial warrants of any kind out against him?"

The two detectives kept shaking their heads.

"Does your PD have anything *bad* to say about Mr. Roger French?" Gallagher said, now venturing into sarcasm. "Parking tickets ... books not returned to the public library ..."

The senior detective cleared his throat and finally said, "The deceased appears to be clean."

Gallagher finally had to let it out, and when he did in his tone there was a certain amount of *tell me again why am I wasting my time with you guys?*

"Yet you fellows are still sticking to the drug-dealing scenario?"

"Meaning what?" the detective retorted.

Gallagher was getting impatient. "Look at this crime scene. The victim was tied to a chair, and by my guess had been connected to that wall socket over there by electric leads ..." Gallagher pointed at the tiny burn marks on each earlobe.

"So," a detective said, "he was ..."

"Right, tortured," Gallagher cut in to save time. "Perfectly standard interrogation technique, of course, if you live in, say, Iran. But, gentlemen, this is Philadelphia ..." Then as he surveyed the body he added, "I think he put up a fight. Maybe reluctant to talk, otherwise no need to turn up the juice on this poor guy ..."

"Talk about what?"

"That's what I need to find out. What kind of information did our victim have access to, other than insurance rates and commercial premium amounts? Anything that might be of unique value to some bad guys?"

"We're not sure."

"How about any unusual contacts he had. Anything there?"

That's when the two detectives looked at each other. After a moment, one of them spoke up.

"Mr. French is the son-in-law to Mr. Rocky Bridger, a retired general."

"Where was the general detailed?"

"The Pentagon."

Gallagher had already done the math. One of the first things the detectives told him when he had arrived was that Roger French had left a message on the voicemail of his wife saying he was going to be late to their daughter's basketball game because he had some "last minute business" to attend to. Gallagher figured the killer could have set up a meeting with French. He had computed the drive time from the crime scene in the swamp in the New York State countryside to that part of Philly. Gallagher was starting to get the feeling in his gut, and in his brain, and literally right in front of his eyes, everywhere, that this crime spree he was witnessing was a trail of carefully premeditated mayhem left by Atta Zimler.

"The Pentagon?" Gallagher yelled out loud, to emphasize the obvious.

Two detectives nodded in tandem.

"Fellas," the agent said, handing his card over to the senior detective, "I would appreciate any updates you can give me on your progress on this case."

When Agent Gallagher was in his car, he called Miles Zadernack, his supervisor. He was glad Miles picked up the call immediately.

"Miles, Gallagher here. That case I've been working on turned up something big. I think it needs a focused, special investigation."

"What do you have?"

"My favorite subject … Atta Zimler. Miles, I think he's entered the United States."

There was a dead silence on the other end for at least ten seconds.

"If that's true," Zadernack then said in a deadpan monotone, "that would certainly be remarkable."

Remarkable? That comment struck Gallagher like something you might expect from a birdwatcher who had just spotted a species he hadn't seen in a while.

"*If* it's true," Zadernack added again for emphasis.

"I think it is. I've been piecing together the trail. It has all the elements of the *modus operandi* of our terrorist assassin."

"Yes, but why would he enter the United States in the first place? Seems highly risky for him."

Gallagher was trying to keep a respectful tone, but it was getting really hard.

"Miles, hey, you've got to be kidding. Please, trust me on this one."

"John," Miles Zadernack said. "I think we need to meet to discuss this. Face-to-face. Here in the office."

"I'm in Philly now, following some leads. That's going to be kinda tough. Time is of the essence — "

"I'm not *asking* you to come back to New York."

Gallagher burst out with, "Miles, you're kidding me — "

But Miles shot back with, "John, I don't know why you keep saying that. You know I'm not a person who kids around. I want you back here ASAP. Then we'll talk."

John Gallagher clicked off his Allfone cell. His chest was burning again. Zadernack had already derailed his investigation of Ivan the Terrible, the talk radio host.

Now this. His first thought was, admittedly, one of base self-preservation. *Am I getting canned? Demoted to a desk job? Reassigned to Montana? Something's coming down. Whatever it is, this is not going to be good for John Gallagher.*

What he didn't expect, though, was something far worse.

TH1RTY-5EVEN

The first seventeen holes flew by. Joshua and his partners were having a good time. The course at Hanover Golf Club was every bit as difficult as Joshua had remembered. When they got to the last hole, Joshua's ball was about ten feet off the green. Campbell's ball was a few feet back on the fairway.

Joshua was laying two strokes on that last hole, which was a par four, and he was ahead of Paul Campbell by three strokes. But the pastor was also laying two on that last hole. Joshua knew that his opponent had played a respectable game, even making him sweat a little at the beginning of the back nine. But Joshua's powerful command of the game was finally edging him away from his competitor.

Joshua carefully eyed his ball, then studied the distance to the green and to the cup. Campbell was watching him.

"I'm starting to recognize that look on your face. You're aiming for a birdie on this last hole, I'm sure of it!" Campbell shouted out to him. "You're going to try to drop that ball right into the cup."

As Joshua pulled out his nine-iron, he smiled and shot back, "It's crossed my mind ..."

"Rub it in! Go ahead, rub it in!"

He took a few practice swings, then set himself at the ball. Joshua looked up and over the wide green for one last second, looking beyond it to the huge sand trap that lay on the other side. *Enough but not too much. Controlled swing. Get up under the ball. Arch it high so it drops a few feet directly in front of the hole. Forget about the backspin this time. Don't focus on the sand hazard. Go for broke.*

Joshua swung a seemingly flawless stroke, catching the ball on the full flat of his nine-iron and scooping it high into the air and sending it toward the green in a graceful curve.

It looked perfectly aligned to head right toward the cup, which was in the middle of the wide, irregular-shaped green.

But without backspin the ball hit the green hard and bounced once and then skipped over the hole and then caught the down-slope on the other side of the green and started rolling away from the pin, now picking up speed.

In an instant, the golf ball rolled off the green, dropping off the little lip of the sand trap where it met the green and rolled down several feet almost to the beginning of the steep sand hazard on the other side.

Joshua kept his cool, as he always did. But he was already adding it up in his head. If Campbell did well in his final stroke or two and Joshua didn't, things could get very interesting.

Campbell took out his nine-iron. He looked relaxed in front of the ball. He swung.

His ball went up into the air and then landed down on the green with a vicious spin, slowing down, but still heading right toward the cup, and then picked up the slight down-slope and kept rolling. Joshua was watching, and now he was concerned.

The ball was rolling up to the cup. But just before it got there it angled off and caught the edge of the round hole.

The ball rimmed the cup and rolled around the circumference once and then dropped into the cup with a clunk.

Joshua was astonished. *Oh man, that was too much . . .*

"Great shot!" Joshua called out. "Now how do we account for that? Divine miracle or minister's luck?"

Campbell was surprised himself at the shot and was laughing. "Don't ask me. I couldn't begin to tell you how I just did that ..."

Joshua had just lost his three-stroke lead. With his next stroke it would be down to just two. And he might be lucky to win by just two. The sand trap was a bear of a hazard. There was ten feet of sand to cross. Uphill. Then to a green that seemed to be fast. And he still had to conquer the moderate up-slope to the pin.

Joshua took out his sand wedge and sauntered down into the sand.

From the top, looking down at him, Campbell was smiling, watching a super competitor in the clutches of a pressure play.

But inside Joshua's head, he had closed out the emotions that tell you how much winning is important — winning at everything — and he was now running on automatic.

It was his own mental formula developed in those situations where he had been up in the thin air, going several hundred miles per hour in a military jet when things suddenly went bad, and he had to make them good — or perish.

Direction, altitude, power, precision, control.

Now ...

With the swing, the full plate of the wedge scooped the golf ball up and sent it arching over the wicked sands, upward, toward the green.

There was enough power behind it to take it completely out of the sand hazard and over the green where it dropped and started traveling fast toward the pin.

Joshua couldn't see the hole from down where he was, so he was "flying by instruments," as he called it, just using the flag on the pin that Pastor Campbell was holding up there on the green as his guide.

Then Pastor Campbell gave a little jump and he swung his fist in the air and laughed.

"Unbelievable!" he cried out. "Great shot!"

Joshua made his way out of the sand, strode up to the green and over to the cup.

There was a quiet feeling of satisfaction as he reached down and felt the ball at the bottom of the cup and then plucked it up.

Bob and Carl, who were playing back, had arrived just in time to see Joshua's magnificent shot.

When the four of them were back at the clubhouse there was a general celebration over Joshua's mastery of the course. At the same time, Pastor Campbell said that it had been the best eighteen holes that he had ever played at Hanover.

The two other men had to run off to meetings, so Paul Campbell and Joshua sat down in the club for a quick sandwich.

"You really forced me to up my game," the pastor said. "But at the same time, hey, I've got to admit ... some of my shots were flukes. I don't think I earned my score today, shooting just two strokes behind you. You, on the other hand, really earned your score. You play the game with a tremendous amount of skill. And discipline."

Joshua smiled as he chewed on his BLT on whole wheat.

Then something occurred to him. He had to say it out loud. "That's it."

"What?" Campbell replied.

"The answer to your little riddle. You said that life was dissimilar to the game of golf."

"Right. So, what's your answer?"

"I think your point was that it may take discipline and skill to achieve things in life. Obviously. But that somehow those things aren't enough."

Paul Campbell stopped eating. He wiped his mouth with his napkin and leaned back.

"I think you're right."

But now Joshua wanted the pastor to close the loop. He asked, "So, skill and discipline are not enough ... but not enough for *what*?"

"For God."

There was silence between the two men. Joshua expected the man sitting across the café table to keep talking. But he didn't. Finally Joshua had to plow ahead.

"Okay. What about God?"

"As skilled and disciplined and accomplished as you — or anyone, for that matter — might be ... regardless of that, it's not enough to please God."

"Sounds like He's hard to please," Joshua shot back with a chuckle.

The pastor replied simply, "Exactly. God is hard to please. Impossible in fact."

This surprised Joshua. "Wow, that's a downer coming from a clergyman. I thought you guys specialized in giving out words of hope."

"Let's put it this way: God won't be pleased with purely human effort as a way to achieve relationship with Him. That'll never work."

"Why not?"

"The Bible says every one of us has sinned and fallen short of the glory that we were originally designed for. We all have an inherent sin flaw, and we act on that. That blocks our ability to connect with God."

"So what's your solution ... to not sin? Act self-righteous? Be pious? Go to church?"

"Nope."

Now Joshua was getting impatient. If there was a problem, then he liked to figure out the solution. Campbell was proposing a tragic problem for the human race, and no solution.

"Then what?" Joshua asked. His voice was loud enough to draw the attention of a group of women eating lunch at a nearby table who turned and looked.

Campbell replied, "Accept the one solution that God's given us. That's the only remedy that will work. The only thing that will enable us to have any kind of relationship with Him. To receive forgiveness for sin. Take us out of the enemy camp and put us into friendship with the Creator of the Universe. That's it. Nothing else will do."

Joshua was looking for loopholes. "So no multiple options available?

Look, if I'm way up in the stratosphere flying at Mach one and I encounter problems with my aircraft, I'm not going to limit myself to one single solution. I'll try multiple strategies to get control of that airplane."

"Let's use a communications model. You're up in that aircraft. You want to contact the control tower. The radio has to be set on the right frequency. If the tower has only one frequency available, it doesn't make much sense to say you don't like that frequency and you'd rather have multiple options ..."

"So, what's the single frequency for God?"

"The Bible makes it crystal clear. The ultimate reason that Jesus came to earth was simple, but pretty mind-blowing. He came to be cruelly tortured and then to die in a Roman crucifixion just outside the city walls in ancient Jerusalem. That's the only way He could be a sacrifice. The perfect Son of God, offered as a perfect payment for the price of my sin — and yours."

Joshua was calculating the odds. Something didn't add up. "There are what ... thirteen billion people who've lived on this planet, something like that? So how could one man, I don't care who he is ... how could one man's blood possibly cover the sins of every single person? Couldn't be done."

Paul Campbell nodded. "You're right. Can't be done."

Joshua chuckled and sized up the man across the table. "Now you agree with me? What's the hitch?"

"Because an ordinary man could never die for his own sins, let alone billions of others. But then, that's the point of those Bible prophecies I was talking about at church. God has given us the guidance from His Word, like landing lights on an airport runway. Pointing the way directly to Jesus as the one and only Savior. God made into man. Fully human, yet fully Divine. Incomprehensible? Yes. But when Jesus was crucified, it was literally the blood of God being shed, which is the only thing that can cleanse the sins of thirteen billion people. Obviously, Josh, God thinks human beings are worth saving. It's that simple. And that profound. The only thing left is how we respond to that."

"So here's my response," Joshua said. "Some things are worth saving. Right? We can agree on that. In my case I want to save my country. I caught what you were saying last night. In fact, you and I have something else in common, beyond a close golf game I mean."

"What's that?"

"We both realize that this may be the last and best chance we have to stop America from being sucked into a global commune. A place where liberty gets destroyed by redefinition. Our borders start to evaporate. Where we have to ask permission of the international community before we take action to defend ourselves. Where the vision of men like Patrick Henry and George Washington gets erased from the memories of our grandchildren. According to what you said last night, if that happens, it could be the beginning of the end. One long, ugly global nightmare. Well, I'm not just going to sit back and watch it happen."

"Nations are made up of people. That includes you. So, you may want to consider looking to your own salvation first, Josh. You may be surprised what God has in store for you once you sign onto His team."

"You want me to do the same kind of spiritual conversion thing that Abby did? Which is fine for her. But what you're offering me, it's certainly not the right time."

"What do you mean?"

"Let's face it. Right now my life is tied up in a complicated struggle. I'm on a mission. Everything I am and all that I have, everything is going to be devoted to that task. My business interests, my energy. Everything. I appreciate what you're saying. But I'm on a different road right now. And I'm not stopping till I've accomplished the mission."

Campbell nodded and said. "You mentioned Patrick Henry. Wasn't he the one who said that God directs the destinies of nations?"

"Sure. But then he rose up, shook his fist at Great Britain, and fought for freedom. I can't wait for divine intervention, Pastor. I need to act."

"Just one thought. Something I didn't get a chance to share last night."

"What's that?"

"God's the keeper of the timetable. He's the only one who knows the exact timing of the end. I've made the Scriptures my lifelong study. You want to know where the United States is mentioned?"

"Sure."

"So would I. And I'm still looking. Why no clear, specific mention of America? Maybe He simply doesn't want us to know the fate of our nation in advance. So we can rise to the challenge. Seek His face while there's still time."

There was a penetrating power in Pastor Campbell's gaze. He was looking into Joshua's eyes with a strange kind of tranquility.

Finally, Joshua stood up from the table, saying he had to get to the office. He smiled and shook Paul Campbell's hand.

But before turning to leave the clubhouse, he had to give some credit where credit was due.

"Great game, by the way. You gave me a run for my money. Let's do it again sometime."

THIRTY-EIGHT

Vice President Jessica Tulrude's feet were killing her. She wished she hadn't worn heels, particularly for the tour down the ancient Roman stone streets of Pompeii. She pretended to listen intently to the tour guide and worked equally hard to keep her smile in place for the small contingent of international photo press.

Tulrude was part of a small entourage that included several officials from the European Union and the deputy assistant to the president of the EU. Tulrude had come to Italy for a joint conference between the EU and the United States on matters of common interest, including global finance.

Before the trip she had had a heated argument with Secretary of State Danburg over who ought to attend the conference. Ever the political survivor, Vice President Tulrude was able to muscle him out of the picture. She knew the public-relations value of the event. After all, her political advisors had told her she needed to increase her international prestige in foreign affairs if she wanted to give her future campaign a bump. This would be just the thing.

The luminaries in the tour group also included a handful of influential international entrepreneurs.

Caesar Demas was one of them. He was strolling in his short sleeves and smiling from behind his custom-designed Georgio Armani sunglasses.

Demas strode up next to Tulrude while he pretended to be surveying the Roman arched doorways and first-century stone houses on each side of the white cobblestone street.

Tulrude was careful not to face him but addressed him in a side glance. "Tell me again, Caesar, who cooked up this ridiculous idea to spend a half day walking through a dead Roman city?"

"I believe, Jessica, it was his eminence, the president of the European Union. This is part of his global media push for an international effort among the nations to jointly prepare for mass disasters."

Demas couldn't see it, but Tulrude was rolling her eyes at that one. When she responded, her voice was dripping with the kind of whiney, cynical tone that her advisors had warned her against.

"So he picks a city ... from the first century ... that was buried by a volcanic eruption, as the photo-op for his pet project on global disasters? Oh pleeease ..."

"Look at it this way. At least it gives the two of us an opportunity to chat for a few minutes in a way that doesn't raise suspicions," Demas said. "I have been meaning to connect with you anyway. Tell you how sad I was that I couldn't work with the White House as an unofficial envoy to negotiate an arrangement for sharing the RTS weapons technology with other nations ..."

"Yes, well all the polls went south on that issue for us. It sounded like a good idea at the time, but in the end we couldn't have survived the political fallout."

"Understood. But you and I now have other things to talk about." Demas patted her on the arm. "Like your political future."

Before Tulrude could respond, she spotted her chief of staff, Lana Orvilla, and a secret service agent walking at a fast clip toward her.

Orvilla handed her an encrypted satellite Allfone.

"Sorry, Madam Vice President," she said, "but we have an urgent call from the Department of Justice. Attorney General Hamburg needs to speak to you."

Tulrude excused herself from Caesar Demas and then stepped away from the group to take the call.

"Madam Vice President," Attorney General Cory Hamburg started out. "Sorry to break into your travels, but we have an important security issue that we need to verify. Both the FBI and our own terrorism people here at the Department of Justice need to double-check on something."

"Certainly. National security always comes first. What can I do for you?"

"There was a directive given from Homeland Security relating to a prime terror target. A known terrorist and assassin by the name of Mr. Atta Zimler."

"How does this concern me?"

"Well, Zimler has been high on our terror list for a number of years. But Homeland Security has asked us to stand down temporarily on any domestic investigations concerning Zimler. When we questioned them about it, they said we should talk to your office."

"Yes, now I recall the situation," Tulrude said. "The White House and Homeland Security have been discussing the problem of mistaken identities in our antiterrorism programs. You know, arresting the wrong people because of a glitch in the system. Similar names. That kind of thing. We simply can't tolerate those kinds of mistakes . . ."

The attorney general was quick to interject, "Yes, that's what they told us too. There was some unnamed diplomat who thinks he may be at risk, you know, to be mistaken for Atta Zimler. This diplomat is supposedly coming to the United States, and Homeland Security is concerned about international embarrassment if he is wrongly taken into custody. Truthfully, I'm a little uneasy about this one. We have no name for the diplomat. Frankly don't even know whether he exists . . ."

"Of course he exists," Tulrude said but refrained at adding anything else. She pursed her lips and started tapping her finger on the cover of the phone. After a few seconds of silence she said, "I'm not sure where you're going with this. How this involves me ..."

"Just so you know," the attorney general continued, "Madam Vice President, this directive is highly irregular. It came from Homeland Security to the Department of Justice. Regarding a potential terrorism investigation ... as you know, protocol is that it should work the other way around. They also told us that Zimler was taken into custody in Europe ... maybe Paris. If Zimler is in custody, okay, fine, no problem ... but we can't get verification of that. Nothing through the normal channels ... zero information from the Paris police ... nothing from INTERPOL — "

Tulrude's reply was curt. "What do you want from me, General Hamburg? Spell it out."

"While you are there in Italy, if you could talk to the EU folks, have their contacts in France put a rush on this intelligence issue. Confirm that Zimler has been caught. We need this information ASAP. Obviously, in the interim we will pull back on any investigation here in the U.S. regarding persons that might be mistaken for this Atta Zimler — "

"Yes, of course. When the timing is right ..." Tulrude assured him. "And General Hamburg? I'll be sure to put in a good word for you at the EU conference."

"Thank you, Madam Vice President."

Tulrude handed the phone back to her chief of staff. The secret service agent was standing right behind her. The rest of the group had wandered farther down the ancient street, all except Caesar Demas, who was lagging behind.

The vice president ordered Lana Orvilla and the secret service man to walk up ahead and said that she would be there shortly. The secret service agent protested politely. He reminded the vice president that her safety was his responsibility. But Tulrude cut him off.

"Agent, would you like to be relieved of your assignment?"

He got the message. His face tightened.

"I'll be waiting for you right up the street, Madam Vice President."

When Orvilla and the agent were at least fifty feet ahead on the old Roman street, Tulrude strolled up next to Demas. When she did, she nodded toward the arched entrance of a stone building where they could talk. The two of them stepped up to the portico, looked both ways for photographers, and then stepped just inside the doorway and out of sight.

"You'll never guess, Caesar, who that phone call was from."

Before Demas could respond, Tulrude plunged ahead. "It was the attorney general," she said. "Calling about this Atta Zimler matter. Now I've gone out on a limb for you. We're delaying any domestic investigation into Zimler for the time being. Just like you asked. So you can tell your diplomatic friend … whoever he is … that he doesn't have to be worried about being harassed inside the U.S. by mistake. But I need you to ask your contacts inside the Paris intelligence office to verify with the DOJ that they've actually got this Zimler in custody, as you told me they did. I mean, really, Caesar, I am taking a serious risk here for you. Just think of the damage to me if you're wrong, and this Zimler actually ends up inside America somehow …"

"Not to worry. I'll have my friends inside French security give the necessary assurances to your Department of Justice people."

"Good."

Caesar Demas moved in closer for just a moment to grasp the vice president's hand.

"My foundation has deposited ten million euros in an offshore account for your election campaign. It will then be dispersed through a variety of American organizations and charities into your campaign. Very clean. We will deposit another twenty million — assuming you can pass the primaries in good shape."

"Oh, I'll get through the primaries, Caesar. Have no doubt about that."

"I'm just reminding both of us of the rules."

Just then something caught Jessica Tulrude's attention. She craned her neck to look closer at the faded paintings on the wall of the ancient building where they were standing.

"Caesar, what kind of building was this? I mean, in Roman times ..."

He laughed.

"It was a brothel."

Tulrude broke out into a loud cackle.

Both of them enjoyed the unspoken humor. Picking that kind of a place to discuss Jessica Tulrude's intentions to run for president.

TH1RTY-N1NE

At Liberty University

"Mr. Jordan, perhaps you could answer that question?"

Cal Jordan had been busy sketching a picture on his notepad. He looked up with embarrassment to find the entire class staring at him.

"Sorry, professor. I didn't hear it."

There were muffled laughs from a few students ten rows back that echoed through the large college lecture hall.

At the front of the class the professor frowned and tried again. "The question, Mr. Jordan, from one of your fellow classmates, was, Why should Congress have the power to force a private citizen to testify in a congressional hearing?"

For a moment, Cal's brain froze.

The professor studied Cal and then expanded his question. "We are studying the powers of the Congress. Mr. Hitchney asked a salient question about the subpoena power of the Congress."

Cal turned around and looked ten rows back until he located the face of Jeff Hitchney, another student in the class. Hitchney, a tall blond sophomore had a twisted half-smile on his face. Cal now realized that the student had planted the question on purpose to embarrass him. Hitchney was the star pitcher on the college baseball team and was the leader of the school debate team. But there was one more thing. He had a keen interest in Cal's girlfriend, Karen Hester. And

Hitchney seemed intent on harassing Cal. After all, how could Karen have preferred Cal over him?

"Mr. Jordan," the professor said, pressing in gently, "I thought you might have some thoughts on the subject considering the fact that your father, Joshua Jordan, is in the news on that exact issue."

Cal cringed. *There it is again. Colonel Joshua Jordan. The man who single-handedly rescued New York City from the perils of incoming nuclear missiles. Wherever I go, I can't escape my father.*

Now Cal struggled to focus and form an intelligent answer. He gave it his best shot. "The power of Congress to conduct hearings sort of assumes, I guess, the power to conduct hearings for the good of the country. And that would assume, I suppose, the power to force people to testify."

The professor gave a quick nod. Then he saw Hitchney's hand up again and called on him.

"Professor, it seems to me that Jordan is admitting then that his father is wrong and that Congress is right. Because he plainly suggested in his answer that the subpoena power is an appropriate exercise of the authority of congressional committees."

Hitchney capped it off with a smug grin.

A few more chuckles from Hitchney's row.

Cal's hand shot up. The professor recognized him. "Yes, Mr. Jordan."

"Mr. Hitchney is correct that I am admitting the power of Congress to subpoena witnesses. But that's not what my father's case is about. What that case is about is the fact that Congress can't force someone to give away trade secrets and business intelligence. Which is what they are trying to do. Plus ... there's something else involved too ..."

The professor asked, "And what is that?"

"Sometimes people refuse to give information to Congress ... or a court too ... for good reasons. Last week we studied the situation about media reporters who refused to testify in court about who their confidential sources were. They said they had a greater right to protect their news sources."

"And what is the greater right in your father's case?"

Cal paused. He now was in the interesting dilemma of having to defend his father's case. He wasn't hot on that idea. Plus the things that his mom and his sister, Deborah, had shared with him about his father's legal situation were strictly interfamily matters. Very private. But Cal had another overriding thought. *On the other hand, there's no way I'm letting Hitchney off the hook.*

"Okay. Here's the deal," Cal replied. "My father invented this laser weapon ... the RTS. Return-to-Sender thing. He never gave the government full ownership of the design. It was still in, like, an experimental phase. Then the North Koreans launched missiles at us. The government used my dad's weapon to stop the missiles —"

Another student blurted out, "Yeah, and melted the North Koreans who may not have even been the attackers ..."

With that a few students gave out a subdued *boo*.

But the rest of the class started their own spontaneous cheer for Joshua Jordan.

As the issue erupted all over the lecture hall around him, Cal was quietly staring at his hands in front of him. *Man, I can't believe this. Why did the professor go into this stuff anyway?*

After the instructor brought the class back to order, he asked Cal to finish his thought.

"The point I was making is just this," Cal explained. "If the government doesn't own the weapon, then shouldn't the businessman who invented it be able to protect his design?"

Hitchney shot his hand up, and the professor nodded for him to speak again.

"Weapons involve national security. That issue doesn't belong to some multimillionaire businessman; it belongs to the government."

Cal didn't wait to be called on.

"Uh, we *are* the government," he said, turning back toward Hitchney. "We studied that during the first week of this class …"

Hitchney didn't wait for the nod from the professor this time. "One private citizen can't decide those kinds of things. That would be chaos. The government is supposed to decide those issues —"

"And what if some of the politicians in Congress aren't trustworthy? What if they let that weapon information slip into the wrong hands —"

"Wow, talk about paranoid," Hitchney muttered to his friends sitting next to him, but loud enough for most of the class to hear.

That is when the professor stepped back into the discussion. "Okay, okay. Good discussion. By the way, I love it when you students decide to exercise your gray matter. I think that's great."

Then the professor turned to Cal again. "Just wondering Mr. Jordan, what's your major?"

"Art."

"Well, if you ever get tired of art, you may want to think about pre-law. You raised some good points today. And you might give some thought to joining the debate team too."

When he said that, the professor smiled and threw a smile up toward Jeff Hitchney, who was trying hard not to look threatened by that last comment.

As the professor continued his lecture, Cal felt his Allfone vibrate. He had set the vibrate mode on Morse code. Home was coded to vibrate dots and dashes for the word *family*. But calls from his father's office were set to vibrate out the code for *SOS* — the international distress signal. That was his own private joke.

This time it was the SOS. He wasn't going to take it. At least not right now, when the eyes of half the class were still glued on him.

□□□

Back in his high-rise office in New York, Joshua Jordan was letting his call go through to his son on his speakerphone while he continued to scan a weapons design memo from his engineering team.

The phone kept ringing. Joshua put the paper down. *He's not going to pick up. So, he knows it's me calling, and he's not picking up. Of course, he could still be in class. Take it easy, Joshua. Give the kid a break.*

When Joshua heard the start of his son's voicemail message he thought about leaving a message. But bad news was best delivered person-to-person.

He decided to hang up and try him again in a few minutes.

Joshua thought back to the call he had just received from Rocky Bridger, a man whose fortitude was usually chiseled out of granite. But when Joshua had picked up his telephone call, his voice sounded different.

Rocky started by saying, "Josh, Rocky. Oh man ..." His voice wavered.

There was a long pause. Then a sound. Rocky's voice was breaking with emotion.

"What is it?" Joshua asked.

"Roger, my son-in-law ... murdered ... Joshua ... my God, he's gone."

When Rocky collected himself, he shared the slight information he had. The police were playing cloak-and-danger with this. But the horrible bottom line was that Roger French was murdered in his office in downtown Philadelphia. The local police were being extremely tight-lipped about the details, though they'd mentioned that the FBI had some interest in the case. But his son-in-law was gone, the victim of a brutal crime, and now Rocky was with his daughter, who was in shock and was inconsolable.

Joshua tried his best to comfort his friend and mentor. But he felt stupid and useless and clumsy.

He had immediately called Abby. He'd always been impressed with her sense of compassion, but this time her willingness to drop everything to go to Philadelphia to help the family was particularly heartwarming.

Then something struck Joshua like a meteor. *Rocky just lost his son-in-law. To a senseless murder. Your life changes in a heartbeat. You can lose them … so quickly. When was the last time I told Cal that I loved him? Debbie and I don't have that issue. She's so up-front with everything. But Cal and I … things have always been uptight. Strained. And the clock keeps ticking. And nothing gets resolved. What if something happened to me? And I didn't get a chance to smooth things out with Cal beforehand?*

That's when Joshua felt the overpowering need to call his son.

He tried again, and after a few nervous seconds, Cal picked up the call.

"Josh, this is Dad."

"Hi."

"How are you doing?"

"Fine."

"Good. Look … I just heard some really bad news from a friend of mine. You know Rocky Bridger?"

Cal fell silent.

Joshua added, "The General from the Pentagon. Longtime friend of mine from the Air Force?"

"Oh, yeah …"

"Well, his son-in-law was murdered a couple of nights ago in Philadelphia. Rocky didn't have any details — why would anyone want to kill Roger?"

"I'm sorry to hear that, Dad. You and Mom mention Roger a lot. But I didn't know him well …"

"Well … I got to thinking, and I just needed to call you."

"Okay."

"And …"

"Yeah?"

"Just tell you …"

There was a pause.

"I love you."

Joshua wanted to elaborate somehow, but ended it there instead.

Taken off guard, Cal could only mumble, "Thanks, Dad."

"Sometime we need to talk, you and I."

"Okay."

"Man-to-man."

"All right."

Cal was thinking to himself, *What is this all about?* But asking that was too risky.

"I mean," Joshua added, "about what happened in New York. The day the missiles came. With you still being in the city ..."

Cal was thinking, *You mean so you can drill me about how I didn't tell you the truth about staying behind in Manhattan with my girlfriend, Karen Hester, who you don't approve of? You mean we need to talk about that? I already admitted all of that to Mom. Can't you just let it go?*

That is when the conversation started drifting away like a rudderless sailboat.

Finally, Joshua was the one who ended it.

"Okay, Son. Just wanted to call. So ... good-bye."

Cal was the last one to speak.

And all he said was, "Good-bye."

Then he clicked off his Allfone.

Some students who had just been in his government class when he took on Jeff Hitchney passed him by and called out his name and gave him the thumbs-up sign.

Cal smiled weakly and acknowledged them.

But inside, he was in turmoil.

FORTY

The owner of the hardware and mining-supply store in West Virginia was gingerly holding onto the box of explosives. He set it down cautiously on the counter. Then he pointed to the contents, so his customer could look inside.

The customer standing in front of him was a man in a flannel shirt with the sleeves cut off. He was wearing blue jeans and boots.

The jeans looked new.

He didn't recognize the customer.

"Which mining operation did you say you are working at?"

"Wyler Coal," Atta Zimler said, concocting the name instantly and doing a good imitation of a slow drawl. "It's a small mine. It's family owned. Just opened up."

"Okay," the hardware man said. "So anyway, these are the solid-pack Bridgewater-type blasting caps. They detonate from an electric spark…"

"Good," Zimler said. "That's what I'm looking for."

"What are you using as your primary explosive?"

Zimler grinned. He had no intention of telling him the truth. His *primary* was military grade plastic explosives he had already obtained on the black market for a pretty penny at a drop spot outside of Pittsburgh. All he needed now was a detonator. Blasting caps set off by an electric charge would be perfect. He had already purchased the remote switches from an electronics shop. Rigging those up with cell phones to send the charge would be child's play for him.

"Primary explosives?" Zimler replied. "Oh, the usual. Now these caps, they won't detonate by accident with static electricity in the air, right?"

"Nope."

"Stray cell phone signals, that kind of thing won't do it?"

"No. You have to send the electric charge directly to the cap for it to blow."

"Good," Zimler said. "My attitude is, when you blast, you want to make sure that your target gets the full force. And only *when* you want it to go off. Timing is everything. Right?"

Something hit the store clerk strange about the conversation, though he couldn't put his finger on it. "Yeah, I guess so ...," he replied.

Pulling out a wad of bills, Zimler paid cash.

Before the store owner handed over the box of blasting caps, however, he grabbed a clipboard and slapped it on the counter. "We're supposed to get this from everyone who wants explosives. Got to put your John Hancock right here ..."

Zimler smiled and acted like he understood the phrase. But he hesitated for just an instant.

He looked at the clipboard and noticed the signatures on it.

"You want me to sign here?"

"That's the general idea."

Zimler signed a fake name. The shop owner handed over the box.

"Y'all be safe now," he said to Zimler.

"Of course," Zimler said as he took the bag with the box of blasting caps in it and then left the store. He had taken a long detour to pick them up, but it was worth it.

▢▢▢

At one point in time, when Zimler had been on his way to West Virginia to secure the blasting caps, he had been going east on the Pennsylvania turnpike. That was before he had turned south toward the

West Virginia border. At that precise moment Zimler was less than fifty miles away from Special Agent John Gallagher's location.

The FBI agent was still stuck in Philadelphia before returning for New York. He had one more stop to make. But it was a crucial one. He knew he had to face Miles Zadernack at FBI headquarters. But hours before he was due at the airport, he had received a call from the Philly police detectives. Surprisingly, the lead detective was good to his word and was calling him with some additional information about their investigation into the murder of Roger French.

"Agent Gallagher, we've got something you might find interesting."

"I'm all ears."

"A video surveillance tape."

"From where exactly?"

"Taken from the video camera in the lobby of the building where Roger French's insurance company had their offices."

"Oh, yeah, I do love lobby surveillance video," Gallagher said with a bounce in his voice.

There was a pause on the other end. The detective didn't know exactly how to respond to this wise-cracking FBI agent.

Finally he said, "Come on over. We're in the viewing room."

When Gallagher hung up he suddenly felt as if he was seeing the light breaking in the distance. With any luck Zimler would be ID'd on the tape. And if that happened, then Miles Zadernack would have to listen to him.

Things were looking up.

FORTY-ONE

In the lobby of Jordan Technologies, Inc., the secretary had the deer-in-the-headlights look. Joshua had warned her that it could happen. But she still hadn't been prepared to come face-to-face with a U.S. marshal holding a subpoena in his hand.

"Madam, do you hear me? I'm a United States marshal. This is a legal document. I have to deliver it to Mr. Joshua Jordan. *Immediately.*"

She glanced down at it. She caught the caption at the top of the document:

By the authority of the Senate of the Congress of the United States of America

To: Mr. Joshua Jordan

You are hereby commanded to appear . . .

The secretary raised her eyes to the marshal and said, "He's not here, sir."

"Where is he?"

"I don't know."

"When is he coming back?"

"I don't know."

"Young lady, you are coming very close to obstructing a federal marshal in the course of his official duties. Do you realize that?"

She swallowed hard before she answered.

"Look, like I said, Mr. Jordan had an emergency, had me cancel his appointments, and left. I don't know what else to tell you."

The U.S. marshal dropped his card on the desk.

"Here's my number. Call me the moment he gets in."

The minute the marshal left the office, she called Joshua. He was in his limo heading down the Boulevard of the Americas in Manhattan. Joshua was on the line with Harry Smythe when the call came in. He put Harry on hold.

"Mr. Jordan," the secretary said breathlessly, "a U.S. marshal just came in with those papers."

"And?"

"I said exactly what you told me to say. Every bit."

"Very good."

"I was a little nervous though."

"Don't worry. I'm sure you did just fine."

Joshua said good-bye and then clicked back to Harry.

"Well, just like you predicted, Harry, they were over at my office trying to serve me with the subpoena."

"I think we need to just face up to this, Josh. Admit service. I'll accept service of the subpoena on your behalf at my office. Then I'll see what can be done legally."

"Harry, I want Abby's input on this."

"Is she there with you?"

"No. She's up in Pennsylvania. She's helping out a family friend of ours. They had a personal tragedy."

"Same old Abby."

Joshua asked Harry to standby while he conferenced her in.

When Abigail's Allfone rang, she was doing the dishes in the French house, while newly widowed Peg French was resting in her bedroom. Rocky Bridger was quietly playing with her and Roger's daughter.

"Abby, honey, it's me," Joshua said. "How are things going?"

"Peg's finally resting. Josh, this is so terrible."

"Have they got any more details?"

"Not much. They just said they have several theories. The police are being very secretive for some reason. But they did say one thing."

"What's that?"

"That he wasn't just murdered. He was tortured before he was killed."

"*Tortured*?"

"Yes."

"Who would have wanted to do that to Roger French? I can't think he would have been mixed up in anything sordid — he was a solid guy."

"No one can figure that out."

"And Rocky?

"He's putting up a brave front. You know him. He's focusing on Violet, Peg's daughter."

"Look, I'm sorry to throw this at you. But I've got Harry Smythe on the other line. I want to conference you in. Just as he thought, Senator Straworth is going to the mat on the RTS issue. They've issued a subpoena. A U.S. marshal was trying to serve it at my office. But I was out."

"Fine. Patch me in," Abigail said. She wiped her hands off with a dishtowel and then found a corner of the dining room where she couldn't be heard.

After Joshua looped all three of them in, he spelled out the issue. "Abby, Harry says we should let them serve the subpoena, then try to fight it out in court."

Abigail jumped in immediately. "Harry, I assume you're going into D.C. federal court with a motion to quash the subpoena?"

"That's the strategy. I just don't want my position weakened by any delay in Josh accepting service of the subpoena from the marshals."

Abigail was silent on the other end. Joshua knew she was digesting it. Then she spoke her mind. "Harry, once Josh is served with the sub-poena, the clock starts ticking. You then have to rush into court. What if you get the wrong judge and your motion is thrown out?"

"Well," Harry said, "then the game's almost over. Josh either turns over all his RTS documents or he goes to jail. Those have pretty much been the two options all along."

"You know Josh," Abigail chimed in. "He won't turn over those documents to Congress. He believes that our national security is too compromised on Capitol Hill right now. And if he goes to jail, his reputation, all that he's accomplished will be tarnished and destroyed."

"The whole thing stinks," Harry said. "I know that. But I don't make the rules."

"Then maybe it's time," Abigail said, "to change the game."

"What are you thinking, baby?" Joshua asked.

Abigail shot back, "Stall this thing. Stretch it out. We only need a few days."

"Days for what?" Harry said. "Josh, when it comes to political battles like this with Senator Straworth, you're in my world now. I know something about that. Most of my practice has been represent-ing senators, congressman, even a stint in the White House Counsel's Office, as you know. Look, I respect you, Abby. You did some great legal work on the Hill when you were practicing law. Cases before the Federal Communications Commission. Other federal agencies. But Josh, you've got to listen to me on this. There are some people up there in Congress who want to *destroy* you. And they will, believe me, if you start playing games like avoiding a subpoena."

"Harry, you're talking about enemies who want to destroy me. That sounds like war, and when it comes to military logistics, you're in *my* world. I don't intend to let a bunch of politicians destroy me."

"Which is why," Abigail said, "we strike first. We hit back first."

"With what?" Harry said, his voice now rising with a tinge of professional arrogance. "The only hope is my motion to quash this subpoena — "

"That's just one strategy," Abigail said. "And frankly, Harry, I think you'll lose that motion. The backup strategy, Josh, is that we buy time. Just long enough to make sure that Phil Rankowitz has got the AmeriNews launched."

"What are you talking about?" Harry said.

"A media project I'm working on," Joshua said. "Something you can't have any involvement in. But Abby's right. That's our offensive."

Abby said, "If we keep the marshals from serving that subpoena on you, then we keep you out of jail just long enough for the American people to read the first issue of AmeriNews. Once they find out the truth, I'm betting they'll vent some outrage to their senators. When that happens, I'm betting that Senator Straworth and his buddies will start thinking about withdrawing that subpoena."

"Josh, *really*," Harry blurted out. "I mean talk about a long shot — "

But Joshua cut him off.

"Harry, I've made my decision. Here's the drill. I'm going to avoid being served with that subpoena. Go into hiding if I have to. Harry, can you still try to get a judge to throw it out?"

"By not accepting service you're putting me in a very uncomfortable position with the court."

"I'm not asking about your comfort. I'm asking if you can still try that legal maneuver if I'm not served the subpoena."

After a moment's pause, Harry Smythe replied, "Yes, I suppose I can."

"Good. Meanwhile, Abby, you and I need to make sure that AmeriNews gets launched ASAP. We need to get to the American public. That's our best hope."

Harry Smythe wasn't going down without a fight.

"So you're simply rejecting my approach? My recommendation then?" Harry said coolly.

"What I am doing," Joshua said, "is going with Abby's plan instead." And then he added something else.

"When it comes to her advice, I'm willing to bank my life on it."

"You may have to," Harry punted back in his lawyerly pessimism. "You've got the federal government coming after your scalp."

FORTY-TWO

Somewhere in Hamad Katchi's brain, all was not well. Even though all around him the azure blue seas of the Mediterranean were calm and sparkling and a gentle four-knot wind was blowing.

Katchi had been on the huge yacht of his partner, Caesar Demas, many times before. This was the first time, though, that Demas had used such a small crew. Only a captain, a first and second mate, neither of whom Katchi recognized, and two other fellows. The last two appeared to be pretty useless. They were thick necked and muscular, looking more like bodybuilders or bouncers than sailors.

The Pakistani-born arms dealer was afraid of boats. He made no pretense of that. It was the general unpredictability of the sea that gave him that unease. The undulating expanse constantly changing. He found the absence of the sight of land disconcerting. As well as the fact that it contained living, teaming creatures under the surface. Things you cannot see. But creatures that can eat you.

Seated in a soft chair on the rear deck next to Caesar Demas, Katchi was trying to look relaxed.

They'd been making small talk.

Then Demas changed the subject. He wanted to discuss their plan to sell the RTS laser weapons technology as soon as Atta Zimler had obtained it.

"We've talked many times about our arrangements to sell off RTS."

"Yes. Any news from our messenger?"

"He's very close. At this point, he's virtually unstoppable."

"That's good to hear."

"So," Demas continued, "we are still of one mind, you and I, that when we are in possession of the RTS design, we should sell it to a group of willing nations. No exclusive rights to just one nation. Right? Didn't we agree on that?"

"Of course. Best way to maximize profit."

"Profit, yes, of course."

Caesar Demas glanced around for one of the crew. Then he spotted one of the muscle guys sunbathing on the upper deck. He was wearing dress slacks but had his shirt off.

"Georgio," Demas called out, "get me a gin and tonic."

Demas looked over at Katchi, but he said no, he didn't want anything except a glass of water.

By that time Katchi was feeling slightly nauseous. Maybe a bit seasick.

After a few minutes Georgio came with the two drinks.

There wasn't any ice in Katchi's water. A small thing. Katchi was going to ask this guy to fetch him some but decided against it.

"So," Demas said, making a sudden right turn in the conversation, "how was your trip to Moscow?"

Katchi was stunned. He hadn't told Caesar anything about the trip.

"Good," was all he said in response.

The rolling sense of imbalance on the ship was now getting to Katchi. He hoped he didn't vomit on the varnished wood deck of Caesar Demas' ninety-million-dollar yacht.

Katchi took a big gulp of water. But it didn't help.

Caesar Demas was casually inspecting the gently rolling blue sea all around, but he wasn't talking.

Now Katchi was getting nervous. He felt as if he needed to give some explanation about the Moscow trip. *If I don't explain, Caesar might think I just didn't consider it a big deal. Which would be good. On the other hand, my silence might make him think I'm hiding something. Which I am. Does Caesar know why I was there? Maybe he does and he's just playing with me. That'd be just like Caesar. Why did I go on his yacht today? I could have come up with an easy excuse. Told him I was sick. That I don't like boats.*

Demas took a slow sip from his glass and wiped his lips.

"About the Moscow trip," Katchi finally said. "I've always had an understanding with you ..."

"Oh?"

"About doing small side deals myself. Small arms. Nothing big. But you gave me the impression that was not a problem."

"Small-weapons deals? Not a problem. Is that what Moscow was all about? Small arms?"

"Yes. Yes, it was."

"Selling to some small-time Russian thugs I suppose."

"Right. A little pocket change. To pay the electric bills."

Katchi tried to laugh, but it caught in his throat.

"Small arms ...," Demas muttered.

"You know. AK-47s. Rocket launchers."

Caesar Demas said, "Hmmm."

"I trust you're okay with that?"

"Oh, yes. I would be okay with that."

More silence.

Then Demas glanced over toward Georgio, who, Katchi suddenly noticed, had worked himself, his shirt still off, closer to them and was standing up.

Then he was joined by the second muscle guy who had a silly smile on his face.

Both of the men had their hands in their pockets. They were looking at Hamad Katchi.

"The Moscow trip was successful for you?" Demas asked.

"Oh, sure. Not a lot of money. But worth the trip I suppose."

Demas made a quick, flitting gesture to the two men, quick, almost indecipherable.

The two men came up to stand on either side of Katchi.

"Please stand up," Demas said calmly to Katchi.

Something wasn't clicking in Katchi's brain. In his business of trading in weapons of destruction and death, he should have recognized what was happening. The survival instinct should have kicked in. Fight or flight.

Except in this case, neither was an option. And the brain was jamming.

"Get up on your feet, Hamad," Demas said again. "And step on the mat."

Looking down, Katchi noticed a thick fabric mat in front of his chair.

He also noticed a life vest lying on the deck. But the life vest was not orange like all the others he had ever seen. It was blue. Like the ocean. Which was strange, because someone wearing it would not be noticed from the air.

Katchi followed Caesar Demas's command and slowly rose, trying to come up with something clever to say. Something to stop the clock from ticking. To stop the bad thing he vaguely felt in his inner gut was about to happen.

He tried to smile. "On-deck calisthenics — "

But he couldn't finish his lame attempt at a joke.

Before he could, the muscle guy with his shirt off had whipped a small handgun from his pocket and fired once into Katchi's thigh.

The explosion of searing pain went through his midthigh. He screamed and collapsed on the mat.

Caesar Demas was still sipping from his glass. Then he bent forward toward Katchi who was gripping his leg and moaning in pain.

"Who did you meet with in Moscow?"

"I told you, just some local gang. Small time operators — "

This time the other muscle guy pulled out his handgun, took aim, and shot Katchi in the other leg.

Katchi was pleading and screaming.

"Did you meet with anyone else?"

Katchi was unable to talk through the pain, but he was shaking his head.

Demas gave a nod to the two fellows.

The two guys strapped the screaming Katchi into the life vest.

Then they tossed him over the side.

Bobbing in the cold Mediterranean as the blood flowed out from the wounds in his legs, Katchi was still conscious. He could see Caesar Demas and the two muscle guys bending over the rails of the yacht.

Demas yelled out to him. "Just tell me yes or no. Did you agree to sell the RTS to Vlad Levko in Moscow? Agree to give Russia exclusive rights to the RTS? Just nod your head up and down if you can't talk. If you tell the truth, we'll pull you in. Fix up your legs."

Katchi nodded his head up and down.

Then a thought flashed through Katchi's mind. *I'm in the sea. Sharks? I'm spilling blood . . .*

It was as if Caesar Demas could read his mind. "No need to worry about sharks. I read an article by a marine biologist that they are very rare in the Mediterranean."

Half a minute went by, but Demas made no effort to pull the man into the yacht. Katchi tried to yell out but didn't have the strength. He tried to lift an arm to get their attention, but it felt as if it were filled with cement.

Then he saw something out of the corner of his eye. Something moving in the water to his left.

But Demas and his two guys saw it first, and they had a better view.

It was a blue shark, its fin cutting the water toward Katchi. It was maybe four or five feet long.

Caesar Demas's last words to Hamad Katchi were, "I guess I need to tell that marine biologist he was wrong ..."

Katchi felt a collision with his leg, like he had just been hit by a car. Then another hit.

Now Hamad Katchi was being pulled down under the water. He was fully in the jaws of the blue shark and it was wagging him back and forth.

The currents of blue water above him and the frothing bubbles from his own silent, underwater screams were the last thing Hamad Katchi saw before everything went dark.

FORTY-THREE

Harry Smythe knew the stakes in this case were as high as any he'd ever handled.

In Washington, D.C., in courtroom number twelve of the U.S. District Court of the District of Columbia, Harry was sitting at the counsel's table. At the other table were his opponents, two assistant U.S. attorneys. They would be arguing the case on behalf of Congress.

If Harry lost his motion for an emergency order striking down the subpoena issued by Senator Straworth's committee, he would have only one tactic left. He could try to get the U.S. Court of Appeals for the D.C. Circuit to take it up and issue an emergency stay against enforcement of the subpoena. But that was a stretch. So his only real chance was right here, in the courtroom of Federal Judge Olivia Jenkins.

Yet there was a sadly inevitable feeling of doom in the pit of his stomach. His arguments would be novel. Too novel. Judge Jenkins didn't like exotic contentions. She liked to decide cases when the issues were clear. When ordinary applications of settled law were involved.

This case was anything but ordinary. The suit that Smythe had filed argued that the court should quash a subpoena issued by a congressional committee — a subpoena that was clearly within that committee's jurisdiction.

Smythe heard the door open from the inner chambers behind the bench.

The bailiff strode in, followed by the court clerk, who slapped a court file on the judge's bench, and then the court reporter followed last.

Less than a minute later Judge Olivia Jenkins entered the courtroom, and the lawyers jumped to their feet.

The rest of the courtroom was empty. The government had secured an order from the judge clearing visitors and bystanders and barring the media on the grounds of national security.

Jenkins was an attractive, middle-aged black woman with a reputation as a smart, no-nonsense judge.

She glanced through the file and then called the case.

Harry Smythe strode up to the podium and offered his arguments. There were only two main points. First, that the RTS design belonged to Joshua Jordan, not the government. It was a matter of patent law and intellectual property rights. Congress had no right to force disclosure of weapon designs that were trade secrets and belonged to a private citizen. Besides, Smythe argued, Joshua Jordan had had no qualms about testifying to the select committee and he had answered all of their questions. The only "line in the sand" he drew was his refusal to produce highly sensitive documents for the design of the RTS weapon to members of Congress.

Judge Jenkins asked the assistant attorneys to weigh-in.

The first government lawyer was brusque. "The contract that the Pentagon had with Mr. Jordan states, Your Honor, that when the weapon was officially accepted by the United States, it would become the property of the United States. Mr. Jordan signed away any special rights he had to the RTS design — "

Harry Smythe shot back, "But the RTS system was still experimental. It was never officially accepted by the U.S. government — "

"You're wrong," the government attorney countered. "When the U.S. government used the RTS weapon to turn back incoming missiles — and used it, Your Honor, with Mr. Jordan's permission and participation, I might add — that was the same as 'accepting' the weapon for purposes of the contract."

Judge Jenkins made short work of that argument. "I'm *not* convinced," she said, "that Mr. Jordan retained any private rights to the RTS weapon design, at least as against the United States of America. He can protect his patent against other private citizens, but not against Congress, which is an arm of the U.S. government. Mr. Smythe, you've lost on that one."

Smythe then launched into his second point. That Joshua Jordan had a concern about the ability of the congressional committee to keep the RTS weapon design information secret.

"That committee had already leaked information to the press," Smythe said, losing his characteristic professional calm. His face was beginning to get flushed as he spoke with an angry passion. "How can we assume that it will not allow the leaking also of this sensitive weapons information?" he added.

"Mr. Smythe's argument concerns me as well," the judge said, motioning to the government lawyers to respond.

The second assistant attorney strode to the podium to address that point. "It seems to me that we could agree on steps to be taken that would ensure the super secrecy of this RTS information," he said. "Once Mr. Jordan discloses it, of course."

Judge Jenkins turned to look at Harry Smythe.

Harry had the premonition already what the judge was going to do. It was all too reasonable. Too practical a solution for the judge not to jump on it.

"Mr. Smythe, what do you say about that?" Judge Jenkins said. "We do confidentiality procedures all the time in contested subpoena cases. Have Mr. Jordan produce the documents to this court. I'll fashion some restrictions on the committee that hopefully they will agree to. Then everybody's happy, right?"

But Smythe knew somebody wouldn't be happy. He knew that

Joshua Jordan had no intention of divulging his RTS design for the eventual use — or misuse — by a group of politicians.

Smythe braced himself as he began to share the bad news. "Your Honor, I doubt that your creative solution will work."

"And why is that?"

Harry was about to pull the pin in the hand grenade. "Because Mr. Jordan is not inclined to comply with the subpoena. He won't divulge his RTS technology. Except to the Defense Department under conditions where he has some guarantee that it won't be used for political purposes and that it won't be shared with other nations."

There was a different look now on Judge Jenkin's face. No longer the mediator, the conciliator looking for a compromise among the parties. Now it was the aggravated judge who had the power to level judgment.

"The government in their response papers says that Mr. Jordan is deliberately avoiding service of the subpoena. Is that true?"

"They have been unable to serve him, Your Honor ..."

"That's not what I asked. Is your client willing to admit service on the subpoena?"

"No, Your Honor. He isn't."

"So Mr. Jordan is in defiance of Congress. He's defying an official subpoena. I wonder, Mr. Smythe, if he will also be in contemptuous defiance of this court?"

"Your Honor?"

"As you know, the government has asked me as part of this proceeding to issue an order that Mr. Jordan produce his RTS data, and failing that to be held in contempt of court, and to be sent to jail until he complies. If Mr. Jordan is ordered to produce his RTS documents to this court, are you saying that he will disobey my order?"

Smythe now had to do a quick legal tap dance.

"Your Honor, with all due respect, you are asking me to commit my client to a hypothetical future situation. The fact is that you haven't yet ordered my client to produce his RTS documents ... we only have the congressional subpoena — "

"Well I'm ordering it *now*," the judge barked. "Your client has exactly forty-eight hours to turn over these documents to this court. Failing that, I will consider — and will probably order — his indefinite incarceration in a federal detention jail. You'd better tell your client he's in deep water right now. I hope he knows how to swim."

As soon as Harry Smythe pushed his way through the reporters milling around in the hallway outside the courtroom and yelled "no comment" to those peppering him with questions, he found a quiet corner.

He called Joshua.

"Josh, we've been shot down by the judge."

"Abby said we'd probably lose."

"The judge ordered you to produce your RTS documents within forty-eight hours."

"Or ...?"

"Or federal marshals put out a warrant for your arrest. Then they haul you in for processing, take your mug shot, remove your personal effects for safe-keeping, and do a strip search. Then they put you in a jail cell."

"What's your next move?" Joshua asked coolly.

"Appeal it. But don't count on a favorable result. More important, Josh, what's *your* next move?"

"What I always do when enemy fire is incoming. Keep my head down and my finger on the trigger."

FORTY-FOUR

Part of her still couldn't believe it was happening.

Darlene Rice had settled in fairly well at the Living Waters Recovery Center in Tucson. From her vantage point, she felt as if she'd been making progress. The question now was whether the rehab specialist thought so too. Now Darlene was sitting across the desk from a female drug counselor named Margaret. It was her first review after having been at the center for several weeks. All of this still felt foreign to Darlene. One good thing, Darlene thought to herself, was that she really liked Margaret. She was kind but tough. A straight shooter.

Margaret looked up from a report, smiled, and began.

"We've finished the assessment. During the days you've been here we all think you've been very cooperative. In the end, you are the one who will be directing your own recovery. It may look like we're the ones in charge, but not really. A person has to understand they have an addiction, and then they have to *want* to get better. From our perspective, it looks to us like you do. That's a really good thing, Darley. We're very encouraged. You should be too."

Darlene smiled back, but she was shaking a little. She wanted to hide her hands, which hadn't stopped trembling since she'd been taken off her excessive prescription meds. Yet somehow she knew this was a place where it was okay. They would understand. Yes, she would have preferred that Abigail be there to hold her hand. But then, maybe it was for the better. Darlene knew she had to learn how to walk the road to recovery from her addiction on her own.

Margaret continued, "We've got a picture now of your situation. I'd like to talk to you about the next steps. First, I noticed that your husband, Fortis — "

"We all call him Fort."

"Okay. Fort didn't come during visiting day yesterday. No big deal. People have busy schedules. But I just wanted to ask some more about him."

"Well, we talked in the interview already about Fort."

Margaret was nodding softly. But Darlene saw that she wasn't buying it. She liked Margaret. She had the wonderful knack of getting down to the truth of Darlene's drug addiction without making it too painful. In other words, she used anesthetic before doing emotional surgery. That was really important to Darlene. She thought, *I've been using drugs to numb the anxiety and fear about so many things. Seeking comfort from pain whenever I could. After losing Jimmy I needed to escape from anything that hurt me. I know that now. But, what do I tell her about Fort ... ?*

"So your husband ..."

Darlene decided it was time to blurt it out, so she said, "Fort hasn't bought into this whole counseling thing. He's very traditional. A private man. He's not convinced I really have an addiction. He doesn't like the idea of a group program where people tell other people their problems. His attitude is — just stop taking the pills. Plus, there is the other thing ..."

"Other thing?"

"The fact that this is a *Christian* drug rehab center. Oh, my, he really does have a problem with that." Darlene gave a little chuckle. "Fort says that 'too many people use God as the front man for all their problems.'"

"But you came here anyway?"

"Yes. My good friend Abby Jordan recommended it. I'm so glad she did. Abby is one of those 'glow-girl Christians.' That's what I call it. You know, they have an inner glow. Like the power light on your curling iron that lets you know it's hot and ready to go. Anyway, she's got a power inside that other people don't have. I'd love to have that."

"Well, we talked about that in the session last night, right?"

"Yeah, and I've been thinking a lot about what you said. It's a little like what Abby used to say to me. Even before she found out about my addiction. Not just solving a problem ... but *transformation.* "

"And remember how that happens?"

"You said it was through the transforming power of Jesus Christ."

Margaret said, "Right. I was an addict myself. Jesus changed my life. Completely."

That is where Margaret stopped talking. She smiled, leaned back. For a moment no one said a word. Then Darlene, whose brow was wrinkled in thought, looked up and spoke.

"You know what? I want that too."

"You can."

"I don't know. I've felt so lost since Jimmy died. I don't even know how to begin."

"Just like there are steps to recovery, there are steps to getting right with God. First recognize that you — like all of us — are a sinner. Not a popular phrase anymore. Not politically correct. But eternally true. The Bible says, 'All have sinned and fallen short of the glory of God.' "

Darlene nodded vigorously. "Oh, I've blown it so many times. Sometimes, it feels like I just can't help myself ..."

"Next, you need to understand that God loves you. He hasn't forsaken you. He's made a plan that can bring you into His family. His Word says that He loved the world so much that He gave His only begotten Son — Jesus Christ — that whoever believes in Him won't perish, but will have everlasting life."

"On the cross. Died for us ..."

"Exactly. The only way our sins can be forgiven. Washed clean. Absolutely clean ..."

"Cleaner than that extra strong stuff with bleach I use obsessively to clean my bathroom fixtures," Darlene said, and they both smiled.

"Cleaner than clean. But you have to do it God's way. Declare that Jesus Christ is the Son of God, that He died for your sins, that He rose from the grave three days later, just as the Bible says."

Darlene took a moment to be sure. She'd been thinking about this for a long while. After she talked to Abby for the first time about the change in her life. And then so many other times after that when they would talk about God and how things had changed for Abby. It was as if a wind had been at her back all of this time, pushing Darlene from behind. Moving her to this point.

"Yes. I believe all that," Darlene said. "I remember what Abby used to tell me. She used to ask me whether I was willing to invite Jesus Christ into my heart, to forgive my sins, and to change my life forever. I'd change the subject. I wasn't ready. But now I am. I want Jesus to be my Savior. I mean ... personally. Not just some religious figure on a cross or in a picture. But to be real ... I want to meet Him in my heart. I don't want to put this off any longer."

They both bowed their heads.

Just then, Darlene had the instinct to get down on her knees. So she did. Margaret followed her to the floor, sitting next to her, both of them resting their arms and hands on the couch.

"I am a sinner, God," Darlene said, with her eyes closed tight, her voice trembling. "No surprise there, right? You always knew that. And I know that. I believe your Son, Jesus, died on the cross for my sins. Then He walked out of the grave because, well, He had to, because He's the Son of God. Not a problem for God's Son to get that done. So, God, I want Jesus Christ to come into my heart. Please have Him come, God. I need Him to save me. Clean me up. Not just the pills. But everything ..."

Her words were wavering and caught in her throat as she continued, "I want Jesus to be totally in charge. A changed life. Transformation. Please, God, I need this so badly ..."

That's when the tears came and the words stopped.

Margaret put her arm around Darlene, whose shoulders were shuddering.

They sat together, on their knees, for a long time. People walked past the office, talking and laughing, but Darlene didn't notice.

A few hours later, Darlene was in her room, still thinking about what had happened. A thought occurred to her. She laughed loudly and yelled, "Oh, yes! I've got to do it!"

She dialed the number by heart.

She got Abigail Jordan's voicemail and said, "Guess what, Abby dear! I prayed a prayer today. And anyway ... I guess I've become a glow girl!"

Darlene clicked off the phone and sat down on her bed. She couldn't wait to talk to Abigail about it.

But then, an instant later, a thought flashed through her mind.

What in the world do I tell Fort?

FORTY-FIVE

Joshua was now in hiding. He had checked himself into the triplex suite at the Palace Hotel in midtown Manhattan. Only two people knew where he was. One was Abby. The other was his long-time private chauffeur, who had booked the room under his brother-in-law's name and paid cash so Joshua's name wouldn't appear on the registry. Then he took one more step to insure he wouldn't be tracked. Joshua's company had been developing a super-secure Allfone, one with signal-cloaking capacity so it couldn't be located via satellite or tower tracing. It was designed for special-ops guys operating in hostile territory, but the Defense Department put the project on hold. Joshua was carrying the prototype with him.

Even Harry Smythe didn't know his location. But he did advise Joshua that while the federal bench warrant didn't rate the kind of priority given to escaped prisoners or violent offenders, this was still a serious business. If Joshua was stopped for a traffic ticket or recognized by a federal agent in public somewhere, the jig was up.

Joshua's plan was to stay undercover until the AmeriNews media service got off the ground. The project was taking longer than Phil Rankowitz had predicted. Then, hopefully, the Roundtable's project would ignite citizens into immediate action. People would learn that Joshua's real motives in resisting Senator Straworth's heavy-handed demands about the RTS system were to protect America. Voters would discover that a gang of Washington politicians were trying to send an American hero to jail. The phone lines at the Capitol switchboard would light up with angry calls from American citizens. Straworth would see his approval ratings drop like a bowling ball in a swimming pool. What else could he do then but withdraw the subpoena entirely?

At least, that was the scenario. But Joshua understood the odds, exactly how many dots had to be perfectly connected for all that to work. The thought of jail didn't worry him. Sure, Abby was probably right that the bad press of being incarcerated could stain his professional reputation and irreparably damage his businesses.

But Joshua had a more tactical worry. *If I'm locked up, I can't run things. I can't direct the decisions that need to be made about the AmeriNews project. And what about the RTS refinements that my engineering team and I were working on? We are just on the verge of solving a potential design problem. I can't afford to be taken out of action.*

Before he knew it, it was dinnertime and he was hungry. Just as he was about to order room service, he noticed the message light flashing on the hotel phone. From the front desk. He dialed them and was told that a note was waiting for him. Joshua told them to send it up. A few minutes later a bellman arrived with a sealed envelope. On the outside were written the words *To the Gentleman in Room 2507.* After tipping the bellman he ducked back into his room and read the note.

Joshua Jordan:

You don't know us. But we know you. It is important we talk. We can help. I am downstairs in the private dining room, the one with the closed doors. It is not visible to the public. I will have dinner waiting for the two of us. Please forgive me for the note, but in the interests of discretion I must not be seen coming up to your room.

The Patriot's Wife

Joshua's first thought was that his cover had been blown. Someone knew where he was. Was this a trap to lure him out of his room? But if the feds were behind it, they wouldn't be using this cloak-and-dagger stuff. They would simply come up to his room unannounced, armed with a warrant. No, this was something else. He knew he had friends in the Pentagon who were quietly supportive of him. Maybe there were others. But one thing was clear. Now that a federal judge had targeted him for arrest, he needed all the help he could get.

Looks like it's time to take a calculated risk.

Ten minutes later Joshua was seated in a private room off the main dining room, behind polished mahogany doors that had been closed, eating dinner across the table from an attractive middle-aged woman.

Joshua took another bite of his filet mignon. He had noticed that his host was fashionably dressed. Though Abby would have recognized even more, like the exclusive Vera Wang dress, and the carat weight of the diamond studs in her ears — likely two carats each.

"Sorry to be so secretive," the woman said. "But I know you're currently undercover, Mr. Jordan. First, let me tell you how much my husband and I appreciate you."

Joshua flashed a quick smile and said, "Thank you," but he immediately had several questions. "Your husband is described in your note only as 'The Patriot.' Do I know him?"

"I don't think so." Then she added, "but he thinks you're on the right track. He wanted you to know that."

"Which track would that be?"

"Your distrust of Senator Straworth. And perhaps a few other members, or their staff, on the special committee investigating the North Korean missile crisis. My husband also agrees with your decision not to give them the RTS design information. Some members of that committee cannot be trusted."

It was clear this woman had a sharp understanding of Joshua's world.

"I applaud you and your husband, whoever he is," Joshua said. "You apparently have a grasp of issues that the media hasn't covered."

She smiled. There was something behind the smile. Her next comment told Joshua a lot.

"Sorry to be so clandestine. But we both need to be cautious."

Her choice of words rang bells. So Joshua pushed a little.

"What is it you came here to tell me?"

"You're in danger."

"That's not very specific."

"I realize that. Let's just say that I'm not talking about the things you're already aware of. Like the crazies out there who don't understand the reasons for what you did. Or the Capitol Hill political bunch that wants to bury you. None of that."

"Then what?"

"We have the distinct sense, from multiple sources, that you are at substantial risk from foreign actors."

Again, her choice of words, the familiar intelligence lingo, rang a bell with Joshua.

"What can I do about it?"

"Nothing yet. I just want you to know we are out there. And if you are willing, then we can set up a meeting so you can be briefed in more detail."

"This is all very interesting ... but I still don't know your name."

"For now I'm just the Patriot's Wife," she said with a smile.

Then she reached inside her little purse, which was exquisitely decorated with white beads, and pulled something out. She laid it on the table. A white business card. All it said was *The Patriot*. And there was a telephone number.

He took the card, fingered it, then looked over at the woman. Now it was time to get blunt. "How do I know I can trust you ... or your husband?"

"That should be simple," she said with a grin. Then she rose to leave.

Ever the gentlemen, Joshua rose to his feet with her.

She reached out and shook his hand. Then before turning to leave, she said one more thing to Joshua. "Perhaps you can reflect on two things. First, we were able to locate you here, even though you took precautions to hide from the federal authorities. The U.S. marshals haven't been able to find you so far. But we did."

"And the second?"

"We haven't reported you."

FORTY-SIX

In the crowded upscale piano bar called Johnny One Note on Park Avenue South, attorney Allen Fulsin was sitting across the booth from his contact. They'd just ordered drinks and were engaging in small talk. But the other man, Bill Cheavers, an executive vice president for the North American Division of World Teleco, was getting impatient.

"Allen, you said you had inside information for me."

"Are you up to speed on the pending negotiation between World Teleco and a media group called Mountain News Enterprises — MNE?"

"It's no longer a pending negotiation. It's a signed media distribution contract. I'm not sure I want to go into any more details than that. Maybe you should talk to our corporate lawyers."

Allen Fulsin laughed coarsely and said, "Oh no, Bill, that's definitely *not* what I ought to do."

"Why not?"

"I'm a lawyer. I know what happens when the pencil-neck corporate counsel inside an organization like yours gets a whiff of this kind of insider information. They get all nervous. They run to the first whistle they can blow. They threaten to call in some federal agency to look into it. All because they don't want to get caught in the middle. Or lose their law license. Or worse."

Bill Cheavers glanced around the bar quickly for any familiar faces. Finding none, he turned to the lawyer across from him.

"Okay. Look, Allen, the only reason that you and I are having this discussion is that you handle my sensitive, personal legal stuff. So let's get to it."

"That media group MNE is a cover."

"For what?"

"A radical group. Don't know the name. But it meets secretly. Some very powerful people in it."

"How do you know this?"

"As luck would have it, a retired former Idaho State supreme court judge named Fortis Rice approached me about this secret group, you know, to feel me out. They meet regularly in some clandestine spot in the Rocky Mountains."

"Why'd he approach you?"

"His group needs some more legal muscle, I guess. I think it's because they liked some of the issues I argued when I was in the solicitor general's office. Frankly, I didn't agree with half the cases I had to argue, but that's Washington. You do what you got to do and pretend you believe in it. I must have been more convincing than I realized ..."

"And this group you mentioned ..."

"Yeah. Full of extreme anti-Corland people. It seems that you either have to be filthy rich or really well connected — or both — to be invited in. I guess they thought I was the latter. I'm sure not the former, though I'm working on that one." And then Fulsin smiled and took a swig from his glass.

"And they don't know you have a connection to me, as my personal lawyer?"

"Naw. The question Rice asked me was whether I ever represented World Teleco. And I said no. Which is technically correct. Very technically."

"But how'd you find out about the connection between Mountain News Enterprises and this secret political group?"

Allen Fulsin laughed again. "Because after Rice talked to me I started digging around like a West Virginia coal miner. Looking for information. And I know how to find it in this town. Hey, when opportunity knocks ..."

Bill Cheavers was putting it all together in his head. Then he had a question to ask. "Which leads me, Allen, to the obvious question: what's in this for you?"

"Just trying to be a good Boy Scout."

"Come on, what do you want out of this?"

"Bill, all I need you to do is to make sure this contract between World Teleco and Mountain News Enterprises on behalf of Rice's group goes nowhere. You don't have to be concerned with how I benefit from it when that happens."

"If we breach a signed contract on a national media buy like this — wow, that could be a real litigation nightmare for us."

"Consider the consequences."

"Such as?"

"This covert group is planning on taking aim against the Corland administration. Real scorched-earth stuff. By facilitating their plan, whatever that is, World Teleco is going to stir up the wrath of the White House."

"We may have to take our chances."

"You definitely *don't* want to do that."

"Why not?"

"The White House could bring down your company's entire telecommunications empire, Bill. Seriously. Along with your World Teleco stock portfolio, your profit-sharing plan. You get the picture?"

"That's a bold claim. Outrageous, actually. I need specifics."

"How about a call from the White House? Would that work for you?"

Bill Cheavers was stunned. He pushed his glass away from him, then he said, "But a breach of contract ..."

"Companies do it every day," Fulsin said. "Have your lawyers find some loophole. That's what you pay them for." Then he bent forward and said, "You've got to stop this media plan from happening." After looking at his watch, Fulsin added, "In one hour you'll get a call from a restricted number. Pick it up. It will be the White House. After that call I think you'll want to pull the rug out from under this Mountain News Enterprises deal."

Bill Cheavers didn't finish his drink. He got up quickly and looked around the bar once more. His last words to the attorney were, "I'll be waiting for that call." Then he left.

Allen Fulsin emptied his glass and exited a few minutes later.

□□□

That was when another man at the bar, who had been watching the two of them, pulled out his Allfone and dialed a number.

A man answered the phone on the other end and simply announced, "This is the Patriot."

The man at the bar said, "I've just eye-balled the rendezvous between Fulsin and a fellow named Bill Cheavers."

"Who's Cheavers?"

"High-ranking executive with World Teleco."

"Okay. Keep on it. Get the information to me in the usual way."

"Will do."

The man at the bar clicked shut his encrypted Allfone, paid his tab, and left.

□□□

In downtown Philadelphia, at the police headquarters, John Gallagher was getting tired of waiting. He was supposed to meet with the detective who was going to show him the surveillance footage of the lobby of the corporate building where Roger French worked. But just before Gallagher arrived, the detective was pulled out on another field investigation.

Gallagher glanced at his watch. *Man, I'm going to have to ditch my plane reservation. I'll never make it to New York in time to meet with Miles first thing tomorrow. Maybe there's a late train I can still catch.*

Gallagher called the ticket office for the express train. Yes, he could still catch the last one, which left in ninety minutes. He booked it over the phone.

That was when the detective strode into the video viewing room where Gallagher had been waiting. He had a uniformed cop with him.

He delivered his weary apologies to Gallagher, then turned to his video forensics officer and told him to start running the footage.

Gallagher's eyes were fixed on the paper-thin flat-screen monitor on the wall.

The time and date were running in the lower right-hand corner of the black-and-white video as the image of an empty corporate building lobby was cast on the screen.

"Sorry they didn't use color footage. But these building owners always go the cheap route."

"No, this is better," Gallagher muttered. "Black-and-white gives you better definition. At least for what I want."

The tech guy then fast-forwarded the video to the point in time two hours before the estimated time of Roger French's death. Then he slowed it down only slightly.

Until they saw the image of a man in a suit entering the lobby.

"Stop there!" Gallagher shouted out.

They froze the frame.

A man of medium height. Well dressed. Broad shoulders. Confident strut. But his head was slightly turned away from the camera.

A shiver crawled up Gallagher's spine.

"Zoom in."

The tech guy brought the image closer. It blurred a little with magnification.

Gallagher stared at it. He had to know. Was it Atta Zimler?

"Okay," he said, "roll it, but very slowly, frame-by-frame."

So the tech did.

The man in the lobby, as he was caught in each sequential, choppy frame, had kept his face turned away.

Then he brought his face back toward the camera.

Gallagher stood up.

"Let me see ya, you stinkin' scum ... show your face!"

The man in the lobby, in the jerky frames, kept looking down, fiddling with the buttons of his suit coat, keeping his face hidden.

"Look at me!" Gallagher shouted out.

And just then, as the man in the lobby was approaching the elevator doors, he gave a side glance toward the watch on his left wrist, revealing about half of his face.

"Stop!" Gallagher yelled out.

The frame froze.

"Bring it in ..."

The tech magnified the frame until a face could be partially seen.

Gallagher walked right up to the screen. He touched it with his index finger.

"I know it's you. I know it!"

Then Gallagher wheeled around. "Can we get an immediate high def JPG image of this emailed to somebody?"

The video forensics officer came out of the control room and looked at the detective, who nodded the okay.

Out of his wallet Gallagher fished an email address for the Facial Identification Unit of the Biometrics Technology Division of the FBI. Then he gave it to the video guy.

"I need this emailed *stat*," he said.

On his way to the railroad station, Gallagher called the private home number of Sally Borcheck, the facial ID guru at the Bureau.

She was watching TV. After nine rings she picked up.

"Sally, it's John Gallagher here."

"Geez, John, I'm here at home in my pj's. What's up?"

"Got a favor to ask. Sorry about this. But it's real important."

"Yeah?"

"I'm having an image of a guy being emailed to your office as we speak."

"Really ... can't this wait?"

"No. It can't. Truly. Life-or-Death. Pleeease?"

"Oh fine," she groaned. "What's the possible match?"

"A guy in our files by the name of Atta Zimler. I need a facial ID match."

"Where's the image from?"

"Lobby surveillance footage."

She groaned again.

"Those are usually pretty lousy."

"You're a genius. You can make it *un*lousy."

"Okay. Give me about an hour to get down to the Bureau. You owe me big time, Gallagher."

"You name it."

"I'll call you on your cell when I've completed the analysis."

"I'm naming you in my will, Sally, really."

"Wonderful," she said. "A one quarter share of nothing is ... let me see ..."

"I'll be waiting on pins and needles. See ya."

Gallagher looked at his watch again. He figured that he just might be able to make that train after all.

□□□

In Manhattan, Bill Cheavers, the World Teleco executive was looking at his watch too. He had settled back in his hotel room, but it was getting late. It was one hour since he had met with Allen Fulsin. *So, where is that phone call?*

He figured that, for whatever reason, his lawyer was lying or exaggerating. Why? He didn't know. Cheavers was just about to turn off his Allfone for the night when it rang.

He looked on the LCD screen. It said *Restricted*. Cheavers couldn't believe it.

When he answered, the person on the other end, a woman, spoke up. "Mr. Cheavers, this is Lana Orvilla. I am chief of staff to vice president Jessica Tulrude. How are you this evening?"

"Good. Thanks."

"Sorry to call so late."

"Not a problem."

"The purpose of my call," she continued, "is because the Corland administration is very concerned about possible antitrust violations being committed."

"Oh?"

"Yes."

"What kind of violations?"

"Well, large telecommunications companies like yours, World Teleco, for instance. We are considering whether it might be appropriate for an investigation to be launched into those kinds of allegations. Bring it to the attention of the Department of Justice."

"I can assure you, that World Teleco has not violated the Sherman Act or anything else."

"I'm sure you're right," she said. "This is just a friendly call asking for your cooperation."

"What kind of cooperation?"

"Any cooperation that you deem appropriate."

Cheavers paused. He had to get it nailed down. If he was going to have his company break a contract with Mountain News Enterprises, he had to know for certain that this was what the White House was asking him to do to avoid an antitrust investigation.

"Please know that I would, of course, be happy to cooperate completely —"

But the vice president's chief of staff interrupted him. "You're friends with Allen Fulsin, the lawyer, I understand?"

"Yes."

"He's a good man. He gives good advice. Don't you think?"

"Absolutely," Cheavers said. That was it. There was nothing more to say.

Lana Orvilla thanked him for taking the call so late and then said good-bye.

Cheavers immediately called the voicemail of the corporate legal counsel in the Allfone media transactions department. He left a message. "This is Bill Cheavers. Please give me your best legal avenue first thing tomorrow for a termination of our Allfone contract with Mountain News Enterprises. We are going in a different direction on that. Please make this the very highest priority. And please send an alert to the operations department about the pending deal that I think they were calling AmeriNews. Tell operations that the deal is being permanently cancelled."

FORTY-SEVEN

John Gallagher finally pulled into Grand Central Station at 7:30 in the morning. The train had been delayed getting out of the Philly station. Then another delay at one of the stops. After grabbing a cup of coffee at a window snack stand, he dashed up the stairs and outside to catch a cab.

His meeting with Miles Zadernack was set for 8:30. With cross-town rush hour, he'd be lucky to be on time.

In the middle of traffic, which was crawling along like a slug, he received a call from Sally Borcheck. She'd finished working on the video image.

"Great timing," Gallagher said. "I need this for a conference. What's the bottom line?"

"Oh, no, I'm not giving it to you," she snapped back. "Not until I go over some preliminaries first."

In the cab Gallagher pretended to strangle his Allfone with both hands.

He said, "Sally, can't we skip that stuff? I'm really in a rush."

"Look, you're the one who caught me in my comfy pj's in front of the TV. I was already halfway into the old version of *The Detective* with Robert Mitchum. I *love* that movie. And they almost never run that one on television. So back off, John — "

"Give me a break here, Sally — "

"No, you give *me* a break. I did you a favor. And I know what's going to happen. You'll use my analysis as the reason for some Normandy invasion you want to launch somewhere. And if things go bad, who do you think the Bureau's going to blame?"

"Me, of course," Gallagher said. "But fine. You win. Give me the drill."

"Okay," she began. "Facial ID in biometric matches depends on the quality of the subject image. In this case, that video clip you sent me was not good."

"But adequate for analysis. Right? Tell me it was minimally adequate?"

Borcheck sighed. "Yeah, minimally adequate. Now there are eighty facial variants we use to create a face print. Skull size, facial measurements, interrelationships between facial structures ..."

"Eighty variants. Good. Moving on ..."

"Range of certainty on the upper scale is measured from sixty to ninety percent."

"And how'd you score this one?"

"Remembering the qualifiers I just mentioned — "

"Sure. Right. What's the score?"

"I rated your video image at a sixty-seven percent certainty that the facial characteristics in the video matched that of the known subject, Atta Zimler."

"*Certainty* ... I love that word."

"Yeah, but it's on the low end of certainty," Borcheck reminded him.

"But only because of the poor quality of the video and the angle that the guy had with his head partially obscured."

"True. On the other hand, with better video and a full face shot, who knows, maybe we'd have much less than a sixty-seven percent match ... in other words, no match at all."

But Gallagher didn't care about the negative possibilities. Right now he had the necessary forensic basis to pursue a full investigation of Atta Zimler's presence within the United States. He was on a roll.

"Sally, I got what I need," Gallagher said as he reached over to pay the taxi driver. "You're brilliant!"

Gallagher rushed his way through security at the Bureau headquarters by 8:35. He was in Miles Zadernack's office at 8:39.

Miles was dressed in his black suit, pressed white shirt, and plain single-colored tie.

Gallagher was crumpled from the all-night train ride and was sweaty.

"Miles, I've got some breaking stuff I need to tell you about," Gallagher said.

"And I have some things to tell you," Zadernack said blandly. "Let's start with my agenda item first."

"Sure."

"You are going to have to remove yourself from any further investigation into Atta Zimler."

Gallagher kept up his grin and nodded his head athletically up and down. He half-expected this. But he figured he now had something he could wedge in the door before his supervisor closed it on him completely.

"Okay, which is what I wanted to talk to you about," he started to say. But Zadernack cut in. It was clear he had a speech and he was going to make it. "You don't understand, John. You are being *removed* from any further investigation. Not just dealing with Atta Zimler, but any fieldwork. For the time being. You're being placed on desk duty here at headquarters. Meanwhile, I'm arranging for you to take some counseling in Bureau professionalism."

Gallagher was getting red in the face. "Wait just a minute —"

"This is exactly what I'm talking about," Zadernack said. "Your attitude borders on insubordination — which is a serious problem!"

But Gallagher was going to bull his way through. "I have a facial match between Atta Zimler and a suspect who just tortured and murdered the son-in-law of a former high-ranking Pentagon general. It *just* happened. Over in Philadelphia. We have a forensic match, Miles. Come on — "

"Our forensics?"

"Yes. Sally Borcheck in biometrics. She did a match from some lobby surveillance video taken at the time of the murder and at the scene of the crime."

"What level of certainty?"

Now Gallagher had to swallow hard. This was the hard sell. "Sixty-seven percent. But this was from *lobby* video. Zimler was clearly trying to duck away from the camera. But we're still within the ranges of certainty we need for an investigation. Enough for probable cause for warrants, wiretaps, you name it."

Zadernack gave his favorite emotionless, plaster-of-paris expression. He spoke in something just above a monotone. But what he had to say was outrageous. "Okay, John. Take a deep breath. All right? Relax. Here's the story. We've been told that Atta Zimler is in custody. In Paris."

"Who took him in?"

"We're waiting for confirmation, but the attorney general himself has told us to stand down. We don't want to risk some false identification of innocent persons. Apparently, some foreign diplomat is entering the U.S. and is worried he'll be flagged as Zimler. That's all I know."

Gallagher shut his eyes and shook his head as he spoke. "No, we wouldn't want that. Sure, maybe a psychopathic terrorist might slip through our fingers and mosey around America slashing, killing, torturing. But the main thing is we treat people nicely — "

"That's enough!" Zadernack nearly shouted. It was a rare show of emotion. Then he continued. "John, it's called 'Bureau professionalism.' You'll learn all about it in your counseling sessions. That's all for now. I've got some other matters to attend to. Thank you for your time. Vera, my secretary, will assign you a desk."

Gallagher felt his brain go numb, like someone had given him a shot of novocaine there but forgot to do the surgery.

He walked out to Vera's desk. She smiled courteously and led him to a cubicle, not even an office. She pointed to a desk. "This will be your work area," she said. Then she left.

Gallagher sat down at the desk. He knew then that he was standing on the banks of a Rubicon. A place where, years later, he would look back and realize he needed to make one really smart decision. Something that would make sense, a path that would insure his future.

He would be retiring before long. He had put too much into his work at the Bureau to trash it all now. So there was a serious question pending: Was he going to throw it all away for a mere sixty-seven percent certainty? The more he thought about it the more it didn't make any sense. *Man, sixty-seven percent isn't even a passing grade. That's flunking.*

Then he drummed his fingers on the naked desk top in front of him. He couldn't shake another competing thought: *On the other hand sixty-seven might be passing after all. Some teachers grade sixty-to-seventy as a D. Right? And then there's the fact that some teachers grade on a curve . . .*

He propelled himself up on his feet. He walked fast, past Vera's desk on his way to the elevator.

"Agent Gallagher?" Vera called out toward his quickly moving frame.

"Gotta feed the meter," he called back and disappeared into the elevator.

When he was on the street he put in a call to Ken Leary over at the CIA.

"Ken, Gallagher here. Got to talk fast. They're closing me down on my investigation into Zimler."

"Whoa!"

"I need any further updates you have on Zimler or the murder of that professor over in Bucharest. And I need it in like, oh, five minutes."

"You're really out there on this one, John. And I don't know how much I can afford to stick my neck out any more than I have."

"If you ever owed me money, Ken, all debts are cancelled. How about that?"

"Actually, you owe *me* money — "

"Okay, forget it. Look, Ken. I really need this. You know how long I've been after this sicko, Zimler."

Leary took a full five seconds.

Gallagher was pacing on the sidewalk, looking around to make sure he wasn't being observed.

Finally Leary spoke. "Look, there's a Korean laundry about two blocks from my office. Yang's Dry Cleaning. Meet me there in ten minutes."

"First, tell me something," Gallagher asked.

"What?"

"Do you have more stuff on Zimler or not? I can't afford to waste time."

"Uh, figure it out, John," Leary said with a laugh. "We're going to discuss possible clandestine information from the CIA about a world-class terrorist, and I chose a Korean dry cleaners as the meeting place. What does that tell you?"

FORTY-EIGHT

Joshua Jordan was locked in a tight embrace with Abby. He was kissing her passionately in the foyer of his Palace Hotel suite.

"I missed you so much, baby," he said, still holding her tight.

"Not as much as I missed you," she purred and then kissed him again.

Then she stopped and moved her head back slightly to tell him something. "Oh, I've had such bad dreams," she said.

"Being there with Rocky and Peg in that house. Helping them with their grief. I'm not surprised."

"Not about them. About us."

"What do you mean?"

"Bad dreams. For a while now. This sense of disaster. Like something bad, impending doom or something. I can't shake it. Last night I dreamed there was this shadowy figure in our condo. Looking through our things. Wanting to hurt us, I think."

Joshua shrugged it off. "Just a dream. That's all."

He noticed her overnight bag on the marble floor and snatched it up and carried it in for her.

He asked her how things were going with Peg as she dealt with her loss, and how Rocky Bridger was doing. Abigail gave him the rundown in detail.

But Joshua saw the exhaustion in her face. "The way you give yourself to other people, Abby … you've got to look out for yourself too."

"I'm fine," she said. Then she looked around the spacious hotel suite. "So, this is home for a while."

"Yeah. Comfortable. But definitely not home. Honestly I'd rather be at Hawk's Nest together, in our rocking chairs, watching the stars."

That sounded good to both of them. But they knew that wouldn't happen for a while. Not until the mess with Congress and Judge Jenkins' order and the AmeriNews project had all been taken care of first.

"Abby, sweetheart, you came here at a good time. Well, sort of."

"What do you mean?"

"Well, good news and bad."

"Let's start with the good ..."

"We've got a conference call with several of the Roundtable folks thirty minutes from now. Hopefully to tell me that AmeriNews will go live later today. I'd like you to sit in on it with me. I need you on this."

"So what's the bad news?"

"The reason I want you on the call is that I received an email from Fort Rice. He now says he has had to bow out as head of our legal section. He says he has a conflict of interest."

"What kind of conflict?"

"Darley followed your advice and checked herself into a drug rehab place. The one you recommended."

"But that's good news."

"Not from Fort's standpoint. He thinks her 'addiction' has been blown way out of proportion. Truthfully, I think Fort is suffering from some embarrassment that his wife needs help. He's a very private, old-school kind of guy."

"You know," Abby said, "I think Fort is going to see that she really does need help."

"Well, it's more complicated than that. Darley's become a born-again Christian at that Center."

Abby's eyes widened; then they filled with tears. "Dear Darley. My precious friend. I couldn't be happier for her. That's so incredible ..."

"Fort is really blowing a gasket over this. He's not real keen on the Christian thing. He holds you partly to blame."

"I'll take that kind of blame, Josh. I really will. Darley is going to get better. From the pills, sure. But she's also going to be spiritually healed, from the inside out. That's what happens when Christ comes into your life. He changes you."

"I don't blame you for anything," Joshua said, taking her hand and squeezing it, "but between Fort and me, there's been a freeze-out. I just find it hard to believe that Fort is bailing out of the Roundtable like this ..."

"Look, Josh, you called him 'old school.' Remember he's a former state supreme court judge. He takes conflicts of interest very seriously. Judges are trained to think like that. If he has a grudge against me, thinking I influenced his wife, and really thinks that will impact his effectiveness on the Roundtable because you're the chairman, then Fort Rice is the kind of guy who would recuse himself. I know it sounds nitpicky, but strangely, I can understand where he might be coming from. Then there's the personal problems he's having with Darley's situation too ... "

"Well, the point is, that's where you come in."

"How?"

"You've got to be the legal representative on the call today."

"How are the others on the Roundtable going to take it?"

"I'll handle them."

Abby was looking around the kitchen in the suite to make herself some tea when Joshua's signal-cloaking Allfone rang. Abby and the Roundtable were the only ones with that special number.

"That's funny," Joshua said. "They're early."

He clicked it on. Phil Rankowitz and all the other members were on the call.

Phil started out. "Josh, we've got an emergency here. Everyone else has already been briefed."

"I know. Fort's taken a leave of absence," Joshua said. "Not important why right now. Says he has a conflict of interest. But we need some legal counsel with us —"

"We'll need it big time," Phil said. "You'll hear why in a minute. Something else is going on."

"I've asked Abby to join us on this call," Joshua went on. "She's a smart lawyer. I think she can pinch-hit."

"I think you're underselling your wife," Phil shot out. "She's got a brilliant legal mind. Let's bring her in."

"Wait a minute," Alvin Leander called out. "Maybe it's my old days from serving on the Senate ethics committee coming out, but speaking of conflicts of interest, don't we have a problem with Abby advising the whole Roundtable while her husband is the chairman?"

"Screw the ethics lecture." The voice on the phone was Rocky Bridger's.

"Rocky," Joshua said. "We're all so sorry about your loss. We'd understand if you bowed out —"

"I'm on this call because I think it's that important," he said. "And as far as Abby being on board, I vote a resounding yes."

Leander backed off that point.

Joshua switched to his speaker phone so Abby could join in.

Phil Rankowitz jumped right to the crisis. "World Teleco has cancelled our contract for AmeriNews."

"What?" Joshua yelled out. "On what basis?"

"They've contrived some ridiculous argument based on the fine print. I've gone over it with our transaction lawyers. They say it's a pretty pathetic excuse. I call it a breach of contract, pure and simple. Call me paranoid, but I see something very political behind all this. They know something about our message. And World Teleco doesn't want any part of it."

"Okay, counsel," Rankowitz said, addressing Abby. "Where do we go from here?"

"Assuming it's a clear breach," Abby said, "we can go into court for injunctive relief. But that's a tough call. No guarantees. Besides, the telecom company can tie us up in litigation for years."

"We don't have that kind of time," Rankowitz said. "Josh, didn't the judge order you to produce your RTS documents by tomorrow?"

"That's the deadline," Joshua replied. "Harry's appealed the order. But he says the chances are nil."

"So I ask again," Rankowitz said, "Abby, what can we do?"

"Give me some time to think this through," she said. "Give me an hour or two."

Everyone on the conference call could hear Alvin Leander grumbling in the background.

"Okay," Joshua said, "we reconvene in one hour. Phil, you set up the same conference call. Patch Abby and me in last."

When the call ended Joshua looked at Abby. She was deep in thought.

"I need some tea," she said. "And some time to think."

She walked into the kitchen and heated up the tea carafe.

Joshua knew enough to leave her alone. He went into the large study and tried to scan some information he had received from his engineers, suggesting improvements for the RTS.

But he was having a hard time focusing. *How am I going to run this company from the inside of a jail cell?*

A few minutes turned into an hour. Joshua looked at his watch and then called to Abby. But he couldn't find her.

He started searching the large suite. Until he found her in one of the bedrooms.

Fast asleep.

He stroked her cheek gently. *You're exhausted. I'm sorry.*

She opened one eye.

"Time's up. I'm afraid we've got our conference call now, honey."

She nodded and worked to open the other eye and then started to rise. Abigail trudged into the bathroom and splashed some water on her face.

Then Joshua and Abigail sat next to each other on the couch in the great room with the Allfone set up on speaker phone for the call.

A minute later the call came in.

Phil Rankowitz began. "Okay, Abby. Let's hear it. Have a plan?"

Abby asked, "Can you get me some lawyers?"

"How many?"

"Four."

"When?"

"By eight tomorrow morning, and they have to be versed in tele-communications law."

"Yeah. I think we can arrange that."

"I thought you said litigation would tie us up for years?" Alvin Leander said.

"It would," Abby replied, "but I'm not talking about a lawsuit."

Beverly Rose Cortez spoke up. "Abby. You can work some magic by tomorrow on this? You really think so?"

"I've got an idea. But it requires one vital piece of evidence."

"What's that?" Joshua asked his wife.

"We need to know something definite about World Teleco's motives. Some hard evidence that Phil's suspicions are right. That they shut us down to keep our message from getting out."

"Digging up that kind of proof," Leander said. "takes too much time."

But Joshua intervened. "Not necessarily. Folks, let me work on that one."

FORTY-NINE

John Gallagher arrived at Yang's Dry Cleaning a few minutes early.

A friendly Asian man at the counter asked him if he had dry cleaning to pick up.

"No thanks," Gallagher said. "But I think my friend does."

Five minutes later Ken Leary strolled in licking an ice-cream cone. He had a big brown envelope under his arm.

The Asian man was at the counter again, smiling. Leary handed him a laundry ticket.

The Asian man nodded and walked around from behind the counter, went to the door, locked it, and flipped the sign to read "Closed," and pulled the shade down over the window. Then he disappeared into the back room.

Leary sat down on a chair with a faded red slip cover in front of the counter. Gallagher sat down in another chair while Leary pulled some papers out of the envelope.

"This is a transcript," he began, "of an interview between one of our agents and Mrs. Elena Banica. The interview took place following the murder of her husband. I can't let you take this. It's bad enough I'm letting you read it. And even worse that it's left our New York station even for a few minutes. So look it over now. This is all I have for you. When you're done, I need to get it back to the office."

Gallagher turned to the first page. He'd read a lot of interrogation

293

transcripts in his career. He knew that a transcript couldn't tell the whole story. There was always the human element that surfaces during that kind of interview. Something that doesn't translate well from the computer keyboard as the Agency secretary types it out. But a few decades of fieldwork with the FBI, inside friendships within the CIA, and an extraordinary degree of gut instinct gave Gallagher a pretty good idea how it all went down. He could practically visualize it.

This particular transcript contained an interview that had been conducted in Bulgaria by an American agent in the Clandestine Services unit. Elena Banica was the young, attractive wife of a much older Dr. Yergi Banica.

When the interview took place, the subject, Elena, was seated in an empty back room in a large cathedral just off the Pasaj Subteran Unirea in Bucharest. She knew a friendly priest there, so she had insisted on that location for the meeting. Considering her former seedy occupation, Elena's demand to give her statement in a church probably seemed ironic to her interrogator.

But the agent questioning her didn't linger on that. The Agency needed to get down to the basement level about Dr. Banica. Elena was the only witness who knew enough about him and who could also be pressured into spilling it.

Next to Elena, on the floor, was a digital recorder, which was recording the conversation. The questions from the agent zeroed in on her relationship with Yergi. His next question was pretty blunt. "Considering the difference in ages, why'd you marry him?"

"Love," she said, but she didn't look at her interrogator when she said that. Elena tried to smile and took a second to tap the ashes from her cigarette.

"What else?"

"Oh, he provided for me."

"Money?"

"He took care of me, yes."

"Were you seeing anyone else while you were with Yergi?"

"No. But you probably don't believe that …"

The agent started talking about the murder.

"Did you see him on the day of his death?"

"I served him breakfast. Spicy sausage. Grilled tomato. Coffee."

Elena spoke the words without expression. Yes, she was tough. Had worked as a call girl in Bulgaria. That was before meeting Yergi. She always thought he knew but was too much of a gentleman to mention it. So one day she discreetly let him see the results of her routine medical check up and blood tests, so he could relax and know for sure she didn't have a disease.

The agent continued to peel back the layers in his questioning.

"Did Yergi talk to you that morning about where he was going?"

"Not then, no."

"Did you know where he was going?"

"I think so."

"So he talked to you about it then?"

"Yes. But only generally. Just that he was selling some information that had come into his possession."

"He had obtained it originally from a Russian agent?"

Elena scrunched up one corner of her mouth. She wondered if the American agent was being honest when he had told her that if she cooperated he would keep her out of trouble. On the other hand, what choice did she have?

"Yes," she replied, "he told me he got the information from a Russian agent."

"Information about an American weapons system?"

"It was … some kind of missile thing."

"What kind of thing?"

"Would send a missile coming to a place … well, would turn it around … with a big surprise. Would go back where it came from. Boom. That kind of thing."

"Return-to-Sender ... RTS? Did he call it that?"

"Yes, I think so."

The agent paused long enough to lean back and size up his subject. He didn't care if she had loved Yergi Banica. That wasn't the point. What really mattered were her answers to his next line of questions.

"So Yergi was going to take this Return-to-Sender information, which he had received from the Russian, and was going to sell it to someone else. Right?"

"That was his plan. Would get big money from that. We would get new house. Close to the beach."

"Did he ever give you a name?"

"For who?"

"I mean the name of the person he would be selling this information to ... in Bucharest ... the person he was going to meet in the hotel. That name."

"No names. No."

"Any description?"

"What do you mean?"

"Man or woman?"

"Man."

"Height?"

"No."

"Weight."

"No. Nothing about that."

"Complexion?"

Elena sighed and took a drag on her cigarette.

"No. Yergi never mentioned that."

"Age?"

"No. He really didn't — "

Then the agent cut her short.

"Anything about his nationality?"

Elena blew a whisper of cigarette smoke into the air. She pursed her lips. One eyebrow went up.

"Say again?"

"Anything about this man's nationality? What country he came from?"

A few more seconds went by. Elena considered taking another drag on the cigarette and raised it to her lips as if she were going to.

But then she stopped.

"Yergi called him 'the Algerian.'"

"'The Algerian'? Are you sure?"

"Yes. That I am certain about."

"Okay. Thank you."

"But I want to tell you one more thing," Elena said.

"Yes?"

"When you find this man who killed my Yergi. Please ..." Elena's chin trembled a little.

"What?"

She managed to stop the trembling. Then she spoke with icy control.

"Kill him good."

That was the last entry that appeared on the last page of the CIA interview transcript.

When Gallagher had finished reading the transcript, he collected the pages and handed them back to Ken Leary, who had by then finished his ice-cream cone. Leary thrust the papers back into the big envelope.

"Thanks," Gallagher said.

Leary was struck by the way his friend had said that. Gallagher seemed intensely deliberate like Leary had never seen him before. Committed. Inflexible. So Leary gave Gallagher another warning, just for good measure. "Look John, I can't deal with you any more on this subject. You're on your own from this point on. I will deny our conversation. All of it. You know that."

"Right."

But Leary had to ask one last question. "You're going to keep after Zimler aren't you? John, do you know what you're doing?"

"Ken, I thought you and I were finished talking about this. Isn't that what you just said?"

Leary smiled and stood up with the envelope under his arm. His last words to John Gallagher were "God's speed."

Then he walked out of the dry cleaners and headed back to his office.

FIFTY

From his position against the railing of the ferry, Joshua Jordan had a good view of the Statue of Liberty as it loomed large on the water beyond the bow of the tour boat. The sky was grey and overcast, and the iron-colored water of the bay was choppy as the ferry left Battery Park Harbor in Manhattan. He felt uneasy about leaving the privacy of his hotel room. Wearing a baseball hat and sunglasses was a start. But he knew he was exposing himself to risk. But the wife of the Patriot, whoever she was, had said that they had inside information about threats against Joshua, and he needed help. Time for another calculated risk. But he couldn't afford too many more. He just hoped he wasn't walking himself out onto a gangplank by agreeing to the meeting.

He turned his focus toward the passengers on the deck and tried to pick out his contact. Joshua didn't know what he looked like, but the voice on the phone had told Joshua that the man known as "The Patriot" would recognize him.

Taking one last look at the business card bearing only "The Patriot" on it along with a telephone number, Joshua wondered if anyone would show up. Joshua had called him immediately after the conference call with the Roundtable. The Patriot had insisted on the ferry for their rendezvous. Not exactly Joshua's first choice.

There was a crowd on the ferry that day. Joshua looked over the sea of faces milling around on the deck.

Then he heard the voice of a man next to him. "You remind me of a man who likes to play chess."

That was the prearranged opening line. The scripted intro concocted by the Patriot seemed melodramatic. But Joshua was required to give him the agreed response.

"I do. I prefer to lead with the knight."

The other man reached out his hand and gave Joshua a crushing, hydraulic handshake. He had a good-natured face, in his early sixties, was medium height, and in very good shape. By all appearances he could have been a banker or a clerk in a men's clothing store.

"Sorry about the secret-agent stuff," the man said. "Mr. Jordan, it's a pleasure to meet you."

"Call me Josh."

"And you can quit calling me the Patriot. My name is Packard McHenry. I'm simply Pack to my friends. So you wanted to talk to me?"

"Your wife gave me your card. It seems that you're a man who stands ready to help. Exactly how, I'm not sure."

"Information, Josh. Among other things. I've got a little group of friends that work with me on matters important to our country. Similar to your Roundtable."

"How'd you know about that?"

"If you knew my friends you'd understand. Retired folks from the National Security Agency. Former members of the Defense Intelligence Agency. Past agents from the Secret Service. Me, I'm retired from … the Company."

"CIA?"

Pack McHenry smiled, didn't reply directly, but asked, "What can we do to help?"

"We've got an emergency. We need to know something about World Teleco. They're shutting down a project of ours. We had a contract with them, but they're refusing to honor it. Our media plan depended on it. And that, in turn, was going to be the linchpin for everything."

"You mean, the linchpin to get Senator Straworth to drop the subpoena, so Judge Jenkins will then not order you incarcerated for contempt of court and of Congress … so you can keep the RTS weapon design protected and solely in the hands of the Defense Department of the United States, so it doesn't get leaked to some less-than-friendly nations? You mean that kind of linchpin?"

Joshua chuckled and said, "So, you really are on top of the game."

"Look, my group likes what you're doing. For the country. So I've had some of my people track you. For your own safety. And also to track some not-nice people who might pose a threat to you. I have intelligence about a meeting arranged by one particular not-nice lawyer by the name of Allen Fulsin, a man you know about because Judge Fortis Rice from your Roundtable talked to him about joining your group. I'm sure Judge Rice thought he was being discreet when he talked to him. But it turns out that Fulsin is one of those well-connected guys who knows all the dirty tricks and can get deep information from only a few leads. So Fulsin did some digging about your Roundtable based solely on the tidbits Judge Rice had given him, got what he needed, and then met with a high ranking VP of World Teleco at a bar. In a corner booth. We've got the whole story. Fulsin warned the telecom company that your message would be criticizing the White House. Exposing corruption. Showing how deliberate misinformation has been fed to the American people. How a media monopoly is aiding and abetting this. And most important to us, explaining how control of our country is being sold off, piece by piece, to a global network."

"But how did you get all this information?"

Pack McHenry pointed to the approaching Statue of Liberty. "I wonder when they started naming a football play after that monument?" he said.

Joshua just shook his head.

McHenry said, "Well, sometime before the turn of the century, at least, a college team ran the first Statue of Liberty. That same play, or some variation of it, is still used occasionally in college ball. I've even seen it used in the NFL. Guess that proves one thing."

"Which is?"

"It's good to stick with the old stuff that works. We followed an old playbook with Fulsin. Did an old-fashioned close surveillance. It paid off. When they set up the meeting, we made sure they were shown to a booth. It was in the evening, and both of those guys are the drinking type. Not likely to take coffee. So we had a listening device placed in one of the sugar packets in the cream-and-sugar basket. I'm telling you all this because it's our first meeting and we're building trust. But don't expect me to tell you any more of our tricks of the trade in the future."

"Understood."

"I'll tell one of my people right now to email you an affidavit substantiating the meeting between Fulsin and the World Teleco executive."

"Here, I'll give you my private email address — "

"No need," McHenry said, "we already have it. By the way, you may want to upgrade your email encryption security program." Then he smiled as he continued. "Just be warned, I'm hoping this doesn't get into court and go public. If it does, our operative who signed the affidavit will have to distance himself entirely from us. That'll be the end of his usefulness to our group. And he's a good man."

"Don't worry. My wife has a plan, but it's not litigation."

"Good."

"But there is something else I need to know," Joshua said.

"Right," McHenry said preempting him. "What my wife, Samantha, told you in the hotel restaurant. About being in danger from foreign actors? All we've got are bits and pieces that don't add up. What we do know is that federal agencies, including the Department of Justice, are all clamping down on this hard. Closing ranks. We can't get any intel on this at the moment. But we're working on it. I do have one recommendation, though."

"What's that?"

McHenry handed Joshua a slip of paper, then said, "Have General Rocky Bridger from your group call this man at this number. They need to talk."

On the slip of paper he had written the name of Special Agent John Gallagher along with his private telephone number.

After that, Pack McHenry pronounced what sounded like a kind of benediction. "We wish you God's speed."

Then he crossed the deck and disappeared into the crowd of passengers.

FIFTY-ONE

Judge Olivia Jenkins was in her chambers bright and early. She flipped open her calendar to see what was pending. She had a full docket. But one case in particular was on her mind. And it would be the first case she would call.

Outside in the courtroom Harry Smythe and the two assistant U.S. attorneys from the government were waiting patiently for the clerk to call them back into the judge's chambers.

Then the clerk poked her head out into the courtroom and waived them in.

When all were seated and the clerk had closed the door, Jenkins began. "Harry, I notice that your client, Mr. Jordan, is not with you today."

"He's not, Your Honor."

"Are you prepared to give this court the whereabouts of Mr. Jordan so he can be served with my bench warrant today?"

"I'm not, Judge."

"What's the reason for that?"

"Not anything I can discuss without breaching attorney-client confidentiality."

"I recognize that," Judge Jenkins said. "But it could be argued that the oath you took when you were first sworn in to be a lawyer — the oath to uphold our system of justice — is equally important. Maybe more so."

"There's nothing more I can say, Judge," Smythe said in his studied calm. "Except that I've been presented with a very ... challenging dilemma."

"You know I could cause you a world of trouble," the Judge said.

"As a federal judge, your power is broad and impressive," Smythe said. "I would only ask that you allow us until the end of today before you issue your bench warrant for the arrest of Mr. Jordan."

"Judge," one of the assistant attorneys interjected, "that would be *more* than forty-eight hours. And your order from the bench the other day said forty-eight hours."

"End of business today," Harry Smythe said. "That's all I'm asking." In his face was the plea for mercy rather than justice.

Judge Jenkins recognized the look. She picked up the case file and balanced it in one hand. Then she ruled. "Okay. End of business today. But that's it. No more extensions. No more excuses. Unless there's been a radical change of circumstances, at that time I will be issuing an order for the immediate apprehension of Joshua Jordan. From that point on he will be treated as a fugitive from justice by the federal government."

Harry Smythe slipped quickly out the courtroom and called Joshua to give him an immediate status report. He got his voicemail and left a lengthy message.

□□□

Cloistered in his hotel suite Joshua wasn't taking any calls other than those from the Roundtable. That day he had been in constant contact with Phil Rankowitz about the AmeriNews project. Phil had his entire wireless tech team ready to pull the switch on the national unveiling of their news service, sending it to half of the cell phones in America. But one thing was missing. The technical support engineers at World Teleco would have to open the electronic gate.

The night before, and first thing again that morning, Phil's media brokers had called the chief telecommunications engineer for the global telecom company, threatening, cajoling, pleading with him to connect the AmeriNews feed to the Allfones that were serviced by World Teleco, just as their contract had required.

"Look," the engineer blew back, "I've been told this is a transaction in dispute. We're not about to throw the on-switch just because you want it. My superiors say no, and I've got to follow orders. Sorry."

Then Joshua got a text-message from Abigail. It said simply, "With lawyers now. Will advise."

Abigail had caught a shuttle flight down to the capital the night before.

Now, in a small coffee shop near the Federal Communications Commission building in D.C., Abigail sat at a table with four lawyers, all of them veterans in communications law. She was briefing them on their legal mission.

"All of you have the affidavit," she began, "of the witness to the conversation between Allen Fulsin and Bill Cheavers, the executive with World Teleco. He lays it all out in there."

"I just have to ask," said one of the lawyers, a middle-aged woman, "about this guy who signed the affidavit, where he got this stuff? How was he able to simply 'overhear,' as he vaguely describes it, this really startling conversation between Fulsin and Cheavers?"

"You can ask," Abigail answered matter-of-factly, "but I won't be answering. Now, let's get to the overall strategy here. There are five commissioners who sit on the FCC. I'll be taking the chairman, Jacob Daniels. I've assigned each one of you to one of the other commissioners. As you know, for some strange reason, President Corland, after he was elected, has dragged his heels in exercising his executive prerogative in appointing a new chairman of the FCC. I think Corland has simply had his hands full with a number of crises. I have a good professional relationship with Daniels, so I will approach him first. If

I think he's amenable to my argument, I will hit the Quick-Tweet—QT—function on my Allfone and instant-message you all with the Twitter 'go' sign to approach your respective commissioners."

"I'd like to go over the legal theory we'll be arguing with these commissioners," one of the other lawyers said.

"Very simple," Abigail said. "You'll remember when all the national news media—all the television networks and all the news-radio syndicates—were required to transfer over to the Internet for the delivery of their communications content. Arguments broke out about who would control it. Who would supervise it. The courts struck down all the legislative attempts to structure a federal oversight. Congress, worried about the economically distressed media and news industry, lifted the antitrust restrictions on those businesses. Internet-based media quickly became a monopoly that now rests in the hands of a few transnational corporations. But remember, the FCC still retains a very narrow, rarely used power over the Internet."

"Right, only in cases of clear viewpoint discrimination by the telecom companies," another attorney chimed in.

"Exactly," Abigail said. "We all know that discrimination by the telecoms against 'politically incorrect' viewpoints over the web does happen. But no one has been able to prove it. Until now. This affidavit is the smoking gun that shows that World Teleco is committing a viewpoint-based act of illegal discrimination against our client and the AmeriNews project."

"Sounds logical," the first lawyer said. But she pointed out, "The Chairman has a great deal of discretion. How do you know he's going to buy this? And how in the world are you going to get him to act immediately? The FCC is known for dragging some issues out for years."

Abigail smiled and said, "Leave that up to me."

"But the chairman is not going to issue a cease-and-desist order by himself," a lawyer retorted, tapping his pen on the table for emphasis.

"No, he's not," Abigail replied. "He's going to want backup from at least two of the other four commissioners, so he's got a majority vote of three out of five." Then she added, "And that's where you fine legal advocates come into the picture."

Fewer than thirty minutes later Abigail was on the eighth floor of the Federal Communications Commission building, in the vestibule of the office of Jacob Daniels, the chairman. In her hand was the file containing the affidavit. Chairman Daniels' secretary had already been given the message that there was an urgent need to speak to the chairman.

After a wait of forty minutes, the chairman's legal counsel strode out. He was a young lawyer, in his early thirties, and he had a pressed smile and an insincere handshake.

"Ms....," he said, searching for Abigail's name.

"Abigail Jordan," she said. "Could you tell me if attorney Cort Windom is still working as Chairman Daniels' chief legal counsel?"

"I'm afraid not. He left about a year ago to practice law with a D.C. firm. I've taken his spot. Can I help you?"

"I used to do a lot of work here with Mr. Windom, representing media clients before the FCC," she said. "I also worked very closely with Chairman Daniels on a number of communications issues. Back when he was a new Commissioner. I haven't seen him since he's been serving as chairman. But I always enjoyed an excellent relationship with Jacob."

"Well ... that's nice," he said blandly.

"Did you get my message ...?"

"Yes. You'd like a meeting with the chairman. I'd be glad to pass your name on to Chairman Daniels' scheduling secretary. Maybe something could be set up a few weeks from now."

"This is an emergency. It can't wait."

The lawyer struck a pose as if his mother had just been insulted.

"I'm sorry. But protocol is that walk-in requests for appointments must first be vetted through the scheduling secretary. No exceptions."

"I assure you this is a matter that Chairman Daniels is definitely going to want to discuss immediately."

"No exceptions," the lawyer said with a strained smile.

Abigail sat back down in the lobby chair.

"Would you like to speak to the scheduling secretary?" he asked.

"No. I'll wait for Jacob."

"Chairman Daniels is not going to take a walk-in appointment with you."

Abigail smiled back at the young lawyer but didn't move.

"Perhaps," he said, "you should come back another time."

She kept smiling. But didn't budge.

"I really don't want to have to call for security ..."

"Then perhaps you shouldn't," she said, gripping her file even tighter.

There was a long, uncomfortable moment as the lawyer bobbed on his toes and Abigail sat stone-still in the chair, the file in her lap.

The secretary at the reception desk was staring at the scene, and her mouth was parted slightly in anxious wonderment. Everyone in that vestibule of the chairman's office knew that something was about to happen.

And it did.

The door to the vestibule swung open, and Chairman Jacob Daniels strode in, his suit coat off and in his shirtsleeves, holding a Styrofoam cup of coffee.

"Had to go across the street to get this," he said absently. "When are they supposed to repair our coffee machine? Does anybody know?"

Then Jacob Daniels swept the room with his gaze, looking for an answer. His eyes locked on Abigail.

He searched for her name.

"Abigail ... uh ..."

"Jordan."

"Yes, of course. With all the news about your husband, how could I forget your last name?"

"Right," she said with a grin.

"We've missed seeing you around here. You did some great communications work for your media clients."

"Thanks. I liked the work. But I've been out of the practice for a while."

"That's the legal profession's loss then," he said. "So, my staff treating you all right?"

Abigail glanced over at the lawyer who was no longer bouncing on his toes. He was now standing perfectly still. Hoping that the shrapnel that would be coming his way any minute would merely be a maiming injury, and not a career-killer.

"Oh, yes," Abigail said flashing another bright smile. "Your staff attorney here has been most helpful."

The lawyer managed a meek smile in return and started breathing again.

"Well, what brings you here?" Daniels asked.

"An urgent matter that I think you will find very interesting," she said.

"It must be important to bring you back here," the chairman said.

Then he pointed to his inner office and said, "Let's talk. I've got a few minutes."

FIFTY-TWO

In crowded Manhattan, up in his hotel suite, Joshua Jordan was caught up in his brain-storming session with Phil Rankowitz. They were laying out the final last steps in their AmeriNews plan. Yet they knew that it all depended on one thing. Abigail still had to get the FCC to order World Teleco to honor its contract and launch the Roundtable's explosively controversial wireless news service to millions of Allfones. But after hanging up with Phil, Joshua had a nagging feeling he was forgetting something. He glanced over his Roundtable checklist for the project. No, everything was on track. Maybe something else. Something personal?

Then he remembered his conversation with Abby. Before she left for Washington, she urged him to give a call to Cal to see how he was doing. He still remembered her words: "Josh, I think he needs to hear from his dad again. He always knows his mom's in his corner. But *you* need to reach out. It's been awhile since we've heard from him. Besides, you said your last call with him didn't go anywhere."

Joshua had been all consumed recently. Maybe Abby was right. Besides, she had a remarkable intuition about the kids. Joshua dialed Cal's number, confident in his signal-cloaking Allfone.

On the campus of Liberty University, Cal's cell was ringing. He didn't answer it at first. He was busy watching his ex-girlfriend, Karen, walking

311

away from him. The ringing continued. Without looking at the caller ID, Cal answered in an angry tone.

There was an awkward pause. Then Joshua Jordan spoke.

"Cal it's, me. Dad. Everything okay?"

"Yeah, sure."

"School okay?"

"Sure."

"Everything else?"

"Fine."

There was another pause. Joshua dug deeper. "How are things between you and Karen?"

Cal muttered, "Wow, two points."

"Didn't quite get that ..."

"Never mind, Dad. Just about the Karen thing ..."

"Tell me."

Cal didn't really want to. But he blurted it out anyway. "We broke up today."

"Sorry. How are you with that?"

"It wasn't my idea. She's getting back together with Jeff Hitchney."

"Gottcha. That hurts. Male ego's a powerful thing. But I know you had some strong feelings for her. Sorry it didn't work out."

"Really? I kind of find that hard to believe ..."

"Just because I had some questions about her. And I thought you ought to be concentrating on your studies — "

"Well, that's not how it came across. Okay? The way I see it, it's just one more way that Joshua Jordan is trying to control the world, including his son."

"That's a cheap shot, Cal. I pay your tuition. I think that gives me some say-so in your school life. Your choice of major. Relationships that might jeopardize your studies." Joshua's voice was firm but not angry. Cal, on the other hand, was having a hard time keeping it together, so he didn't talk. His father filled in the blanks.

"Look, let's keep this civil. Adult. You're not a child, Cal; you're a man. So I'm going to talk to you that way. You and I need to be able to converse about things with the drawbridge down. Okay? You have a problem with me, that's fine. I can take it. Speak your mind. But I'm going to keep speaking mine. Don't cop an attitude with me just because I let you know that your compass is going whacky and your trajectory is off. All right?"

"Fine."

"Is that a yes?"

"Yes, sir."

"One more thing."

Cal was listening.

"You need to know something. More important than anything else."

"What's that?"

"Your father loves you. Get that down pat. Nothing's ever going to change that."

"All right."

Just then there was a beep on Joshua's line.

"That's my next conference call coming in. Gotta go. Remember the last thing I just said, Cal. Okay? It's important."

"Okay, Dad."

Then the call ended. An instant later, as Cal was staring at his cell phone, he realized that he'd screwed up. For the second time recently, his dad told him he loved him. But Cal hadn't reciprocated. He wondered, *What is my problem anyway?* Down deep Cal knew he should have said something. To let his dad know how he really felt. Of course Cal looked up to him. But more than that, he harbored a towering sense of awe for his father. But there was always so much other turmoil getting in the way between the two of them. Whenever his dad reached out, which wasn't often, well, he didn't know how to handle it. So he'd go silent. Maybe it was time for that to change. *Next time*

I talk to him, I'll let him know how I feel. And that I love him. Respect him. I'll tell him that, no matter what.

Cal was now walking back to his dorm room.

□□□

On that day, Cal's sister, Deborah, was busy with her class schedule up at West Point. As for the rest of Cal's family — for Abby and Joshua — they had been immersed in their own struggles. But every one of them was oblivious to the danger that was stalking them — and getting closer.

At that precise moment, Atta Zimler had arrived at a point a mere two miles from his destination. And he was closing in.

He knew parking might be a problem. His ability to get his utility van out fast was a high priority. Like everything else, he had a plan for that too.

The timetable was perfect. He knew that shortly his target would be in his grasp. He would then secure the RTS design documents. And the pleasing thought of the fortune that would be wired to his offshore account, to be added to his already huge balance from the upfront fee paid by Caesar Demas. But this wasn't just about money for Atta Zimler. He was a man with a planet-sized ego. When he says he will kill a man, the man gets killed. When he says a certain thing will get done, it gets done. He considered himself a force of nature. Unstoppable. Unremitting. Merciless.

Zimler had his tactical file on the seat next to him. Photographs. Schematics. Maps. Escape routes. And most importantly, of course, his deadly tools of the trade were carefully laid out in the back of the van.

Thinking forward about the final coup de grâce, Zimler knew that there would be lots of blood before it was over.

But he had a sense of amused satisfaction when he considered exactly how it was going to be shed.

FIFTY-THREE

FCC Chairman Jacob Daniels had only one person in his office. Abigail Jordan. No staffers. No other legal counsel. Just the two of them.

Abigail tried to look poised. But inside she was having a tough time holding it together. She knew how high the stakes were for Josh. And she was also smart enough to know how improbable her whole strategy seemed. One thought dominated her mind, no matter how she tried to stay focused. *How in the world are we going to pull this off?*

Was she really going to convince the FCC to issue an immediate cease-and-desist order against one of the largest telecom companies in the world by the close of business that day?

While Chairman Daniels read through a copy of the affidavit she had presented him, Abigail took a moment to acquaint herself with his office. She hadn't been there for years. It was spacious but eclectic. There was a large couch, several ornate credenzas, and two Victorian Art Nouveau book cases, which looked like antiques. Four chairs were arranged around an unusual coffee table, which had wrought iron legs and a table top fashioned out of a layer of white Jerusalem stone. Abigail was in one chair and Chairman Daniels in the other.

She took her two fingers and tried to press a crease out of the affidavit that she was holding. The sworn statement was courtesy of their "Patriot" friend, Pack McHenry's surveillance man, who had taped Allen Fulsin's meeting with the World Teleco executive at the New

York bar. That affidavit was the only evidence Abigail had to present. Suddenly the three-page document looked pretty thin.

Daniels finished, flipped back to the first page, looked up, and tossed the affidavit onto the coffee table.

Abigail smiled.

He glanced discreetly at his watch. Abigail took a breath, and like a runner putting her feet in the starting blocks, she readied herself silently. *Okay, here we go ...*

Then she started her pitch.

"As chairman of the FCC you've always spoken out boldly about the potential for a media monopoly to develop."

"Sure, of course. But I don't think the right people were listening."

"I recall you saying the worst-case scenario would be a dictatorship of a few media giants controlling the news for the entire nation."

"Yeah, true," he said with a grin. He was glad someone remembered his remarks. "I knew all the news networks would eventually migrate to an Internet platform. So then the question was how were we going to prevent censorship of the news if only a few telecoms controlled the wires and no one had jurisdiction to police the Internet? See, my goal was not content control or even regulation. Forget that. I always felt that the free market generally ought to prevail over the web. I just wanted to make sure that America's news wouldn't be censored, that unpopular viewpoints wouldn't be blocked by a few powerful telecoms."

Abigail lunged in. "This situation with World Teleco is a perfect chance to vindicate your position. We all know that President Corland could and probably still will replace you."

"I've always wondered why he didn't simply ask me to resign. Standard procedure. I would have done it, of course. Just like all the other chairmen before me. But he didn't. So here I am."

"Not by accident," Abigail suggested cautiously. She hesitated for only a split second before she spoke what was really on her heart. "I think God directs events. Destinies. He opens historic opportunities. The fact you're still chairman could be one of them."

"You think this AmeriNews – World Teleco dispute is that important?"

"Yes. It goes far beyond just the flagrant illegality of World Teleco. If you're willing to order them to obey the contract with us, and do it today, the dominoes will start toppling. The playing field for news and information could suddenly become a level surface. Not to mention some other crucial consequences that I'm not free to share."

FCC Chairman Daniels glanced at the affidavit lying on the coffee table. "I've got to admit," he said, motioning to the document. "There's some powerful stuff in there …"

"You've always said that you were looking for the right case to exercise your very limited but important power to keep the Internet open. I remember your words: 'Keeping the channels of communication free from the tyranny of the few who would exercise absolute control over the many.' "

"Yes, I did say that once," Daniels said. In his voice was a longing, like an almost ready-to-retire major league pitcher who figured he'd never make it to the World Series. "Well, at least you're right about one thing. The White House's going to get rid of me. Maybe even tomorrow. Or the next day. But it doesn't look like it's going to happen today." Then reaching over and snatching up the affidavit again, he said, "So for today, I'm still chairman."

That is when Abigail realized what was going on. She was straining to hear what was coming next.

"Okay, Abby. You get me two other commissioners to back me up, and I'll do it. I'll tell World Teleco they can't violate that contract for the AmeriNews service without serious consequences from the FCC. But I need at least two other commissioners so we've got a majority. Which means you'd better get hopping — "

"My lawyers are outside the commissioners' offices right now," Abigail said.

"You know Commissioner Winston won't support it," Daniels said. "Neither will Johnston, I don't think. Talk to Commissioner Susan Copple. She's worth a try. Commissioner Justin Lattig is almost certain to support me on this. Though I think he may be out of town. Giving a speech somewhere. You'll have to check with his office."

"We will."

"Now, I don't have to remind you that from this point on protocol says I can't discuss this with you any further. At least during the time I put this on official emergency circulation among the other commissioners."

"Understood."

"But hopefully we'll have an answer for you today."

Then as Abigail rose to leave, Daniels got up, shook her hand, and added one more thought. "My father was a Rabbi, as you probably know," Daniels said. "He used to quote the first century Jewish scholar Gamaliel: 'Secure a teacher for thyself.' I've gathered a few teachers for myself over the years. Abby, today you were one of them."

Abby was ecstatic. She rushed out of the chairman's office and with one hand sent a Quick Tweet to the Allfones of her other four lawyers, each of them perched outside an office belonging to one of the other four commissioners. It read: "Daniels is a go — secure support from two more commissioners."

All four lawyers simultaneously grabbed their briefcases and swept into the offices.

Even though he was in his office, Commissioner Winston refused to meet with the lawyer. Through his assistant he relayed that he had absolutely no interest in taking action against World Teleco.

In Commissioner Johnston's office, the lawyer was able to make a quick pitch to him personally. But the commissioner begged off diplomatically. "I won't support any immediate action on this," he said. "What I will do is consider joining in on a future Notice of Proposed Rule Making procedure perhaps in the months ahead. But only with a full hearing. Complete public notice. That sort of thing. But I'm not going to vote for a full-court press on that telecom company today under these conditions."

Commissioner Susan Copple had been slowed down in traffic on the Wilson Bridge coming into D.C. from Maryland. The lawyer assigned to her was able to get a cell phone call back from her within the hour.

Copple said she was philosophically in agreement with Chairman Daniels, but she had to discuss it with her legal staff before making any official decision. "Maybe sometime after lunch, we'll try to review this," she said.

As for Commissioner Justin Lattig, he was returning from a speech in Nashville. His plane was scheduled to touch down at 1:00 in the afternoon, but it had been delayed. His staff called him on his cell. Then they relayed a message to the lawyer from Lattig himself. "Tell Abigail Jordan that I will do nothing unless she and I discuss this personally. Face-to-face."

All of the lawyers reconvened together over a working lunch at the Monocle on D Street, just off Capitol Hill.

Abigail tried to be upbeat but the strain among the lawyers was palpable. The two additional votes had not been confirmed. Two Commissioners had already turned them down. Copple seemed a possibility. But Lattig was still out of reach.

"Look Abby," one of the men lawyers said. "This might be doable ... maybe ... but trying to crunch this into a deadline by end of business today ... I mean, we're all seasoned FCC lawyers ... but what you're asking is, well, probably impossible. Sorry. Just telling it the way it is."

"Nothing's impossible," Abigail snapped back. She took a deep breath and laid her menu down and looked around the table. "You're some of the best media lawyers in the nation. Every one of you. We can do this. I know it."

Abigail ordered a Cobb salad. But as the waitress was taking the rest of the orders, Abigail quietly added it all up in her head. She knew that in a few hours, unless World Teleco was reprimanded and AmeriNews was launched and the Capitol was swamped with angry callers, unless all of that happened and happened perfectly, the subpoena would not be withdrawn. And Judge Jenkins would end up signing an order that would turn her husband into a fugitive from the law.

At 1:00 in the afternoon the lawyers dispatched themselves to their appointed places. Two of them at Copple's office, two waiting in Lattig's office for the Commissioner to arrive from Reagan airport. Abigail stationed herself outside the chairman's office.

Then they waited. First one hour. Soon the clock on the commission wall was edging its way past 2:30.

The first to weigh-in was Commissioner Copple. After meeting with her legal staff, she called the two lawyers into her office to discuss it personally.

It was a thirty-minute session, with the commissioner's lawyers peppering Abigail's lawyers with questions, hypothetical "what ifs," and caveats, while the commissioner sat back and observed. What kind of precedent would this set? Shouldn't there be a full hearing before this kind of drastic action was taken? Did the FCC have the statutory authority in the first place? Was a single affidavit enough to face down a mammoth telecom giant? Finally, the commissioner herself was ready to speak.

"I'm inclined to support Chairman Daniels on this," Susan Copple said, "but only after I speak to the chairman myself. I still have some concerns."

That was good enough for Abigail's team. They messaged that to Abigail and the rest of the team.

By 3:00, one of the staffers of Commissioner Justin Lattig poked his head out into the lobby and addressed the two waiting lawyers. "Sorry," he said, "but Commissioner Lattig's plane just landed. He's so late that he won't be coming in at all today. He's on his way to another speech he has to make tonight in Winchester, Virginia, all the way over at the western edge of the state. I'm sorry about that."

The lawyers walked up to Abigail who was still outside the chairman's office and told her the bad news. But she wouldn't accept it.

"Did you tell Lattig's staffer how urgent this was?"

"We did, but we have no way of knowing if he ever told the commissioner."

Abigail raced up to Jacob Daniels' office and managed to get him to come out to the lobby for one final plea. "I told you, Abby, I can't discuss this any more with you — "

"Jacob, can't you at least call Commissioner Lattig and ask him to join us in a conference call from his limo?"

Daniels took a step closer to Abigail and whispered, "Already tried that. The guy's got his cell phone turned off." Then he reached out and squeezed her hand, said he was very sorry, and slowly returned to his inner office. Abigail grabbed her briefcase and stormed out of the building, down to the parking ramp to her rental car. Now all she could do was change her ticket to an earlier flight. Get home to Josh. Let him know she'd failed. And see whether by putting their heads together they could figure out some kind of Plan B. Even though she already knew there was no Plan B.

She was able to enter Interstate 66 from the government center of D.C. much more quickly than she would have guessed and was heading west. But she didn't have the heart to call Joshua. Not yet. How could she? *Lord, why did You bring me this close to a miracle ... just to have everything collapse?*

Tears were starting to come. Then the traffic slammed to a halt, both lanes. *Great. Now I'll be late to the airport. I'll be lucky to get a flight out tonight. This is a disaster ... forgive me, God, but I am so utterly ...*

Then she noticed something off to her right, on an entrance ramp that fed onto the Interstate. A black limo. It slowed as the driver was obviously sizing-up the veritable parking lot of stopped traffic. But a truck about twenty cars ahead of Abigail managed to swing into the adjoining lane creating a gap. The limo driver sped quickly down the ramp trying to race into the space.

Abigail's eyes lingered on the long stretch limousine and noticed the government license plate. It read "FCCOM 2." Commissioner Lattig would have to be heading west on I-66 to get to his next meeting in the western corner of the state. She couldn't believe it. The black limo squeezed into the traffic lane amidst angry drivers and honking horns. The line of traffic was still stopped.

Think. Think, she said to herself. The limo had a twenty-car lead ahead of her. Once the traffic finally opened up she would never be able to catch up.

Abigail swung her car sharply out of traffic and into the emergency lane on the right. Hit the button of the dash for the flashers, and put her car into park. She grabbed wildly at her briefcase, breaking a polished fingernail in the process, but finally laid hold of the folder containing the affidavit. She yanked it out and climbed out of the car and locked the door. Then something told her to do one more thing. She'd brought her gym bag with her, hoping to work out on the treadmill at her hotel. *Oh why not,* she muttered. She popped the trunk and took her high heals off, threw them into the trunk, and frantically tied on her running shoes.

But that was when the traffic suddenly started moving.

No! No! she yelled out. A female driver in the car in the next lane eyed her as she started jogging down the freeway safety lane and shook her head as she slowly eased past.

With the file containing the affidavit in hand, she picked up her pace alongside of the line of snaking traffic, heading in the direction of the black government limo. She was now only twelve cars from the limo. But the traffic started moving a little faster, up to seven miles per hour. She pumped her arms and went into a bigger stride. The traffic jam was breaking up. They were now up to nine miles an hour. Then ten. Abigail was now into a full-speed run and sweat was beading up on her face. The limo was just two car lengths ahead. A male driver next to her yelled something at her, but all she could hear was the word "crazy" as she ran past him.

Help me, Lord! She yelled out loud as she was tiring and couldn't close the two-car gap between herself and the limo cruising just beyond her reach. The traffic slowed just slightly. She kept running. As a tour bus up ahead slowly bullied its way from the right lane into the left, a bottleneck in traffic brought the traffic to another standstill. Abigail rushed up to the rear passenger window. Commissioner Lattig saw someone at his passenger side door and quickly slid over to the far side of the back seat with a startled look. She waved the file in front of the window. Then a look of slight recognition broke over his face. Lattig scooted over the seat and lowered the window half way down.

"Aren't you ...," he started to say.

"Abigail Jordan, yes," she managed to say between gasping breaths.

"What in the world — "

"An emergency matter before the FCC."

Though traffic was still stopped, a car right behind them blasted its horn. Lattig ignored it.

"Oh," he said absently. "I wasn't told it was an emergency — "

"It is. We have two votes in our favor," she said breathlessly. "The chairman and, I think, Commissioner Copple. All we need is your vote ... against World Teleco ... it's an outrage, Mr. Commissioner ...

has to be done this afternoon. Here's the proof of deliberate viewpoint discrimination and censorship committed by World Teleco ..." With that she stuffed the file containing the affidavit through the half-open window of the limo. Then she added, "Your staff said you demanded to see me in person. So here I am ..."

"In person? Oh, that. Yes. But not about this case ..."

"Then what?" Abigail blurted out almost in a shout.

"Well, to tell you something personal. About your husband." Lattig lowered the limo window down all the way. Lattig's face was fully in the open window of the limo. "I wanted you to know that I think your husband is a hero."

Abigail couldn't help herself; she started to laugh and cry at the same time.

"Now, about this case of yours," Lattig said. "Get in, get in. Let's talk." With that he swung the door open. She climbed in just as the traffic started moving again.

ooo

At 4:10 in the afternoon, after conferring personally with Commissioner Copple and talking on the phone with Commissioner Lattig from his limo, FCC Chairman Jacob Daniels wrote a note to himself in his daily journal. At the top was the date and time. The entry read:

On the World Teleco matter, concerning their denial of service over the Internet to AmeriNews ...

Then he lifted his pen off the paper for a moment. He was considering the outcome. And all that might follow. Then he finished his note.

After consulting with Commissioners KC and JL, I have made my decision. I will so order World Teleco to honor their contract with AmeriNews. Commissioners KC and JL concurred, making it a majority vote.

At 4:16, Chairman Daniels had a phone call with Bill Cheavers, executive vice president for the North American Division of World Teleco. It was not a pleasant call.

Cheavers threatened the chairman with leading a "conspiracy to drive World Teleco out of business." Daniels calmly replied that he had no such intent. "Unless, of course," Daniels continued, "you violate our cease-and-desist order and fail to honor your service contract with AmeriNews. In which case we will revoke the authority of your company to do telecommunications in America, which you and I both know I have the power to do — and I have the votes."

"I'll appeal," snarled Cheavers. "You'll lose. You'll look stupid. Then the president will finally get around to yanking you off the FCC."

"All that may be true," Daniels said. "But not until Wall Street and NASDAQ react to your corporation being suspended from doing business. I wonder what the record is for the fastest, deepest drop for the stock of any American Corporation. You folks at World Teleco might just break the record."

□□□

At 4:31 p.m., on the order of World Teleco executive Bill Cheavers, AmeriNews was launched to half of the Allfones in America. The headline read:

An American Hero Persecuted: Senator Lies about Joshua Jordan's RTS Missile Defense System

The subheadline read:

Treason in Congress?

By five minutes before 5:00 that afternoon, the Capitol Hill telephone switchboard in Congress became so overloaded from the outraged calls of citizens that it was rendered inoperable. At 5:25, Senator Straworth was called into an emergency caucus with his party members.

Senate Majority Leader Russell Beyers spoke for them all: "Straworth, you've got a cyclone by the tail here," he said. "This subpoena issue involving Joshua Jordan is now threatening every one of us in the party. You need to withdraw that subpoena — and now. Make this all go away."

Senator Straworth puffed his chest and refused, yelling so hard that spittle flew out of his mouth. "I'm not afraid of a political tornado."

"I come from Oklahoma," the majority leader intoned calmly. "You don't. We know a little about the power of a tornado. It can suck a man clean off the surface of the earth." Then he added, "And if that doesn't remove you, your fellow senators will."

By 5:30, Senator Straworth had ordered the official withdrawal of the subpoena that had been issued against Joshua Jordan, retroactively. And advised the clerk in Judge Jenkins' court accordingly.

Harry Smythe was dispatched to the federal courthouse to try to catch Judge Jenkins and get her to vacate her order against Joshua Jordan on the grounds that the entire dispute with Congress had now been rendered legally moot.

◻◻◻

Joshua, Abigail, and all the members of the Roundtable had been patched into a conference call to receive the news.

Jubilation rang out. Phil Rankowitz was so overjoyed he could hardly speak. Even Alvin Leander was laughing, saying he was still in disbelief that they pulled it off.

After the celebration died down and the call ended, Abigail called Joshua back so they could talk, just the two of them. She explained that she'd received a private telephone call from Harry Smythe, who said there was just one remaining problem — and Joshua and Abigail needed to know.

"The only bad news," Abigail said, "is that Judge Jenkins left the courthouse today without rescinding her order for your arrest. The clerk wouldn't bother her at home. So Harry will be down there first thing in the morning to speak to her. I would have thought she'd have withdrawn the warrant against you as soon as she knew the congressional subpoena — the legal basis for this whole dispute — had been withdrawn."

"Harry'll do the right thing," Joshua said with an air of confidence. "I'm not worried. I think the victory's been won, darling. And I owe it all to you. Your strategy was absolutely brilliant."

"I give God the credit, Josh, honey. He does the miracles. Even when we've quit looking for them."

FIFTY-FOUR

At his country villa north of Rome, just off of the Via Salaria, Caesar Demas was about to get down to business with his guest from the Middle East. He'd already given him a short tour of his four-thousand-square-meter gardens, the mahogany-lined fifty-stall horse stables, and the restored ancient Roman road that made up part of his three-kilometer-long gated driveway. Now he and his visitor were seated in the gold room, so named for the dark wheat-colored walls, with the stunning view of the rolling hills of his estate. Demas was seated in one brown leather chair, his guest in the matching chair next to him.

Now that refreshments had been served, Demas motioned for the servants to leave the room. But before exiting, the head butler bent down next to Demas' ear and whispered, "Excuse me, sir, but Mrs. Demas is wondering whether you will be able to address the matter of the vineyards today. Your chief of operations in your Tuscany property resigned a week ago. Your wife is worried that there is no one to oversee all of the vineyard work."

Demas turned to the butler and gave him a withering look.

"Do not — I repeat — do not bother me with those trifles. Do you understand?"

"Yes, sir," the butler whispered. "But what do you want me to tell Mrs. Demas?"

"Tell her anything you want. Now please leave."

The butler nodded courteously and was about to exit, but then Demas thought of something and motioned for him to come back.

When the butler bent down next to Demas again, his master whispered in the butler's ear, "Remember that I want her to be accompanied at all times. I don't want her left on her own. Understood? And please have her escort, who will be helping her with her wheelchair, send me instant messages regularly. I want to know all of her whereabouts and everything about her activities."

The butler nodded once again and swept out of the room.

Then Caesar Demas turned his attention to his visitor who was sipping tea.

The delegate from the Republic of Iran smiled appreciatively now that they were finally going to address the reason for his visit. With his hand he gave a quick stroke to his closely cropped beard and straightened his white silk waistcoat.

"I had expected Hamad Katchi to be part of this discussion. We had dealt with him previously on this."

Demas said, "Unfortunately, we have many enemies." Then he folded his hands, took on a sad, reflective expression, and added, "I fear Mr. Katchi may have fallen prey to some of them. He's disappeared. We haven't been able to locate him. I am so concerned that they may have liquidated him."

"That would be a terrible loss."

"Yes, to all of us."

"Well, then we shall talk, you and I, about these important matters. The RTS specifications ...," the Iranian said, "will be delivered ... when?"

"We will have possession in the next forty-eight hours. Delivery after that will follow with all possible haste."

"Will technical assistance be guaranteed?" the Iranian asked.

"That's part of the package. We have some physicists and weapons designers who are prepared to help you integrate the RTS into your existing weapons systems."

"The matter of exclusivity has been of great concern to our president," the Iranian said. "We do not want the RTS to turn into a kind of global discount item available to any banana-republic or no-name island."

"Of course not," Demas said, offering to refill his guest's teacup.

The Iranian smiled but held a hand up to say no thank you.

Demas continued explaining. "To reiterate. The RTS technology will only be available to cooperating nations or international unions that are members of our soon-to-be-established League of Ten."

Then he remembered something else and added, "And remember that another benefit is that your nation, and others in our League, will have the benefit of the anti-RTS avoidance technology we expect to develop as soon as our scientists analyze the RTS operating principals. So, you will not only have the benefit of returning incoming missiles to their point of origin, but your nation — and those inside our ten — will also be able to send your missiles into nonmember states, like the United States or their allies ... and the wonderful thing is that you'll be able to bypass their RTS system."

The Iranian beamed and said, "Very good. That is all very good."

Caesar Demas smiled back. Then he had a private thought. *So glad I chose Atta Zimler for this. Truly reliable men are hard to find.*

□□□

In a different time zone, in a very different part of the world, Cal Jordan was in his dorm room at Liberty University, changing into his gym trunks and a T-shirt. He was glad, now that he'd thought about it, that he was going to play some basketball with his buddies to get his mind off things.

And he was also glad he had heard from his dad. *Who knows, maybe he and I will start connecting. Maybe things are going to be better between us.*

Cal was going to turn off the lights in his dorm room before leaving, but suddenly they started to dim — and then they went out completely.

He flicked the switch a couple times. Still no lights. *Nice. I wonder how long it'll take maintenance to get this fixed. I've got a lot of studying tonight.*

Then he heard a knock on the door.

He swung open the door.

A man in a grey maintenance jumpsuit stood in his doorway.

"Sorry to bother," the maintenance man said. "We're cutting the power to some of the rooms. These old fluorescent lights in the ceiling have to be replaced one by one. It's your turn."

"Lucky me," Cal said, then added, "hope this doesn't take long. I'm supposed to shoot buckets in a few minutes with some friends."

The maintenance man gave a look that lacked full understanding at something in Cal's answer, but he flashed a quick smile anyway. Then he rolled a large covered utility cart into the dorm room. A few students wandered past the open door, looking in with some curiosity, before the man closed the door behind him.

"I've got my portable ladder and tools in here," the repairman said, pointing to the cart.

"Okay, well, do your thing," Cal said and took a step toward the door.

"Could you just help me for just a second?"

"Sure."

"I just need you to catch that big lighting fixture when I hand it down. Won't take too long. If you look up there at the fixture in the ceiling, you'll see where the bulb fits in at both ends. Just be careful not to dislodge the long light bulb when I hand it down to you. The bulb could break. It has some toxic contents inside."

"Doesn't sound too hard," Cal said.

Then Cal took a step into the center of the room and craned his neck to look up at the light fixture.

"I think I see what you are talking about," Cal said as he was studying it.

Right behind him, dressed in the grey maintenance jumpsuit, Atta Zimler was smiling.

He stepped up closer to Cal Jordan, and as he did, he had a satisfying thought.

This is almost too easy.

FIFTY-FIVE

Vice President Jessica Tulrude didn't notice the mild look of panic on the face of her chief of staff. In her working office in the West Wing of the White House, Tulrude had been going over her daily agenda with Lana Orvilla. But Orvilla was squirming and finally had to speak up and announce that she had an item of her own to bring up.

"Madam Vice President," she started out, "you mentioned a minute ago that the senators backed down and withdrew the subpoena against Joshua Jordan on the RTS weapon issue — "

"Senator Straworth had a deal with me. He broke it. All bets are off with that slob."

"Well," Lana tried to suggest, "doesn't this back-tracking by the senators hurt them much more than you ... I mean — "

"Are you crazy?" Tulrude shrieked. "I've been the one telling the president to say that we don't need exotic defense weapons systems. My language exactly. That's the official White House position that's been given to the media. We're promoting defense budget cuts, re-member? We are also concerned about international criticism over our nuking those North Korean ships with their own missiles. About the potential for civilian casualties if we use this RTS again in the future. We've taken sides in this political catfight. We took sides against RTS. Against Joshua Jordan's defiance of Congress. Remember, Lana, I'm running for president soon. You keep forgetting that."

"Which relates to what I wanted to discuss — "

"Time's a-wasting. Spit it out."

"On the day of the attack on New York City," Lana began, "when we first found out that the missiles were coming. You had enough confidence in me to include me in your briefing with the Pentagon. Things were scary that day. I have to admit I was pretty frightened — "

"This isn't a rerun of the *Oprah* show, Lana. Where's this going?"

"I have a brother ... don't know if I ever told you this. He works in New York. Manhattan. He's a tech engineer for a radio program."

"Bottom line, Lana! Is there a point to this story?"

"I was worried about him, that's all. In the private meeting with White House staff after the two-minute Pentagon briefing, you said basically ... 'The Pentagon's going to green-light this RTS weapon and use it against the North Koreans. I don't think it'll work, but what choice do we have?' ..."

"I never said that."

"Madam Vice President, you did say that, almost word for word — "

"Well, even if I really did say that, I *didn't* say it — if you know what I mean. Lana, in our letter to Senator Straworth's committee, we said that the White House did *not* authorize the use of RTS, nor did we know it was going to be used. We can't now say, oh, gee, sorry we lied, just kidding — "

"So I was worried about my brother, Ted, who works for the Ivan Teretsky radio show in New York. The radio host's nickname is Ivan the Terrible ..."

Now Jessica Tulrude was starting to put the pieces together. She stared at her chief of staff with a horrified look, now allowing her to finish her awful confession.

"I was in shock. You said RTS wouldn't work. So I panicked and snuck off and called my brother at the only number I had, the direct studio line, and yelled something like 'go down in the basement, protect yourself, missiles are heading to New York,' or something like that."

"Okay, your brother's family. We can keep him quiet . . . ," Tulrude snapped.

"No, you don't understand. It wasn't my brother who answered. It was some other man. I think it was that Ivan guy, the radio talk-show host who picked up the phone when I blurted all that out."

Tulrude was shaking her head, and her face was wincing as if to say, "No, you poor excuse for a human being, you couldn't have been so stupid."

Then she exploded.

"You gave classified information to a talk-show host! Do you realize that? And what's worse, the reason you tried to call your brother was because you heard me say that RTS is our only hope but I didn't think it was going to work. That means that I knew that RTS was going to be used. That means that they can prove that the White House authorized RTS, you idiot! If someone traces that call from you to this radio guy, it's going to reach back to me. It's going to destroy me politically!"

Orvilla stammered a little and said, "But . . . but the president was responsible for making the decision, wasn't he? Not you — "

"The president had just suffered another one of his blackouts, you imbecile. Don't you remember? Are you brain-dead?"

There was a silence in the room. Orvilla began to regain her composure now that her boss had just made a confession of her own that even her chief of staff hadn't heard before.

"You never told me the president has blackouts . . . ," Orvilla said in a controlled voice.

"I told you — "

"No. You never did. You've told me he was 'indisposed.' 'Unavailable.' 'Dealing with personal issues.' On that day when the missiles were coming you simply told me to 'shut up' when I asked why the president wasn't in those meetings."

Jessica Tulrude studied her chief of staff closely. She felt a very personal sense of rage wash over her as she entertained her political dilemma. *Just one more dangerous person I will now need to control.*

□□□

In his cubicle at the FBI office in New York, John Gallagher ate a breakfast burrito and considered his options.

The Ivan the Terrible radio-show investigation had been off his mental radar for a while. First, because Miles Zadernack had taken him off that project. Second, because he had a much bigger fish to fry. But Gallagher was now convinced that Atta Zimler was inside the United States. Though he still had to answer the most important question of all: Why had Zimler ventured into such dangerous territory?

It had to be something big. He was sure of it.

Then a phone call came in on Gallagher's cell from Rocky Bridger. After that, he was even more sure.

Gallagher asked him, "Who told you to call me?"

"My friend Joshua Jordan did. He got the lead from another friend."

"Does that other friend have a name?"

"Josh didn't give me the name. Just said he went by the title 'the Patriot.'"

Gallagher clicked with Rocky Bridger's involvement in the Philly torture and death of his son-in-law, Roger French. A murder that Gallagher had linked to Atta Zimler. So Gallagher got up from his cubicle and quickly scurried down to the men's room so he could finish the call without being overheard.

"I'm so sorry about your loss," he said. "I assume the Philly police interviewed you?"

"They did. But I don't think the investigation's making much progress."

So Gallagher decided to ask a few questions himself. After all, Bridger is the one who called him. He didn't actively violate Zadernack's order to get off the Zimler investigation. It didn't take Gallagher long to get into the details of Bridger's connection to Joshua Jordan. Including his meeting with Joshua regularly in some kind of political group, though Bridger refused to refer to the Roundtable by name.

Then Gallagher asked, "Did you ever confide information to your son-in-law, Roger French, stuff about Joshua Jordan? Location of his home? Business information? Description of his family? Private information like that?"

"He knew I was Joshua's former commander and that I was good friends with the Jordan family. I would have mentioned some things about that in casual conversation. Why?"

Gallagher didn't like doing it, but he had to admit the obvious. "You talked to your son-in-law Roger French about Joshua Jordan. Jordan's a controversial guy with access to powerful defense information. Then Roger French is tortured and killed. Maybe for that kind of information. Nothing's certain. But that's a theory."

As Gallagher thanked Bridger for calling, he knew that he'd just delivered a blow to the retired general — right in the solar plexus. Bridger took it like a man. But Gallagher figured that he had to be dying inside, knowing he may have inadvertently contributed to his son-in-law's death.

After the conversation, the FBI veteran stayed in the men's room for a few more minutes, piecing it together. He had followed the news, as most people had, about Joshua Jordan and his Return-to-Sender antimissile system. The FBI agent knew from Ken Leary's last meeting with him in the laundry that Zimler was interested in getting his hands on the RTS technology.

His predicament was excruciating. If he dumped all of this information on Miles, his supervisor just might see the light. On the other hand, Miles was a rulebook guy. He had the edict from the Department of Justice to stop all active investigations into Zimler within the continental United States. In the end, there didn't seem to be much hope that Zadernack would buck that line of authority. Even if he was willing to think about doing that, all he would do would be to slowly go up the chain of command. Go to the division chief, up to deputy director, maybe even up to the director of the FBI himself, and then over the Department of Justice, and up the ladder again, ad nauseam.

And by then, it would be too late. How many more bodies would be found? How much blood spilled? How much American defense intelligence stolen by a sociopathic terrorist?

Gallagher bent down over the sink, splashed some water on his face, and grabbed a paper towel. As he looked in the mirror and saw in his pale, sagging face the visage of an aging FBI agent nearing the end of his career, he decided to give himself a five-second pep talk.

It's the ninth inning in the World Series, John. Step up to the plate . . .

□□□

Rocky Bridger had been troubled by his conversation with John Gallagher. He was already starting to feel the overwhelming avalanche of guilt that he may have led his son-in-law into some kind of a deadly trap. He also felt that he needed to warn Joshua that something might be happening.

But the two men had barely broached that subject when Joshua's phone beeped. He looked at the LCD screen. It read, "Liberty University Office of Security."

He put Rocky on hold and took the call.

"Mr. Jordan?" a man on the other end asked.

"Yes, that's me."

"I'm with school security. We are trying to locate your son, Calvin. There is some concern about his whereabouts. We wondered if you had heard from him today."

"No. The last time I talked with him was yesterday. Is there a problem?"

"Well, Cal didn't show up to a basketball game with some friends. We're also checking into a report from some students in his dorm building about an unauthorized person who apparently entered his dorm room. Look, Mr. Jordan, don't worry. I'm sure he'll turn up."

After that call, and before reconnecting with Rocky, Joshua had to collect himself. He had to settle himself from the deeply unnerving feeling that something was terribly wrong. He flashed back to the warnings that Pack McHenry had given to him about "foreign actors" coming after him.

He now felt an enveloping dread. Should he have been focusing on keeping his family safe in the last few days rather than fighting all those other battles? Was this situation with Cal part of the threat against him? What did they mean by "an unauthorized person" in his dorm room? And that led to just one more, devastating question that Joshua had to ask himself. About his failed responsibility to his son. It was a question that didn't have a clear or easy answer, but it sliced into his heart like a serrated knife.

What have I done?

FIFTY-SIX

The minute that Abigail landed at JFK, Joshua called her and explained that Cal was missing. Abigail was frantic and peppered him with questions. Joshua answered each of them patiently, sometimes several times. Yes, Joshua had tried Cal's cell phone, but it had been turned off and was going directly to voicemail. No, campus security had not come up with anything else beyond their initial investigation: that an unidentified and unauthorized person, dressed as a maintenance man, was seen by students in Cal's dorm entering his room with a large utility cart shortly before he went missing. Cal was supposed to join friends in a basketball game but never showed.

The school's security had asked Joshua if he wanted the local police in Lynchburg to get involved. He said he did.

When Abigail arrived at the hotel and finally burst through the door, Joshua recognized the same anxious apprehension on her face that he was harboring inside. He said he had nothing new to report in the twenty minutes since they last talked.

But as he heard himself saying that, he exploded. "I am *not* just waiting around for something to happen," Joshua snapped. "I'm going to break this open. I'm getting answers ..."

Abigail ran her hands through her hair, stood up, and put up her hand toward her husband like she was a cop at an intersection stopping traffic. "We can't barge into this until we get more facts," she said.

"We could create more obstacles for the police, end up hindering them rather than helping them."

There was something Joshua was going to say in reply, but he utterly forgot it because of the next sound he heard.

His Allfone. He snatched it up.

The voice on the other end was like a man's but had been digitally altered. It was low and metallic and computerized.

The voice started by saying, "Do not hang up."

"How did you get this number?"

"Off your son Cal's Allfone, of course, Mr. Jordan. This is not a joke. This is real. I have your son."

Joshua waved wildly at Abigail to come over to the phone and listen in.

"Your son is safe ... for now," the voice said, "but if you contact any law enforcement agent — police, FBI, or anyone else from the government — I will know it. And if that happens, then your son will have to be hurt ..."

Abigail had to cover her mouth with both hands to muffle her cries so the caller wouldn't hear.

"To be more specific, if you make that mistake," the voice continued, "then I will take a rusty saw and cut off your son's head. And I will videotape it, as he screams for his mommy and daddy. And then I will place it on VideoNet so that not only you but also millions of others can see it."

The voice ended by saying, "I will call you in several hours. You will be required to follow my instructions carefully if you want to see your son Cal again. Now, Mr. Joshua Jordan, you should be ready to produce for me every design document relating to the RTS antimissile weapon, the laser operating principles, the spec sheets, the engineering drawings — everything. When I call back I will give you the exact specifics on how you will deliver this to me."

"My son!" Joshua yelled into the phone.

"You're not listening," the voice said. "I already told you that your son is safe. For now. When I call back I will show that to you. I will give you proof."

Then the call ended.

Joshua immediately hit the call-lookup function on his Allfone. But when he did, it simply read: "Unauthorized Function."

Abigail was sobbing.

Joshua was in a fury. He screamed into the air. But beneath his rage was a deep current of terror and grief. He wanted a face to hate, a person to crush, not some electronic voice. When he'd been an Air Force Special Ops pilot he'd been trained to drop bombs on incredibly hostile, clandestine targets with deadly accuracy. But where was his target this time? He'd been trained in survival skills and basic hand-to-hand combat if he crashed behind enemy lines. But where were the lines now? Who was the enemy?

Through her tears, Abigail managed to say, "We need to plan this out — "

"I need to kill that monster, whoever he is!" Joshua shouted, pointing to his Allfone.

"We need to save our son!"

Joshua reached out to his wife, and she fell into his arms. They held each other tight in a heart-pounding silence for several minutes.

Then Joshua let her go and said, "We're wasting time."

"What ... what do we do?" Abigail said. "He says he'll know if we contact the authorities. We can't take that chance."

"Listen, I was on the phone with Rocky Bridger when the Liberty campus security people called me about Cal. When we reconnected Rocky explained something to me. At the suggestion of Pack McHenry, the Patriot I told you about, Rocky went ahead and talked with an FBI agent by the name of Gallagher. Rocky says after talking to him he now feels that his son-in-law's murder was somehow connected to me and the RTS design documents."

"What are you saying?"

"I don't know. I don't know. Maybe we need to put our heads together with Rocky. Maybe we can all piece this together."

"And do what? This maniac has our son. He's holding all the cards." Joshua's response had a finality to it that his wife had never seen before. "I'm going to save my son. Whatever it takes."

"Josh, is he really safe right now ...?" Her voice caught, and she choked up with grief.

Joshua held her gently by the shoulders and looked her in the eyes. "I believe he is. I really do. The kidnapper needs to give us proof that he's still alive. Right now he's safe. He has to be."

Abigail wiped her tears and nodded.

"We need to get Rocky down here with us," Joshua said. "Immediately. We have to call him. But not on my cell phone. The kidnapper now has my prototype cell number and may be tracing my calls. I can't afford to trust my high security Allfone anymore."

"We can't use mine either, for the same reason," Abigail said. "I'll go to the hotel business center on the second floor. I can use that phone. They have private work areas. What should I tell Rocky?"

"That we need him at this hotel as quick as he can get down here. And not to tell anyone where he's going. That our son's in danger. And it has to do with the things Rocky was telling me this morning on the phone."

Abigail paused for a second before she left. She was trembling. She said something, whether a prayer or something else, maybe a simple unburdening from the depths of her heart, Joshua wasn't sure. But Abigail seemed to be saying it even from the hollow, emptiness of her grief. And there was also a kind of strange resolution in the way in which she said it.

"Not my will but Thy will be done."

Then she walked quickly out of the hotel suite and closed the door tightly behind her as she left.

When she was gone, Joshua pulled out the Patriot's business card with Pack McHenry's number on it. He stared at it for a long time, tempted to get in touch with him. Until he finally decided against it.

No rash moves. Cal's life is on the line.

FIFTY-SEVEN

Cal Jordan was starting to regain consciousness. He guessed he was in a moving vehicle. A van or a truck. He was lying on a hard surface with a black hood over his head and duct tape over his mouth. His hands and feet had been bound so tightly that it felt as if the circulation was slowly being cut off.

As his head cleared Cal became aware of the dull pain in the left side of his neck. And some oozing from a needle prick there. He didn't know anything about the drug Nembutal, but he was certainly feeling the aftereffects of being injected with it. Even worse was the severe headache pounding inside his skull like a jackhammer.

But after assessing the pain and confusion, fear set in. *What's happening? I was in ... my dorm room. Someone was there with me. Something about the lights ... in the ceiling ... we were looking at the ceiling. How'd I get here? Okay, I'm tied up. In a van or something. There was a guy in my room. He must have done this. I've got to get out. Now.*

Cal struggled, but it was impossible to budge. Not only were his wrists and legs tied together, but his neck, torso and legs were strapped down to the floor of the van. As he tried to free himself, his breathing got labored. It was difficult for him to suck in air because of the tape over his mouth, and he tried to breathe through his nose but as he frantically tried to do that he panicked and hyperventilated and nearly passed out.

There was the sensation of movement, and the sound of road

underneath tires and braking, and momentary stopping. Then it started up again.

For a moment, when he thought the van would stop, Cal felt somewhat hopeful that it all would end soon. But just as quickly, his perspective changed into something dark and dreadful. As if he had just walked past the warped mirrors of a carnival fun house.

What will happen when the car stops? I've been kidnapped, but by who? What do they want? Money. Mom and Dad would pay ransom for me. I'll be okay. Just can't look at the kidnappers — I'm okay as long as I can't identify them.

Then the van started slowing down again. And it stopped.

But this time the driver put it into park and turned off the engine.

Cal's heart was thumping so loudly inside his chest that he wondered if it was creating an echo in the van.

In that split second something became clear to Cal. His assumptions about his own faith were now being spread out onto a table of terror. Everything he thought he knew about God and his relationship with a Savior who guided his steps and indwelled his life. All of that was now being tested in the very center of the fire. He had once survived the mad riot of humanity in the train station that day when the missiles were coming. But even that didn't compare with this. Nothing was like this.

He summoned his simple knowledge that there was an unseen Lord. And that He would surely listen and answer. He formed the words in his mouth and said them silently. *Oh, God, protect me. Please.*

A minute later came the sound of the double doors opening in the rear of the van.

Someone was climbing in. Then the doors slammed shut. Even with the black hood over his head Cal could tell that a bright light was now filling the area in the back of the van where he was strapped to the floor.

The hood was yanked off, and the duct tape was pulled off his mouth ripping the hairs off his upper lip.

A face was staring at him, backlit by the painful glare of a photographer's lamp.

"I will give you a minute to get used to the light," Atta Zimler said.

Cal thought he could recognize the voice. It sounded like the maintenance man in his dorm room. Then he could see the man's face better. Yes, it was him.

Then Cal saw that the man had set up a tripod with a camcorder on it. Zimler was holding the hard copies of two e-newspapers.

"Cal Jordan," Zimler said with a strange nonchalance. "You are going to make a little movie for your father. You are to say your name into the video camera. And today's date. And that you have not been harmed. Then I want you to beg for your life. Because if your father doesn't give me what I want, I will kill you, Cal. And I will videotape it all and put your execution on VideoNet so that millions of people can enjoy it. Do you understand what I have just told you?"

Cal was terrified and couldn't speak, but he nodded his head.

Zimler screamed into his face, "Say it out loud — say that you understand me!"

"I understand you."

"Good," Zimler said with a weird pleasantness to his voice. Then Zimler added, "You know, Cal, this is going to be very interesting." And he smiled at Cal. "Do you know why?"

Cal, still dumbstruck with terror, could only shake his head no.

"I'll tell you why," Zimler explained. "Because when this is over we are going to find out something important about your father, the great Joshua Jordan. I've really wondered about this ... which does he love more? His son or his country?"

□□□

Less than a two-hour drive from Cal's location in the back of Zimler's van, Joshua Jordan's legal fate was being debated. In the federal court building in Washington, D.C. Harry Smythe had managed to arrange a short hearing before Judge Jenkins. Only one assistant U.S. attorney representing Congress bothered to show up.

"I am requesting," Smythe said, "that you drop the bench warrant for arrest issued against my client, Mr. Jordan. The basis of the warrant — that he had ignored a lawful subpoena issued by a committee of the U.S. Senate — is now moot because that subpoena has been withdrawn by Senator Straworth, the chairman. I would also emphasize that the government has no objection to our request."

"All that is very interesting," the judge snapped back, "but that doesn't bind me in my decision. I have the discretion to execute my bench warrant regardless of the validity of the original basis for contempt charges. You're a good lawyer; I'm sure you recognize that — "

"I do," Smythe shot back. "But equity and fairness — "

"Is something for me to decide," Judge Jenkins said, finishing his sentence. "And I've decided that this court needs to satisfy itself that Joshua Jordan has due respect for the rule of law. Particularly in light of his defiance of Congress and his disregard for this court. I'd like to address Mr. Jordan personally, here in my courtroom. Is he here?"

Smythe shook his head and prepared himself for another humiliation.

"He's not, Your Honor."

Harry Smythe had called Joshua earlier to suggest that he attend the court appearance with him but got his voicemail. He left a message but never heard back from Joshua, which was unusual. Smythe was now left without an explanation for the judge and had little to placate her.

Judge Jenkins took a minute to collect herself, but she wasn't able to fully hide her fury. "If your client doesn't have the respect for this court to appear personally to request the bench warrant be withdrawn, then I have no compulsion to withdraw it."

"But, judge, you've put both me and my client on the horns of an intractable dilemma," Smythe complained.

"That's your problem," Judge Jenkins countered. "The bench warrant continues in full force and effect. I've already ordered a small army of federal marshals to hunt down and arrest Mr. Jordan. Good day to you, Mr. Smythe."

FIFTY-EIGHT

As a retired general, Rocky Bridger had several friends who owned helicopters. He was able, on short notice, to get one of them to chopper him down to Manhattan. They located a helipad within a block of the Palace Hotel.

During their two-hour wait for Rocky to arrive, Joshua and Abigail remained frozen in the hotel room, sitting next to Joshua's Allfone.

But no call came in.

Then Abigail turned to Joshua and made a surprising suggestion.

"You wanted Rocky here," she began, "so that he could help us figure out the practical logistics of this horrible situation. And I agreed. But now I also want someone else here to help me figure something out."

"Figure out what?"

"The spiritual logistics," she said. "I need Pastor Paul Campbell here with me."

"Abby, is that really necessary?" Joshua unloaded. He had been mentally consumed by Cal's situation and how he might be rescued. Joshua didn't need outside interference. "We need to keep this to a small circle of people we can trust."

"Which is why I need my pastor here. He's trustworthy."

"Look, this is no place for a pastor. We're wading into war here — "

"Then consider him a battlefield chaplain. This is the scariest thing we've ever faced. Even worse than your spy-plane missions. This is our son's life we're talking about. Our son ... The decisions we make right here could either save him or kill him. Please, Josh, please understand ..."

That's when Rocky Bridger buzzed their hotel suite and said he was on his way up.

Joshua turned to Abigail. His beautiful wife's face was twisted with emotion. She was a smart woman, but more than that she had a habit of being right about things that she was the most passionate about.

"Okay," Joshua said to Abigail. "Call Pastor Campbell. Tell him only that we have an urgent personal matter to discuss with him, and we need him over here. But he can't tell anyone where he's going or why."

She smiled and wiped her tears away with the back of her hand.

Then Joshua made the point again. "I hope that guy keeps his mouth shut."

The doorbell rang, and Rocky Bridger was standing in the door-way. Abigail greeted him with a long hug, thanked him for coming, and then scurried past him on her way down to the hotel business center to call Pastor Campbell.

As Joshua reached his hand out it suddenly struck him that Rocky looked shorter and older as the two men clasped hands firmly and just stood there for a few long moments.

They studied the anguish in each other's eyes. Rocky had just lost a son-in-law, and he had come from a house where he had been trying to comfort his heartbroken daughter and his granddaughter. Joshua's son was now being held hostage — his life hanging by a thread. And it appeared clear that those two tragic attacks were related. They were both tied to Joshua's RTS technology. This was a toll that Joshua had not counted on.

Joshua briefed him again, this time in detail, about the information from the Liberty University security staff and then what the hostage taker had said on the phone.

"And the kidnapper hasn't contacted you further?" Rocky asked.

"No. He just said to wait for his call."

"Let's be straight here, Josh, I'm no expert in hostage situations. You know that ..."

"That's not how I remember it. That situation with that downed pilot in Ecuador who was captured by FARC rebels — you managed to get that guy rescued pretty smoothly ..."

"I had a whole lot of help ..."

"You're still the best man in a crisis I've ever known."

"Well, then are you willing to take some advice from this old general?"

"You know I am."

"You need to spread your net a little wider."

"How?"

"I know you're concerned that someone has been helping this criminal."

"He's got to be plenty connected. I heard from my Patriot friend that foreign interests were after me because of RTS. And we figure that this lunatic tortured your son-in-law to get information about my family. Then he takes my son. The breadcrumbs stretch from my son's college dormitory room all the way across the planet to some unknown international terrorists who are probably orchestrating this."

"I'm not exactly saying we ought to call the FBI and report a kidnapping ..."

"Then what?"

"It's like the 9/11 scenario," Rocky said. "Failure to coordinate intelligence sources can be disastrous. I think we need to bring in that guy you sent me to — Gallagher. He seems to be working this from the other direction. He's trailing a suspect, and he doesn't know where he will hit next. Gallagher just knows that it points in your direction. This could be the link."

"And what if he feels obliged to run this up the command, and it leaks out to the kidnappers' contacts — whoever they are — that's a chance I don't think we can take."

"All I know is that after talking to Agent John Gallagher, I had this feeling."

"About what ?"

"I've spent my whole career taking and giving orders," Rocky said. "A *lot* of order taking way back at the beginning. Then you get your stripes, and later some stars and ribbons, and finally you're giving more orders than you have to take. But it all comes down to chain of command. I recognized that tone when I spoke to Agent Gallagher. The guy's not exactly following orders — not to the letter — but he's still trying not to buck it either. But he's way out there at the outer perimeter. With his toes on the edge of the cliff."

"So, you think we need to bring him in?"

"Yes. I think he knows who murdered Roger. I also think he'll have an idea who your kidnapper is. Likely the same scum did both. Gallagher has the big picture — unlike the local detectives who interviewed me. Gallagher knows a lot; I'd bank my retirement on it."

"Then the question is — will the kidnapper find out?"

"What if he does?"

"No, no, then he kills Cal ..."

"Maybe not."

"I can't even take that risk."

"Cal may be at the same risk whether you contact Gallagher or not."

"But I have to go with what I know. The caller says don't contact the police or the FBI."

"But if Gallagher is out there on the perimeter, like I think he is, maybe he's pursuing this on a discrete channel, in a sequestered way," Rocky said, "in which case the chances are less that our hostage creep will find out. And if this is the same monster who killed Roger ... then I want Agent Gallagher to know what we know. I want Roger avenged as much as I know you want Cal to be saved."

"You really think we can risk bringing Gallagher into this?" Joshua asked again. His eyes were closed as he tried to calculate the incalculable, picturing his son on a sacrificial slab. One wrong move and the blade goes down and the blood starts flying.

"Yes, I do," Rocky said. There wasn't a shred of hesitation.

"And I agree."

Joshua opened his eyes and saw Abigail standing at the entrance of the great room of their hotel suite.

"I think Agent Gallagher has proven himself so far, whoever he is," she said. "We need outside help on this. We can't ensure Cal's safety just ourselves. This kidnapper has already killed Roger. Maybe others we don't know about. And once he gets what he wants from you, Josh, there's no guarantee he'll let Cal go."

"So, we're talking calculated risks ... with our son's life," Joshua said.

"That's all we've got to go on," Rocky said.

Abigail added her own thought.

"That ... and the power of prayer."

Joshua looked into the eyes of his wife. Underneath her pain and fear, she still had a kind of quietude, and it shocked him to his core. He glanced over at Rocky. But a thought had been plaguing Joshua from the beginning, hanging in the shadows, and now it came tumbling into the open.

He dug into his pocket and retrieved the card from the Patriot, Pack McHenry.

But before he could say what was on his mind, he was diverted by a distinctive sound.

He turned around to look right at the spot where his Allfone was lying.

It was ringing.

FIFTY-NINE

Joshua scrambled to the Allfone and picked it up.

On the screen it said: "Video Message. Yes? No?"

Joshua tapped Yes on the screen.

Abigail and Rocky looked on as an image started to load.

It was Cal. They could only see him from the shoulders up. He was sitting against a plain backdrop of some kind. And there was terror in his eyes.

Then he lifted up the print versions of two e-newspapers, one in each hand.

One was the *Washington Post* and the other was the *Boston Herald*. The camera zoomed in on the headers, and both of them bore that day's date.

Then Cal put the newspapers down and glanced to the side as if he were getting instructions.

He bent over toward the side and whispered something to an unseen person.

Then in an instant a hand flashed into the frame and struck Cal in the face, and he gave a yelp and blood started running from his nose.

Abigail shrieked.

Joshua was standing up with his fists balled together, his face contorted in rage. *Why don't you come right here to me, you twisted maggot! Let me get my hands on you.*

Then on the small screen, Cal collected himself, and with a crimson stream running from both nostrils, he looked into the camera. "I'm not hurt," he said in a voice that was close to a monotone, like he was following a script. "I am being held hostage. Please do exactly as this person asks. I am begging for my life. Mom and Dad, just like you were told, if you don't give up the information on the RTS I am going to be killed. My death will be posted on the Internet …"

Just then Cal choked on his words and he had to stop. Then he took a deep breath and finished.

Looking straight at the camera, Cal gave a final message.

But this was not scripted.

"And Dad, I have something to say to you. I want to say I'm sorry I didn't tell you that I loved you in those last phone calls that we had together. I'm sorry for that because I really do — "

But he was stopped by a fist that flashed across the screen and bashed him again in the face, and he fell out of the frame of the picture.

Two seconds later, the image on the Allfone went dark and the call ended.

Abigail was struggling to control her weeping. Rocky let out a long, anguished breath.

But Joshua, still simmering with rage at the person who had struck his son, was feeling more and more like his world was on a fast landslide off the side of a mountain. And he wondered if he had any power to stop it.

The test pilot and spy-plane hero, who had defied fear and faced unparalleled dangers, was feeling overwhelmed by a tide of terror and helplessness.

Then Joshua cleared his throat and began speaking, his voice cracking a little. "We still have yet to get instructions …"

"On how he wants the RTS data delivered …," Rocky finished the thought.

Abigail asked the obvious question that was hanging in the air, filling the room. "Is he going to kill Cal? Is he? Tell me ..."

Neither of the men spoke up.

"I know that's not a fair question," she said. "But I don't *care* about what's fair. I need to know ..."

Joshua stepped over to her and put his arms around her and held her.

"That rough stuff with that guy hitting Cal like that on camera," Rocky said. "That was for your benefit, Josh. He knows you're military. He thinks you need to see that he means business. Just a show of force, that's all. I think Cal is still okay."

"Rocky," Joshua said. "Do you have your cell with you?"

He did.

"Good," Joshua continued. "You call Gallagher on your phone. Then you can hand the phone to me after you've given him the intro."

□□□

Special Agent John Gallagher was in his cubicle when the call came in.

"This is General Rocky Bridger."

Gallagher hustled toward the men's room, trying not to make eye contact with Miles Zadernack's secretary. But when he blew into the bathroom he saw two pairs of feet in each of the two stalls. He went back outside and down the hall.

"Can't talk much at my end," Gallagher said in a hushed voice and trying to smile casually and nod at the agents who strolled past him in the corridor. "You play the part of the guy who does all the talking. I'm not going to have much of a speaking part."

Rocky Bridger gave him a quick briefing. Joshua's son had been taken hostage; the guy in charge wanted the RTS documents in exchange. He relayed the video with Cal holding two of that day's newspapers as proof he was alive. Then Rocky handed the phone to Joshua.

"Have you talked to the police or FBI?" Gallagher asked.

"No. This guy is giving us strict orders not to, or he kills my son. We think he's got inside information."

John Gallagher replied, "That's routine." Then he added, "Listen, the Bureau's official position on hostages is this: when the kidnapper says, 'Don't call the cops or else,' he's usually bluffing. Or if he isn't, we still feel we can keep him from knowing until it's too late for him ..."

But the FBI agent knew he was only giving the textbook answer. In most hostage situations the bad guy has nothing to lose by making that kind of demand. But this case was far from textbook. Gallagher had the sick feeling that there was something very rotten somewhere very high in the United States government. Exhibit A was that mind-blowing directive to Gallagher, the Bureau's number-one expert on Atta Zimler, to stand down from investigating Zimler's entrance into the United States. Did the guys who hired Zimler, whoever they were, have that kind of influence?

"Maybe, but we can't take chances. Rocky thinks you know this guy. Is that right?"

"I'm not sure I can share that with you ..."

"We need help. We've got that video that proves my son's still alive. Can you help us?"

"Not sure," Gallagher confessed.

"Please ..."

"Any delivery instructions?"

"No, not yet. We're expecting some soon."

There was a silent pause.

"Call me when you get those instructions."

Joshua was feeling desperate.

"Agent Gallagher, is that it? All you can say? All you're going to do?"

"Well, let's put it this way," Gallagher replied. "Yeah, that's all I am going to *say* ..."

Then Gallagher clicked off his cell and walked back to his cubicle.

He rubbed his forehead for a moment. His chest was burning and he wished he had a shot of milk to calm things down. Maybe there was something in the lunchroom. He strode down there and swung open the door to the refrigerator. He was in luck. An almost-empty milk carton sitting way in the back. He put it up to his lips. *I think I'll avoid checking the expiration date on this.*

But as he took the last gulp, his mind was whirling.

The puzzle pieces showed Gallagher that Zimler was working this RTS mission from a foreign base of operations, starting in Bucharest. He had to assume that Zimler had been hired by some heavy-duty international guys. And they could have some powerful American connections.

Gallagher felt there was only one chance for him to help the Jordans. And go after Zimler. But it all had to do with Zimler's next move, and Gallagher had a pretty good guess what it was going to be.

Gallagher still had the empty milk carton in his hand as he looked over at the trash can five feet away. But his attention was broken by a voice.

"I know what you are thinking ..."

The comment came from Miles Zadernack. He was in the lunchroom picking up a cup of coffee. Gallagher gave him a feeble smile.

Then Miles switched gears. "So, I hear that you've signed up for the professionalism class."

"Yes, Miles, I did."

"That's good."

Miles stood there with his cup of coffee, looking as if he still had something on his mind. Gallagher had his cell phone in one hand and the milk carton in the other, wondering if his supervisor was a mind reader.

Then Miles added, "Now, John, can I give you a serious warning? I know what you're planning. I can tell what's on your mind right now ..."

Gallagher said, "Oh?" But inside he was really worried that the jig was up. Miles had found out that he was still pursuing Zimler. He braced himself for it.

Miles broke into a slow, forced smile. The two men stood there looking at each other.

Then Miles laid it out. "Yeah, every time you try those long shots with your little milk cartons or your leftover chili dog trays or whatever, you miss the trash can. And in the process you spill food on the floor. It's not fair to make other people clean up after you. We all have an obligation to keep this room picked up. *Professionalism.* Remember?"

Gallagher nodded, and Miles Zadernack took his cup of coffee and left the lunch room.

Now alone, Gallagher turned and from five feet away threw the empty milk carton in a looping hook shot. *Swoosh!*

"Three pointer," Gallagher said to himself.

SIXTY

Thirty minutes later, in the Jordan's hotel suite at the Palace, Joshua's Allfone was ringing again. He picked it up and put it on speaker. He heard the distorted, digital voice of the kidnapper again.

"Your son is a little weakling," the voice said. "He doesn't handle pain very well. I hope for his sake that you decide to cooperate with me."

"I hope for your sake," Joshua bulleted back, "I don't get you alone in a room."

"You are such a big American hero. How about I kill your son right now, Mr. Hero? Would that be good? Would you like to hear him scream some more?"

Abigail frantically waved her hands at Joshua and mouthed the words *no, no, no*.

Zimler continued. "Now, let's talk business. You will produce your design documents on the RTS system. And make sure they explain two things. First, the mirror-image method that the laser uses to capture the flight-trajectory pattern on the inboard guidance computer of the incoming missile. And second, I want to see the system for remotely reprogramming that trajectory one hundred and eighty degrees."

"How am I supposed to get this to you?" Joshua asked.

"You will email all of them to me at an encrypted address I will give you. When my experts analyze them and tell me that they are complete, I will release your son."

Joshua didn't hesitate a second. He blasted back.

"I can't do that."

"I have your son. Remember that. You have no choice."

"No," Joshua snapped, "you've got it wrong. The files are too big for email. If you want the RTS documents, we arrange a meeting place. An exchange. That's how it's going to be done."

Abigail was dumbfounded, and her eyes widened in astonishment. But Rocky Bridger was nodding.

Then there was silence. And the silence on the other end lasted so long that everyone feared that the caller had dropped off the line.

A sense of panic started to rise up in Joshua. What if he had just torpedoed the negotiations? What if the kidnapper had decided to call it all off? Then Cal's life would have no value to the hostage taker. Which meant that Joshua had just moved Cal one step closer to an execution.

Suddenly the silence was broken with the sound of Cal screaming in the background.

That is when the digital voice came back on.

"Your son is crying because I have just broken one of his fingers with a pair of pliers. I thought about cutting it off, but I didn't want to bother changing into my butcher shop outfit."

Joshua steeled himself. *Hold it together man. We've got to outsmart this guy.*

Abigail was covering her face as she sobbed silently.

"If you try to play the tough guy again and make demands of me, then I will start cutting off body parts. Now you listen to me … this is what we will do. You will save the documents on a flash drive and put that in a metal fireproof briefcase and come to Grand Central Station in exactly two hours and thirty minutes. When you are there, I will call you and give you more instructions."

"What about my son?"

"You'll get proof that he is still alive. But you'll also see exactly how he's going to die if you don't obey me ..."

Then Zimler added. "But before anything else, you are going to prove that you can deliver what I want. So get a pen and get ready to write."

"I'm waiting."

Then Zimler gave him an email address. "You are going to email a couple of the RTS documents to that address. If you don't convince me you've got what I want, then I'll let you know where you can find your son's body, and I disappear."

Then he hung up.

Rocky turned to Abigail and said, "Josh played it exactly right. I know you were concerned ..."

"What just went on?" she asked sharply.

"Abby, I had to," Joshua shot back. "We can't risk it with some remote, electronic delivery ..."

"You start giving up everything by email," Rocky said, "and Cal doesn't have a chance. The only hope is keeping this creep cornered. Keep him in close quarters. Within eyesight. Force him to make an exchange. The closer we stay to this guy the closer we are to Cal."

Joshua dialed Agent Gallagher again on Rocky's cell, and when he picked up he bulleted out, "The kidnapper just called. He wanted everything by email. I said no ... demanded a face-to-face exchange. The RTS stuff for my son."

"Good move on your part. Smart ..."

"So he said that the drop-off is to happen at Grand Central Station. I'm supposed to be there in two-and-a-half hours with the RTS documents. Then I get further instructions. But it seemed like he already had that drop-off idea in his head ..."

"Two steps ahead. That's exactly the way this guy works ..."

"You know him?"

Gallagher didn't bite at that, but asked, "Anything else?"

"Yeah. He wants me to email a couple of RTS documents just to prove I can deliver what he wants."

Joshua gave him the encrypted email address, and Gallagher wrote it down.

"So are you going to send the email?" the agent asked.

"Do I have a choice?"

Gallagher didn't bother to say the obvious. That any RTS documents that Joshua might send would probably be classified.

"Okay. I'm going to do what I can," Gallagher said.

"I need to hear more than that," Joshua snapped back.

"I would too if I were in your shoes," he replied. "You're going to have to trust me. Just know that I'll be looking over your shoulder. Don't ask me to explain."

After hanging up, Joshua had the sinking feeling that maybe Cal was just beyond his reach, outside his ability to rescue. But he had one more call to make, and he didn't hesitate for a second.

When he dialed the number, the man on the other end simply answered, "Patriot."

"Pack McHenry?"

"Who's calling?"

"Joshua Jordan."

"Sounded like you."

"I need help. We've got an emergency ..."

"Interesting. Because we were just going to call you," McHenry said.

"Why?"

"We've just received some solid intel that federal marshals are on their way over to your hotel. They're probably already there in fact."

"Marshals?"

"Yeah, to take you into custody. They've got an arrest warrant from a federal judge."

"This can't be happening."

"Yes, it is. Count on it."

Joshua said. "I've got a situation with my son. Life and death. He's been taken hostage … I've got to get out of this hotel …"

"No way. You'll run right into them. I'm sure they're crawling all over the grounds of the hotel."

"I can't afford to get arrested. My son needs me — "

"You said … *taken hostage*?"

"I'll explain everything."

"First give me your room number at the hotel."

Joshua gave it to him and McHenry told him to call him back in exactly two minutes.

Then he asked, "By the way, what floor are you on?"

"We're on the twenty-fifth floor …"

"I think that'll work …"

"What?"

"Just stay in your room. Don't answer the door for anyone … unless it's a delivery guy with a box who says the words, 'Airmail delivery for Mr. Jordan.' If it is, answer it, take the box, and open it. And about your son …"

"Yes, what?"

"We'll see what we can do to help."

□□□

While Joshua was finishing up his conversation with McHenry, downstairs in the lavish lobby of the Palace, two armed federal marshals, wearing conspicuous blue jackets with the words *U.S. Marshal* printed on the back, were at the front desk. Three other marshals were spreading out around the premises.

"I'm sorry," the man at the front desk said. "No one has checked in under the name of Joshua Jordan."

"I'm sure the room is under a different name," the marshal said. "I want to see all of the recent check-ins."

Then he spotted the head bellman. The marshal called him over and pulled out a photograph of Joshua.

"Have you seen this man here at the hotel in the last few days?"

The bellman studied the picture for a moment; then he nodded his head and said, "Saw him when he came in. Maybe up on one of the floors ..."

"Can you tell me on what floor of the hotel you may have seen him?"

"I think so ..."

Just then a man in a brown delivery uniform, carrying a box, entered the hotel lobby and strode up to the elevators.

Then he waited for the doors to open. When they did, the delivery man walked into the elevator and punched the button for Joshua's floor. The marshal who was still with the bellman glanced over just in time to see the elevator doors close.

SIXTY-ONE

Abigail kept looking at her watch, wondering when Pastor Campbell would show up. Rocky Bridger grabbed the tourist book off a coffee table and flipped to the page that had some pictures of Grand Central Station. He was already trying to figure out why the kidnapper had picked that spot.

Joshua called Pack McHenry back and then rushed to tell him everything that had transpired. He also told him that he'd called FBI Agent Gallagher but hadn't received any commitments about what he would do to help.

"Don't worry about that," McHenry said. "Gallagher's a good man in a tough spot."

"You know him?"

"Not directly. Gotta go. I've got a lot of homework to do for you."

Just as Joshua was ending the call, the doorbell rang.

"Maybe that's my pastor," Abigail said and started for the door. But Joshua stopped her and signaled that he would answer it.

"Federal marshals are on their way over here," Joshua whispered. "We need to check this out carefully ..."

He looked through the peep-hole and saw a delivery man in a brown uniform holding a box the size of a small microwave.

Joshua swung open the door.

"Airmail delivery for Mr. Jordan," the delivery guy said and handed him the box. Then he quickly added, "You've got to hurry, Mr. Jordan." Then he turned and sprinted down the hallway.

After locking the door, and with Abigail and Rocky looking on, Joshua ripped open the box.

"What in the world ...?" Abigail started to say as she looked inside. Joshua pulled out of the box what looked like a huge spool of cable encased within a black plastic cover with two handles on each side. At the bottom of the box there was a nylon vest for a grown man with heavy metal hooks attached.

A note in the box read:

Attach the end of the cable to something secure. One handle of the reel is to hold onto — the other is an emergency brake. Put on the vest, attach it to the cable, then lower yourself out the window and hit the release button. Enjoy the ride. The Patriot.

"So this is how he thinks I'm getting out of here?" Joshua said.

"When was the last time you did a rappelling exercise down a sheer cliff?" Rocky asked.

Joshua said, "Not since survival camp in the Air Force Academy."

The doorbell rang again. This time, after two seconds, they heard someone pounding on the door. "Open up. Federal marshals!"

"I think you're about to get a refresher course," Rocky blurted out.

In the background they heard more pounding and warnings of "Open up! Federal marshals! We have a warrant! Open the door ..."

"You've got to be there for Cal," Abigail shouted. "Rescue him. Contact us."

Rocky stuffed his own Allfone into Joshua's pants pocket.

Joshua pulled the end of the cable out of the reel and looped it around a doorknob. Then he ran over to a window in the far bedroom. But the window swung outward only a few inches. It was locked from opening all the way by a safety bracket. Joshua grabbed the window and rammed it furiously back and forth.

"Stand back from the door!" one of the marshals yelled from his position in the hallway.

"Better hustle," Rocky shouted. "They're going to break down the door — "

With one final push Joshua busted the bracket and the narrow French window swung all of the way open. Joshua strapped himself into the vest, clipped it to the bottom of the reel, and then lowered himself out the window slowly, his feet steadying him on the window sill.

He looked down and saw miniature traffic and tiny pedestrians twenty-five stories below.

"Oh man. This looked like a good idea when it was in the box," Joshua muttered.

Then he hit the release button and the big reel of cable started slowly letting out cable in a steady roll. Suspended by the unrolling cable and holding on to the handles, Joshua rappelled himself downward with his feet on the side of the hotel building about five feet at a time. From his position high in the air he could see Grand Central Station off in the distance, six blocks away.

Hold on Cal, he said in the air. *I'm coming.*

Floor by floor, he was descending along the side of the Palace Hotel that faced Park Avenue.

When he was about twenty feet from the ground, he could tell a crowd had gathered below him on the sidewalk. Someone was yelling at him.

When his feet were on the pavement, a few of the pedestrians started applauding.

A twenty-something guy in the crowd, with a backward baseball cap and carrying a duffel bag, kept shouting and pointing at Joshua. "I'm telling you, this is Magic Marvin! I seen the ad in the subway. The guy doing the escape stuff and all those magic tricks over at the Garden tonight. Way to go, dude!"

Joshua hit the "retract" button and the reel flew out of his hands, trailing the sling along with it, zipping upward twenty-five stories until it stopped outside the window of his hotel suite.

"Now I've seen everything ..."

Trying to locate the voice, Joshua swung around. It was Pastor Paul Campbell.

"I can't wait to hear about this one!" Campbell said.

"You have a car?"

"Just parked it down the street. On the way to your hotel —"

"Let's get out of here," Joshua shouted. "You've got to drive me somewhere."

"I hope you can fill me in," Campbell said as the two men started jogging toward the parking structure across the street. "Abigail said you folks are in a crisis."

"That's putting it mildly. Amazing coincidence that you came by when you did," Joshua said as they ran down the parking ramp entrance.

"I don't believe in coincidences," Campbell shouted back, jogging next to him. Then he added, "But I do believe in the providence of God."

"Okay," Joshua said back. "I'll take that."

SIXTY-TWO

As their car roared up the parking ramp, Joshua continued to give Pastor Paul Campbell a crash course on the hostage crisis with Cal. They pulled the car up to the ticket booth and quickly paid the parking fee. Then Campbell wheeled the car out onto Park Avenue.

"Over to my office. I'll give you directions!" Joshua shouted.

"Not to Grand Central Station?" Campbell bulleted back. "I thought that's where you said your meeting takes place! It's only a few blocks from here."

"No. We need to get over there in ..." Joshua glanced at his watch ... "exactly one hour and fifty-eight minutes ..."

Campbell pulled his wrist watch off and handed it to Joshua.

"Why don't you synchronize my watch with yours? That's what you do in these kind of situations, right?"

"Yeah," Joshua said and tried to force a smile, but it was tough to make that happen. Somewhere in the back of his head he was thinking of how far out he was in this crisis, way out there where the air was thin. Without a parachute. With almost no backup. But now it wasn't his own life at stake, like it had been all of those years doing test piloting and spy-plane missions. Now it was Cal. He had to shut out the faint voice, the echo that threatened to knock him off kilter and jar his concentration. He had always been a deliberate, cold-as-steel decision maker. He had been all his life. But now the voice kept whispering doubt.

Are you sure you know what you're doing? This is your son's life ...

Joshua set Campbell's watch and handed it back to him. Then he said, "With crosstown traffic we should be there in about twenty, thirty minutes. Okay, turn right at the first chance you get, and get off Park Avenue."

Then Joshua called his office and the receptionist answered.

"This is Joshua. Who's in the office now?" Joshua barked.

"Uh, just … well, let's see … do you want to know who from R&D or …"

"No. Just tell if we have any visitors …"

"Those federal marshals came by. About two hours ago. I told them you were out, and I didn't tell them anything else, I swear. Really. I told them that I absolutely didn't know. That no one else knew. Couldn't help them — "

Joshua broke in and said, "Okay. Do you have this number I'm calling from in front of you on the reception phone caller ID?"

"Yep, sure do."

"Call me back the instant anyone arrives at my office."

"Will do."

"I'll be blowing into the office shortly. I can't be bothered or interrupted. Understood?"

"Yes, sir."

Then he clicked off Rocky's Allfone.

"I know you're a praying man," Joshua said to Campbell.

"I am."

"I need you to pray that Cal gets rescued."

"I already have."

"And please make it good."

Then there was a pause as Joshua ran his hand through his hair as he looked out the window. Joshua added, "I've got a decision to make. In just a short time …"

"You mean the part about sending the email …"

"No. I already know what I'm doing about that. I've got the documents picked in my head. Enough to let this guy know I've got what he wants. But nothing that will give the bad guys the technology they need to replicate the RTS."

"Then what?"

"It's the other stuff I'm worried about. The full set of protocols. The schematics. The exact specifications for the laser functions. The data-capturing module. The software for remote reading of incoming missile-guidance systems."

"So that's what would enable them to duplicate what you've done—"

"No question. If I give them those documents, our enemies could set up a missile-defense system against the U.S. very quickly. They could not only create their own defense that could return our missiles back to us, but they could figure out how to bypass our RTS system if it ever gets implemented. And deliver nukes to our shores that would be unstoppable."

"You're the weapons expert, I'm not. But doesn't America have the technology edge on all of this anyway?"

"Look, everybody thinks that," Joshua said with a sharp edge to his voice. "The dirty little secret is that research and development have been pretty much halted with President Corland's edict against any 'exotic new missile-defense systems.' The Department of Defense has had its hands tied. That's why my RTS laser has become so controversial in the political circles. It makes Corland's Administration look bad. It falls in his forbidden 'exotic' category, yet it saved New York City. So it became a kind of embarrassment. Can you believe that? This whole thing is so stinking, rotten political ..."

"So, what's your plan? With Cal, I mean, and the RTS documents?"

Joshua looked over at the pastor. He wished he had his Roundtable assembled at that moment. The whole gamut of experts and patriots sitting around the table with him. Advisors. Friends. Instead, he was stuck in the car with this Christian minister who was way out of his league. But it would eat up precious time to try to loop in the others. And then there could still be a chance of that somehow being leaked to the kidnapper. Since they'd already had a breach of security on the Roundtable, with the lawyer Allen Fulsin, could there be others?

Joshua knew he had to overcome his pride and his "my way or the highway" approach. At least the pastor was a good guy, intelligent, and cared enough to stick his neck out and get involved.

Then a thought crossed his mind. Funny it hadn't hit him immediately. *This guy knows I'm technically a fugitive from justice right now. Yet here he is driving me around in his car. Helping me out. Geez, that could be potentially damaging to his position as a high-profile clergyman. Gotta give the guy credit for that ...*

"Pastor, I'm on the horns of a terrible dilemma."

Campbell nodded and waited for more as they pulled up to a stoplight.

Joshua continued. "I give this guy the RTS documents, then my nation is put at peril. I swore on my life I would never let something like that happen. Never. Everything in me fights against that thought. But if I don't ... well you know what I am facing. I'd never do anything to hurt Cal. I can't ... but I just ... I don't, uh ..."

Then Joshua's voice trailed off as his throat choked up and his eyes filled up with tears. He turned away and looked absently out the car window as he tried to pull himself together.

"I try to imagine what you're going through," Campbell said. "But let's face it. I can't even pretend. Can't even come close."

He pulled the car forward after the light changed and kept driving. Campbell was looking ahead, studying the street signs while addressing Joshua at the same time. "How well do you know your Bible?" he asked.

Joshua shrugged. "Some, not as much as I should. Not nearly as much as Abby — "

"The story of Abraham and Isaac. Remember it?"

"Uh, I don't know," Joshua said unenthusiastically.

"God tells Abraham to sacrifice his son Isaac. As an offering. As a show of faith …"

"Yeah. Right." Then an instant later Joshua shot back with, "So what's the point? That I should help sacrifice my own son? Is that it? You're kidding, right?"

"No," Campbell said calmly. "I mean the other part of the story."

"What other part?"

"How it ended."

Joshua was silent. His eyes were glancing vacantly out the window, but he was riveted on the pastor's words. Then he asked, "Meaning what?"

"God stops Abraham's hand. Instead, God says that Abraham has passed the test. Then God shows Abraham something that has been tangled up in the bushes …"

"What?"

"It was a ram. God provides the ram. Caught in the thicket of the bushes a couple of feet away from Abraham. God saves the boy and provides His own ram for the sacrifice."

Joshua finally turned away from the window and looked over at Campbell. "What are you getting at?"

"God is an expert in rescue."

Then a moment went by while Joshua thought about that.

Campbell added, "Maybe we need to pray for God to provide a ram for us."

Now their car was only a few blocks away from Joshua's office.

Joshua asked, "So, why didn't God make Abraham go through with it? Killing his own son as a test of faith? Could have forced him to do it …"

Campbell clicked on his turn signal and pulled into the turn lane for the avenue that led directly to Joshua's office.

"Good question," Campbell finally said. "But God would only

allow *one* Son to die as a sacrifice for the sins of others. And that would happen a couple of thousand years later. When God's own Son would come to earth as an itinerant preacher and die on a Roman cross in Jerusalem. Dying for me. And for you." Then as Joshua's office building came into view two blocks away, Campbell added, "And dying for your son, Cal, too."

Joshua fell quiet.

The car pulled into the private parking area reserved for "president." The two men scrambled out of the car and started sprinting across the parking lot. But then Joshua started slowing down, almost to a stop. His eyes were fixed on something somewhere, but it wasn't clear to Campbell what that was or what was going on.

Campbell slowed down to match Joshua's pace.

Now Joshua was standing still.

Campbell had to ask the obvious. "What is it?"

Joshua looked up and then saw Campbell's face as if he had just noticed him.

"Well," Joshua started to say. There was almost a flicker of a bitter smile in the corners of his mouth. But there was something else in Joshua's look. A dreadful, serious recognition of something down deep. The kind of thing only birthed when a person is in the very hottest place inside the furnace of affliction. "I've just figured something out."

"What?"

"Where we can find the ram."

SIXTY-THREE

Joshua and Pastor Campbell sprinted into Joshua's office, past the receptionist who blinked at them wide eyed.

In his office, Joshua accessed his private computer. He typed in the code:

ReturnToSenderHighSecurityUltimateProtocolsJoshuaMissileRDX143TSC
.DoD.DefenseAdvancedResearchProjectsAgency.U.S.A.

In a few seconds the computer screen filled up with a long index listing the RTS weapons design documents.

Joshua keyed in two introductory RTS documents that included only executive summaries and then sent them to a segregated file for email delivery.

He pulled out a piece of paper with the encrypted email address that Atta Zimler had given him in the last phone call. Then he typed in the email address. Finally Joshua attached the documents to the email.

Then, with his fingers poised over the keyboard, taking a short breath, he looked over at Campbell. The pastor was staring at the ground. His lips were barely moving.

Keep praying pastor, Joshua said to himself.

Joshua clicked on the Send key.

A second later the screen read Sent.

"Done," Joshua said. Then with a wry look on his face he muttered, "I've just committed my first act of treason."

"No harm, no foul," Campbell shot back. "You said that those documents won't reveal anything essential."

"Right," Joshua said. "I don't think they will." Then he added with a desperate honesty, "I hope."

Then Joshua said to Campbell, "Step outside my office, please."

The pastor gave him a curious look but quickly nodded.

With a somber expression, Joshua said, "I don't want any witnesses to this."

Campbell left the room and closed the door behind him.

Joshua snapped open a metal security briefcase so he could start filling it. He knew exactly what the kidnapper wanted. He had all those documents. He had them in the document index on his screen at that very moment. It would take about ten minutes for him to print every one of them all out on the ultra-high-speed printer next to his desk. And then to put them in the briefcase and snap it shut. On the other hand, just a minute or two to download it to a zip drive.

"God, please help me," he said quietly. Then he added, "I hope I know what I'm doing."

Nine minutes later he came out of his office. Pastor Campbell was waiting for him.

"Let's go," Joshua said.

As they hurried down to the car, Joshua heard a beep on the All-fone. A text message from Abby. She was sending it from the business center in the hotel.

Handled the fed. marshals. Not happy. Did sweet talking & quick thinking.

"Good woman," Joshua said out loud.

The end of the text said,

Can't stay away. Need to be there. Rocky & I will be outside the G C Station to be onsite. Will make sure not followed. Am praying. Love you. Oh God help us.

Joshua told the pastor that they needed to hustle back to the Grand Central Station. They needed to be there early. He couldn't risk being a minute late. Then they would wait for the next contact from the kidnapper.

Traffic was bad going back. Joshua glanced at his watch every thirty seconds or so.

"We are only going to have a fifteen-minute window or so," Joshua said.

"I'll drop you off at the main entrance, where the cabs drop off passengers," Campbell said. "Then I'll try to park close by. Here's my cell phone number if you need me. I'll stay put in my car until I get further instructions from you."

Campbell gave Joshua his card with his cell number written on it.

Everything was bumper-to-bumper. They seemed to be hitting all of the lights just wrong. One red light after another.

As they crawled along in the traffic, Joshua gripped the metal briefcase to his chest.

Is this going to work? Joshua kept wondering. Then he would push it out of his mind. It had to work. There were now no other options.

Finally Campbell pulled his car up to the main 42nd Street entrance of the terminal building, with its three huge arched windows and tall pillared colonnade.

Joshua was going to exit the car, but Campbell reached over and stopped him by grabbing his arm.

Campbell's eyes were closed. A car behind them beeped its horn. But Pastor Paul Campbell ignored it. He would deliver his benediction, his prayer, and nothing would stop him.

"Dear Lord, in Your Word, the Bible, this is what it says: 'The Lord spake to Joshua … saying … Have I not commanded thee? Be strong and of good courage; be not afraid, neither be thou dismayed: for the Lord thy God is with thee whithersoever thou goest.' Amen."

Joshua opened his eyes and nodded over to Campbell and then reached out and shook his hand.

"Thanks pastor. Keep praying. That I can save Cal. Somehow. Please. That's all I want. Just to save my son."

□□□

Outside the Grand Central Terminal, a white unmarked New York Police van with tinted glass was parked on Park Avenue, facing away from the columns of the imposing front colonnade of the train station. To help it blend into the street scene, a parking ticket had been stuck on the windshield underneath the wiper. Inside, two men were waiting, tense and focused, watching the front of the train station in the side-view mirrors. One of them was FBI Agent John Gallagher. The other was NYPD Detective Lou Cramer, veteran of the city's counterterrorism unit. The two men had known each other for years.

Cramer adjusted his earpiece, waiting for some word from his police spotter who had located himself on one of the upper floors of the Lincoln Building with a good view of the train terminal. But no word yet.

"Good to be hunkering down together again," Cramer said.

Gallagher simply answered with "yeah" and a visible nod. But they both knew what the other was thinking. The tensions between the FBI and the NYPD had been legend. But blown out of proportion. Then it came to a head all over again years before, way back in 2009, with the terrorism arrest of Najibullah Zazi. The charges said he planned on blowing up the New York subways. The press had another field day with that one, about the supposed feud between the departments. The truth was that Gallagher from the feds and Cramer for the NYPD had quietly worked that case together, in the background, out of the limelight. They had to laugh at the headlines. That was the last time they were partners on a joint terror case.

Until now.

Then Detective Cramer got a message in his earpiece. He nodded and listened. Then he signed off and turned to Gallagher. "Joshua Jordan just stepped out of a car in front of the terminal. He's carrying a briefcase."

Joshua was on the walkway outside the train station. He glanced at his watch.

He cast a long look around the surrounding area and noticed Abigail and Rocky standing next to a newspaper vendor's booth on the sidewalk about a hundred feet away.

Joshua gave a quick, restrained wave with two fingers from his waist.

Abigail clasped her hands over her heart and made a movement toward him.

He could read her face, her body posture even from that distance. Fear, longing, hope. All of it wrapped up in that single moment. That one furtive glance between husband and wife. Standing apart, but bound together by the same unthinkable crisis.

But Joshua immediately shook his head no as Abigail instinctively took a half step toward him. At the same time Rocky simultaneously reached out and gently took hold of her arm.

Joshua gave a short nod to them both and started toward the main entrance doors.

Inside the police van, Detective Cramer turned to a male and a female cop who were in the back of the van. Both were dressed as tourists. "Okay, you're on," he said.

The two cops in street clothes scampered out and started strolling casually but quickly toward Joshua's position near the entrance doors. The man was pretending to read a New York City tour guide map as he and his female partner approached a passerby, but they were shrugged off. Then they walked up to Joshua.

"Say," the man called out to Joshua, pointing to the map, "can you tell me where the Empire State Building is from here?"

Joshua was about to shoo them off, but then the man slipped a small plastic electronic earpiece into Joshua's hand. He could tell it was a sophisticated omni-directional earpiece that could send two-way communications.

"Put this in your right ear, Mr. Jordan," he whispered. "We're police; we're here to help."

Then the man and woman smiled, laughed, and thanked Joshua loudly for the directions and walked away.

Joshua discreetly inserted the small earpiece deeply in his ear.

He waited. Nothing.

Then a voice.

"Mr. Jordan, this is Lou Cramer, detective with the NYPD. We're going to be assisting you today. Let's work together to rescue your son."

"How'd you know ..."

"Don't worry about that now, sir."

"What do I do?"

"Go through with the meeting. We'll be watching you."

"What if he picks up this conversation?"

"No chance. This is a special frequency. If he tries to scan us electronically all he'll get is white noise."

"You should know that I'm still waiting for his next contact with me."

"Fine. Good. You need to speak out loud, audibly if you get any leads or tips on where your son might be. We'll pick it up from here."

"This guy is smart. I don't think he's going to be telling me where Cal is."

"No, that's true. At least not directly."

"Then what?"

Inside the van, Gallagher scratched a note for the detective to read. After looking at it Detective Cramer nodded and then said to Joshua, "We've got some other resources available. Ways of trying to help you. And Cal. Just relax, and go with the flow. We're going to be with you every step of the way, sir."

Then the detective turned the microphone off at his end.

Gallagher asked, "You've got sharpshooters?"

"Right. All of our crisis team guys. And the bomb squad just in case, standing by. Don't worry, John, we've got this covered."

"You don't know his guy. Atta Zimler's the best. He can smell a trap. Almost impossible to catch. I ought to know. I've been tracking him for years."

"Even the best bad guys have a bad day. Let's hope this'll be his."

"So Lou," Gallagher added, "as far as my involvement in this deal is concerned ..."

"Yeah, I know the drill. We called you. You didn't call us. Got it. You're here only at our request. And only as a consultant."

"Exactly," Gallagher said. "As you can see, I'm not carrying ...," indicating he hadn't brought his favorite 357 Smith & Wesson with him.

"I understand. Now relax, John."

But Gallagher couldn't. His chest and esophagus had the feeling of being crushed in a burning hot industrial press.

Gallagher pulled a small bottle of milk out of his suit-coat pocket, screwed off the cap, and took a gulp.

"Ulcer?" the detective said.

"What are you, my doctor now, Lou?"

Then Gallagher glanced down at his watch. He muttered, "Come on, you freak, we're waiting for you. Everything's ready. Come on in. Into the trap. Do it ... do it ..."

SIXTY-FOUR

A tidal flood of human traffic was flowing in and out of Grand Central Station, oblivious to the catastrophe that was waiting within.

Inside the main concourse, on a bench in a corner, a man who appeared to be an Amtrak officer, with a well-trimmed beard and tinted glasses, was working on a small laptop. Atta Zimler took pride in his disguises. This would be one he'd have to use for this particular assignment.

The screen on his laptop had side-view protection. Only he could read it. On the screen was a diagram of the interior of the terminal. Along the sidebar were several boxes. One said "E-Com Scan." He touched his index finger to the box and hit a keystroke. The screen revealed two blinking dots. One of them was less than seventy-five feet from his position. He touched his finger to the screen where the dot was blinking.

Then he inserted the earpiece in his ear. And started listening. A man was talking about an electrical wiring problem.

Zimler glanced over toward the position on the diagram where his computer screen had located the source of the electronic communication. Through the crowd of travelers he spotted a man dressed in a green maintenance uniform, crouching by an electric outlet with a toolbox next to him.

Then Zimler touched the other blinking dot; this indicated a location in another part of the building, much farther away. His wireless transmission scanner was picking up a police radio. He listened in. An officer was making a routine call-in of his position as he strolled through the concourse.

As an extra precaution Zimler clicked on the second box on his screen that read "PublicVideoFeed." In the lower corner of the screen a small box appeared. It was blank. He tapped the second blinking dot with his finger, and the box lit up with a grainy black-and-white picture that was capturing the feed from a terminal surveillance camera in that part of the terminal.

Zimler watched as the officer, on routine patrol, bent his head slightly to the side toward the little walkie-talkie on his collar, signing-off. Zimler had his eyes glued on the image in the corner of his computer screen as he saw the officer then stroll slowly out of the building to finish his shift for the day. Then he minimized the image and went back to the main screen with the diagram of the terminal.

Putting his finger to the part of the diagram that showed a small storage room, he selected it by tapping it with his finger. The image box on this screen was empty. Then he went to a third box on the side of his screen. This one read "PrivateVideoFeed." He clicked it on. Then he tapped the storage-room location again.

Now the image lit up in the little video box in the lower corner. Zimler hit the Zoom function so he could get a closer look. Then he tapped it again for an even closer image. Now he was able to read the yellow LCD screen connected to the bomb he had carefully constructed. He had fitted it with high-grade plastic explosives and armed it with the blasting caps he had purchased at the little mining supply shop in West Virginia. There was a small digital clock in the corner of the bomb's LCD screen. It was blinking with the words "Set — Ready."

Zimler took out a digital detonator control that looked like a tiny television remote. He was ready to press the Clock function. Then he looked back at the video image on his laptop computer screen that showed the inside of the storage room, with the close-up of the LCD screen on the bomb.

He pressed down on the Clock button. The LCD screen clock on the bomb now lit up and started counting down: 30:00 ... 29:59 ... 29:58 ... 29:57 ... Zimler put the remote detonator in his pocket and pulled out two Allfones.

Everything was in place. Now all he had to do was locate his delivery man.

□□□

Outside the terminal by the main entrance doors Joshua was starting to worry. The time had already come and gone when he was to receive some contact from the kidnapper. He checked his own Allfone to make sure it was working and the battery was good. It was.

Then he also checked the other Allfone, the one belonging to Rocky. There were no messages. His brain was racing. *Come on. Come On. Where are you? Let's go.*

That was when he suddenly became aware that someone was approaching him.

The guy had a long, dirty coat, a scraggly beard, and he was wearing a bandana on his head. He looked like a homeless guy.

Joshua took him to be a panhandler looking for a couple of bucks. He reached in his pocket to pull some money out to send the guy on his way. But when the homeless man was only a few feet away, Joshua noticed that he already had money in his hand. He came right up to Joshua and stopped. Looking at his hand, Joshua thought to himself, *The guy's holding a hundred dollar bill.*

Then the homeless man reached his other hand out to Joshua. In his hand was a small paper bag.

Joshua took it. He could feel something inside the bag, something hard and square. For a moment Joshua's brain was telling him not to open it. It could be anything. The whole scene was painfully bizarre.

But just as quickly he knew that he had to play along. The detective had told him to "go with the flow." He didn't have any choice. Joshua Jordan, the man who was accustomed to calling the shots, making the key decisions, controlling the scenario, now knew this was all bigger than him and was ultimately out of his control.

At least for right now.

Joshua reached into the bag and pulled something out. It was an Allfone.

At that point the homeless guy stuffed the hundred dollar bill in his pocket, gave a quick worried look back toward the terminal, as if someone was watching him, and then hurried aimlessly down the sidewalk.

Now Joshua read the message on the screen of the Allfone.

It read: "Click on Video."

Joshua took his index finger and pressed it down on the video key of the Allfone.

The little screen on the handheld lit up with an image. And when Joshua saw it the ground seemed to sway underneath his feet. Like the beginning tremor of an earthquake. He told himself to focus, but his heart was breaking.

Steady, Josh. Steady.

What was he seeing? Was he really watching this?

It was a live video image of Cal. He was tied up. His mouth was covered with tape. There was something around his neck. Like a bulky electronic collar of some kind. There was a series of small packs, each about the size of a deck of cards linked together in the collar. Joshua had seen this before. His military experience told him what it was.

Dear God . . .

The collar contained several blocks of plastic explosives, maybe Semtex.

Then the image automatically zoomed in. Joshua was able to see now the digital clock attached to the bomb around his son's neck. It was ticking. It read: 25:14 … 25:13 … 25:12 …

The image disappeared and a message flashed on the screen of the Allfone in Joshua's hand. It read:

> Want to save him? Bring the RTS package to the grand staircase on the west side of the terminal. Come alone or you will see your son explode.

Joshua held onto the Allfone. With his other hand he gripped the metal briefcase. He stepped toward the doors, got bumped by business travelers and tourists going in and out of the railroad station. All of them except Joshua oblivious to the potential disaster that was ticking away, second by second.

As he entered the terminal he kept thinking one thing, repeating it silently, over and over in his head.

The ram in the thicket. The ram in the thicket. The ram in the thicket.

SIXTY-FIVE

"My son's got a bomb rigged around his neck." Joshua was talking out loud so Gallagher could pick it up through the earpiece-microphone in his ear. He was making his way through the crowd to the great hall of the terminal.

"Any clue where he is?" John Gallagher snapped back.

"Looks like some room somewhere ... not sure where ..."

"What are you doing now?"

"He wants me at the grand staircase at the west end of the terminal."

Gallagher grabbed his personal Allfone so fast he almost dropped it. He had Pack McHenry on speed dial.

"All right. You patriot guys think you're geniuses. Time to pony up. Atta Zimler's got to be inside the building, very near the west-end grand staircase. The guy always works alone so the hand-off will be to him. You've got the photos of Zimler. I'm sure he'll be in disguise. Have your remote camera people video scan the suspects in that area to our computer screen here. I'll confirm which one is Zimler."

At that moment, two of Pack McHenry's associates started strolling through the crowds in the great hall heading to the west end, each with micro-video cameras on their lapels. Each time they saw a suspect they pressed the remote in their pockets and took a snapshot.

The pictures started flooding onto the screen in the van.

"So, who are these guys taking the pictures?" detective Cramer asked Gallagher.

"Uh, private contractors …," Gallagher said, trying to keep a straight face as he said it.

Cramer gave him a funny look. But Gallagher was too busy to notice. He was frantically pressing the delete function for each of the pictures on the screen as he viewed and then rejected them.

"None of these people are even close to being Zimler," Gallagher growled.

Then he saw one that piqued his attention.

He hit the zoom.

On the screen was an Amtrak officer with tinted glasses and a beard, sitting in a corner, hunched over a tiny laptop. Gallagher zoomed in closer. Then even closer.

"Good disguise," Gallagher said, pointing to the image.

"That him?"

"I bet it is," Gallagher said.

"Let's go in, then, right?"

"Wrong. My guess is he's got Cal Jordan wearing that Semtex necklace at a position in the terminal very close by. We've got to find out where."

"Close by? How'd you know that?"

"Zimler employs multiple backup plans. Having Cal close to the action as a hostage gives him leverage if things go wrong."

Then Gallagher picked up his Allfone again. "Okay," he said to Pack McHenry, "the Amtrak guy with the computer, on photo marked jpg14b, is our guy."

McHenry said, "Fine. The next voice you hear is our cyber-intelligence chief."

"Agent Gallagher," the voice said. "I am positioned right outside the terminal in an ice-cream truck. I've dispatched a contact to get in close to Zimler to make a nonintrusive surveillance of Mr. Zimler's computer. As I understand it, you have reason to believe he may have data on it revealing the location of the hostage?"

"Yeah. The guy's a cyber-nut. Probably has it in his computer. But he's going to have it all encrypted. Don't know how you can break through. We've only got minutes here ..."

"We don't invade the digital signal," the voice said. "We go asymmetrical. If it's on his computer screen, we'll get it."

"You've got to be sure of this," Gallagher shot back.

"Agent Gallagher," the voice said. "Mr. Zimler's laptop screen, like any monitor, emits digital signals. It refreshes itself almost a hundred times a second. We scan those signals, run them through our own computer, and decipher them; if you exclude the standard monitor emissions, what's left are the pixels that form the image on his screen. Very soon we'll be seeing exactly what he's seeing." Then the voice said, "Wait ... okay, we're inputting now. We just need his laptop to stay open and the screen loaded with his images for just another minute or two to produce the image. We've got to keep his laptop live."

Inside the terminal, one Patriot operative, now standing twenty feet away from Zimler, appeared to be absorbed in watching a sports event on a small handheld TV. Inside the device, the electromagnetic sensor was picking up and reading the digital signals from Zimler's laptop monitor.

ㅁㅁㅁ

For Zimler, the last scene of the last act was ready to be played out. He had already received a confirming email from an Iranian weapons contact, verifying that the introductory RTS documents emailed from Joshua Jordan were authentic. Now he was studying the location of Cal Jordan on the screen one more time. He clicked on the location of the storage room. Then he zoomed in closer to read the clock on the bomb around Cal's neck. It read 19:28 ... 19:27 ...

Zimler suddenly looked up and began glancing around the room, as if sensing something. He checked his watch. Looked around again. He noticed a man watching a little remote TV. The man was standing a little too close. Hurriedly, Zimler started to reach down to log off his laptop, but something happened.

"Excuse me," a woman said, tugging behind her a small roller suitcase. She was trying to address Atta Zimler. "For the life of me I can't find the listing for the departure time for the train to Dover. Can you help me?"

"No, I'm sorry. Go to the information desk," Zimler said as he again began to reach down to his laptop.

"I already did," she insisted. "But they couldn't help me at all."

"Please, I'm not the right person . . . ," he blurted out.

"But you're an Amtrak official, right?"

For a moment, Zimler was blank-faced as he stared at the woman. Then he quickly caught himself and smiled. "Of course, yes. But train schedules are not part of my job."

"Well, I'm so disappointed," the woman said in a huff and walked away. As she passed the man watching the little TV, their eyes connected, just for a millisecond, in a side-glance of camaraderie. She kept walking until she was out of sight.

□□□

"Okay, so where are we on this?" Gallagher shouted into his Allfone.

"Just a second. Not sure." It was the voice of the cyber-intelligence expert. "We've got some kind of image, but . . ."

Inside the terminal Atta Zimler had turned off his laptop, folded it up, snapped it shut, and stood up. He was holding the little laptop with his left hand. He reached down with his right hand, and snatched up a titanium briefcase that had been on the floor next to him. There was a hefty weight to it.

Then he started walking toward the west end, to the grand staircase.

Joshua Jordan was already there, shifting from foot to foot, waiting, with his briefcase in his hand. He was scanning the room for his contact person.

Then John Gallagher heard the voice of the computer expert. He had his Allfone on speaker, so Detective Cramer heard it too.

"Okay, we've got the image off of Zimler's laptop. He was looking at a diagram of the terminal. There was a blinking cursor over a small room ... maybe a storage room of some kind ..."

"Where?"

"Runs north to south, just off of the grand hall ..."

"Got it," detective Cramer exclaimed. He radioed his bomb squad to break into every storage room along that part of the terminal.

"But tell them to keep it quiet," Gallagher shouted to Cramer, even though he was only two feet away from him. "If Zimler sees a bunch of NYPD guys wearing padded bomb suits running amok in the station, so help me, he'll detonate ..."

SIXTY-SIX

"I'm here at the staircase." Joshua was reporting as he stood at the bottom of the marble spiral staircases. A few people brushed past him, but all of them kept on going. "I haven't been approached yet. Don't know where he is … what's happening with Cal?"

"We think we've got him located in the terminal."

"Thank God …"

"We're sending in some bomb experts."

"What if our bad guy sees them?"

"They're going to be as discreet as possible. We think your kidnapper's dressed like an Amtrak official. Probably carrying either one or two briefcases or laptops. Something like that."

"Okay … wait … I think that's …"

Just then Joshua caught sight of Zimler, dressed in his Amtrak uniform, quickly descending the staircase toward him, carrying two briefcases, one small and one large.

Once again Joshua turned his eyes down to the Allfone that Zimler had furnished him with the video-feed of the ticking bomb.

It read: 09:36 … 09:35 …

"He's here," Joshua whispered.

Inside the unmarked police van on the street, Gallagher was saying, "What did you say? Hey, Jordan say it again." The ambient noise inside the terminal was making it difficult to pick up Joshua's audio.

"Mr. Jordan," Zimler said, "what a pleasure." He was now standing next to Joshua Jordan. Joshua was sizing him up. The other guy was about an inch shorter. Maybe twenty pounds lighter. He looked like he might be in good shape. But that was it. Joshua was considering his options. *If I have to take this guy down myself I may be able to do it.*

Inside the van, Gallagher was trying to figure out what was going on. He wished that these Patriot guys had more remote cameras to sweep into the area and take videos of the action. But they had already used up four of their agents, two on video surveillance, one holding a little TV while picking up the emissions from Zimler's computer, and a woman posing as a passenger late for the train to Dover. No one wanted to spook Zimler by having a familiar face hanging around him.

But then the FBI agent had a fleeting thought. He pictured Joshua Jordan, military hero meeting up with the guy who was holding his son hostage. He knew Zimler's unassuming appearance. He also knew he was as deadly as a coral snake.

Gallagher clicked on the microphone.

"Joshua, this is Gallagher. One last warning. Do *not* underestimate this guy physically. He's a very dangerous dude."

Zimler stood next to Jordan and scanned the room, moving in a three-hundred-and-eighty-degree turn.

"I think you've brought some friends with you today," Zimler said, testing him. "I warned you what I would do if that happened."

"You think I'd be that foolish? Now, give me my son."

Zimler and Joshua stared at each other.

Joshua looked down at the video picture on the Allfone. The bomb now said: 07:19 … 07:18 … He desperately needed to move the negotiations.

"Turn off the bomb."

"All in good time."

"I said deactivate the bomb." He moved a half step closer to Zimler.

"You haven't given me the RTS documents. You're the one wasting time here."

Joshua handed him the metal briefcase he was carrying.

But Zimler wouldn't take it.

Instead he said, "Not here. Not now. Follow me. And remember, I have the power to stop that bomb. Or to detonate it. You try anything out of the ordinary, and I will reduce your son to a pile of bloody, charred gristle. "

Then Zimler turned and started walking through the terminal.

"Where are we going?" Joshua asked.

"You want to see your son? You can see your son. Right now. I'll take you to him. The two of you can be together."

Panic struck. Joshua realized that the bomb squad might be there by now. Zimler could blunder right into that. That would spell disaster.

"You mean where Cal is … with the bomb around his neck?"

"Of course," Zimler said coolly as they walked.

"Negative on that!" Joshua said and stopped in his tracks.

Zimler stopped. He switched his laptop to his other hand, the one already holding the big titanium briefcase.

The two men stared at each other. Zimler pulled his remote detonator out of his pocket. When he spoke he moved up to Joshua's face and hissed with a demonic intensity. "Look at this, Mr. Jordan. This is your son's life I'm holding in my hand. One push of the button, and he's nothing but red smoke."

"I'm not going in the same room as the bomb," Joshua stammered.

Suddenly Zimler stepped back. A smile flickered over his face and he chuckled.

"America's hero," Zimler spat out, "is a coward! You don't want to be near the bomb. Is that it?" He laughed again. Then he said, "Fine, follow me."

Zimler led Joshua down to a corridor. He stopped at the door to a utility closet. He pulled out some keys, tried one, it failed, tried another, and then it opened. He pushed Joshua inside and flicked on the light and closed the door. Inside the four-by-four-foot room, filled with mops and a cleaning cart, he turned to Joshua and said, "Open the briefcase."

Joshua glanced down at the Allfone: 04:03 ... 04:02 ...

"Stop the bomb!" he cried out.

"Show me the RTS documents!"

Now was the moment of decision. Joshua knew that he had no choice but to entrust himself into the hands of the God that his wife prayed to. The Lord of all history that Pastor Campbell preached about.

He silently prayed for what would happen next.

At that moment, Joshua took a deep breath and released everything he held dear.

He crouched down to his metal briefcase. He whirled the combination on the locking mechanism, and it clicked open. Then he lifted the briefcase chest high and, facing its contents toward himself, he popped it open. He was taking his time. Hoping the bomb squad had reached Cal by now. That they were disarming the bomb even as he was cloistered in a utility closet face-to-face with the kidnapper.

"Show it to me," Zimler said.

Joshua turned the opened briefcase to Zimler to show him the contents.

Zimler looked inside.

And he smiled for a second.

But in the next second his smile vanished and his face took on a look of merciless hate that was almost otherworldly.

"What is this?" Zimler spit out.

Atta Zimler was looking inside the briefcase. He was staring at the yellow cover of a New York City telephone book. Then he raised his eyes, filled with fury, toward Joshua.

"Who do you think you are? Who do you think you are?"

Joshua replied quietly. With the voice of total resignation.

"I'm the ram in the thicket."

SIXTY-SEVEN

Atta Zimler was still holding the detonator in his left hand. With his right he set his little laptop and the titanium briefcase on the ground, robotlike, emotionless.

Then with the speed of a coiled snake his right hand struck out at Joshua's neck and grasped it, squeezing with the strength of a vise grip until Joshua couldn't breathe.

Joshua dropped his briefcase to the floor and took both of his hands and tried to pry Zimler's grasp off his larynx. He struggled but wasn't able to loosen Zimler's grip. Joshua was astonished at his opponent's strength and was gasping for air.

Then Zimler let him go and stepped back. He raised the detonator high enough so that Joshua could see it.

"Say good-bye to your son —"

"No, you'll have to get the data directly from me. I can give it to you ..."

"How? You fool ..."

"I will give you my password ... you've got your own laptop there," he said pointing. "You can access the documents directly from my computer remotely ..."

"I told you I wanted the documents ..."

"This is better. You will have electronic access. To all of it ..."

Joshua looked down at the video image on the Allfone. The timing clock on the bomb read: 00:49 ... 00:48 ...

Zimler was staring at Joshua with the look of a killing machine considering its options.

Then Joshua looked at the LCD screen on the Allfone again. It still read: 00:48. Joshua looked a third time. The clock had stopped. He realized what had just happened. *The bomb squad made it to Cal.*

He glanced down at the image on the screen of the Allfone again. Now he saw hands reaching over the timing device this time and pulling wires out.

Joshua looked up at Zimler. The assassin saw something in Joshua's face. Not the look of a victim. But of someone who now was thinking himself to be the victor.

Zimler gave a crooked smile and held the detonator in the air. He was now no longer concerned about the RTS documents. He was going to make a point.

"My reputation is priceless," Zimler said. "Can't have dolts like you thinking you've won the game ..."

He pushed the trigger of the black detonator remote. And waited. No sound.

Zimler grabbed the Allfone out of Joshua's grasp and looked at the screen. He saw the hands of bomb-squad officers untying Cal Jordan.

Zimler stared him in the eye with the look of dark fury. Joshua stared back. In his face was the iron resolve of a father.

"You don't get my son," Joshua said. "Not now. Not ever ..."

"Joshua. Joshua." It was Gallagher yelling to him through his earpiece. "We've got Cal. He's safe. Did you hear that? He's safe."

Joshua whispered a single word. It was barely audible. Only he knew what that meant.

"Isaac."

Zimler heard it and looked Joshua in the eye, stone cold.

Gallagher announced, "Now we're coming after you. We've been tracking the ear bug we gave you. They have a fix on your location ..."

There was something in the tilt of Joshua's head as he listened to that. Something that gave himself away.

Zimler saw it. He yanked a 9mm pistol out of his pocket and stuck it against Joshua's cheek.

Then he stuck his finger in Joshua's left ear. Finding nothing, he did it to his right ear. He fished out the earpiece. Zimler threw it to the ground and stomped on it.

"I may not have your son," he said to Joshua. "But I still have you."

Still pointing the handgun at Joshua, he took his titanium briefcase and pulled out a pair of handcuffs and clicked one end through the hand grip opening in the molded titanium case. Then he clicked the other handcuff onto Joshua's left wrist.

Zimler pulled a second little remote, this one stainless steel, out of his pocket. He pushed the Start button on the countdown clock of the bomb he had inside the titanium briefcase now locked to Joshua's wrist.

The LCD screen on the edge of the briefcase read: 03:00 ... 02:59 ... 02:58 ...

"Hey, Joshua, we lost your signal. What happened? Where are you?" Gallagher was yelling into the microphone, but no one was listening. Then he turned to Detective Cramer and cried out, "Okay, this is it. You gotta get Joshua out of there *now!*"

Standing next to Joshua, Zimler demanded, "Give me the password for your email system."

"No, my son's safe now. The rules of the game have just changed ... you lose ..."

"Are you insane? I've got this briefcase rigged to blow in a few minutes. Give it to me, and I'll stop it ..."

"You're not getting my RTS documents."

"Then you'll die."

That was something that Joshua had prepared for down in his gut, all along. But he was anguished. His world was collapsing. He wanted to say good-bye to Abby. To say something to Cal and Deb. But no time...

Joshua looked down at the briefcase and ran his hand along the surface. He recognized the material.

"Yes, titanium," Zimler said. "Nearly impossible to break into from the outside. But at the temperature of eight hundred degrees Fahrenheit — when a bomb explodes in it — it breaks apart into shards rather well. So if you're going to be a hero, you may want to avoid crowds. Difficult, though, in a place like this. Good-bye."

Zimler tucked the gun in his pocket and fled the room. Fifty feet away he ducked into a men's room and into one of the stalls. He ripped off his theatrical beard and his Amtrak coat and tinted glasses. He looked at his watch. Now he had to get out of the station.

The LCD screen on the briefcase handcuffed to Joshua said: 02:05 ... 02:04 ...

Joshua burst out of the utility room, yanking wildly at the handcuff on his wrist. He couldn't squeeze his hand out. He looked for a knife, something sharp somewhere. Couldn't he cut his hand off?

He started running down the corridor leading to the trains.

He started yelling, "Bomb, bomb, get away from me! There's a bomb in this case! Get away ..."

Crowds around him started screaming and tripping over themselves to get out of his way.

He saw a tunnel leading to the tracks. Away from the building. Away from the masses. He had to get there. Joshua was sprinting with the briefcase dangling from his wrist. An Amtrak security guard lunged at him. Joshua knocked him backward and kept running.

Now he was breaking into the train yard. Trains were lined up on several tracks with passengers climbing in.

He whipped his head around looking for a vacant space. He looked down at the LCD screen. It said: 00:56 seconds.

Abby, I love you. Cal and Deb, I love you.

He spotted an empty track at the far end. He sprinted over toward it. Then he heard someone calling his name.

It was Agent John Gallagher, running and shouting, "It's Agent Gallagher, FBI!" He was about a hundred feet behind him and had spotted him.

"Joshua, wait …," the Agent yelled.

"This is a bomb …," Joshua yelled back. "Stay away."

"We can help!"

"No time …"

The LCD screen said: 00:36 …

A train engine pulling a single empty car was approaching. Joshua rushed up to it on the platform overlooking the track.

Something triggered in Joshua's brain.

Caught in the thicket.

He looked back at Gallagher. Then Joshua made a frantic decision. When it happened Gallagher saw it and his jaw dropped open.

Joshua leaped down into the path of the oncoming train engine.

Someone on one of the other passenger platforms screamed out.

Down on the railroad tracks, Joshua draped the five-inch chain of the handcuffs over the metal rail with the briefcase laying on the other side of the track. Then he jammed his body as far as he could away from the oncoming train, over against the side of the retaining wall.

With a deafening screech the engineer slammed on the train's brakes. The train kept sliding forward, spitting sparks, passing inches away from Joshua's left hand, over the handcuff chain on the rail, smashing it apart and separating him from the briefcase bomb.

The train was slowly grinding to a halt, its metal brakes locking down against metal. The train came to rest with the back half of the empty passenger car directly over the suitcase bomb. Joshua scrambled wildly to his feet and leaped up to try and grab the upper platform and pull himself up. To get away from the force of the blast that was only seconds away. But he missed. He jumped up again, catching the platform above him with his fingertips. He yelled out in an animal grunt, bringing his knees up and trying to push up with his knees.

It's going to blow.

Arms aching, he made one last exhausted effort, kicking, pulling, fingernails digging into the cement platform. Now his hands were flat on the surface of the platform and he was pulling himself up. His head. His torso. Then up to his waist. He belly-flopped onto the platform. Joshua stumbled to his feet and started running toward the station and away from the bomb.

Faster. Faster.

Then it happened. An unearthly roar of smoke and fire and percussion blew up from the tracks. The blast of the bomb picked up the passenger car and jackknifed it into the air and heaved the car and the locomotive against the cement embankment with a hellish, crashing groan of smashing steel and sparks.

Still running on the platform, Joshua caught the full force of the combustion and was catapulted into the air, flipping and tumbling along the platform like a rag doll. Screaming passengers on the parallel train platform panicked and ran into each other and tripped over their baggage while others threw themselves to the ground. Down on the tracks, black billowing smoke poured out from the train engine, which was now on its side as diesel fuel spilled over the scene. The engineer pulled himself out of the open window and then leaped down to the tracks in a frenzy. He was hobbling in pain as fast as he could down the track away from the demolished train. Then the diesel fuel caught fire and a ball of flames enveloped the train and the empty passenger car in a raging inferno.

John Gallagher had been thrown to the ground by the outer cyclone of the blast. When he picked himself up and stumbled to his feet he looked down the platform and spotted the familiar body that was now tangled in a heap. Gallagher bellowed out a single word in a hoarse cry.

Joshua!

PART FOUR
Red Sky at Dawn

North Korea and Iran are already known to co-operate intensively in developing nuclear capable missiles. So what is to stop them helping each other with their nuclear programmes?

"Iran, North Korea and the Bomb — Spinning New Dark Tales."
The Economist (September 12 – 18, 2009)

Under [Iranian President] Khatami, with continued Russian assistance, the Iranian missile program was in fact accelerating.... Russian assistance was contributing to many key aspects of the Iranian missile program: the warhead, the fuselage, and guidance systems.

Dore Gold, former Israeli Ambassador to the U.N.,
The Rise of Nuclear Iran (2009)

And you, son of man, prophesy against Gog, and say, "Thus says the Lord God: 'Behold, I am against you, O Gog, the prince of Rosh, Mesheck, and Tubal; and I will turn you around and lead you on, bringing you up from the far north, and bring you against the mountains of Israel ...'"

Ezekiel 39:1 – 2, NKJV

SIXTY-EIGHT

Two Weeks Later

Agent John Gallagher sat on the edge of a fake leather chair in Joshua Jordan's hospital room. He was feeling slightly out of place, although Abigail was there, and she was trying her best to make him feel like part of the family.

Debbie had been pumping Gallagher for information about his life as an FBI agent. He patiently shared a few interesting incidents, though he was not a guy to share war stories. So after awhile, Abigail told her daughter to give him a rest. So Cal and Debbie leaned back to watch the TV hanging by brackets from the ceiling. Cal was used to the cast on his broken finger by now. They were laughing at a silly TV commercial. Life was getting back to normal.

"So, you get out tomorrow?" Gallagher asked.

"Maybe," Joshua replied. He was in multiple casts. As he spoke, he tried to shift his position in the bed without tangling up the IVs. "You know how they play the medical game with you. Waiting until the last moment before you find out if you're going home."

"He's rushing his recovery, of course," Abigail said with a smile. Then the smile disappeared. "Josh had a hairline fracture of the pelvis. Broken collar bone. Fractured wrist. Multiple lacerations from the shrapnel. One of them punctured his back about one inch from his spinal column. Any closer and he'd be paralyzed."

"All things considered," Gallagher said, "you oughta be dead. You're a lucky guy."

"No, not luck," Abigail said with a tender kind of ferocity. "This was a miracle. This was God. The Lord wanted Josh alive."

Gallagher looked over at Joshua who was thinking it over.

"How can I argue with that?" he finally said. "I'm here, right?"

"Well," Gallagher said at last. "I'd better move along. There's a chili dog out there somewhere with my name on it." Then he got up slowly and stiffly.

"Agent Gallagher," Abigail said, reaching out and taking his hand. "Thank you. Thank you for being there for my husband. And helping to save our son."

John Gallagher didn't like the whole emotional scene, so he nodded quickly and turned to leave.

But Joshua had a question for him. "This Atta Zimler guy. What happened to him? I read in the news that he just disappeared. Vanished. It's troubling to know he might be out there somewhere."

When he said that, Cal stopped looking at the TV and looked over at his dad.

"I wouldn't worry about Zimler," Gallagher said.

"Oh?"

"No. We have some pretty good intel that the guy may have been killed overseas. Here's hoping ..."

"Anything you can talk about?"

"Not really. I'm in enough trouble."

"Hey, are you kidding? You're a hero," Cal interjected. "I saw them give you that commendation on TV."

Gallagher smiled. Sure, he got a Bureau commendation. But the next day, in the office, Miles Zadernack dropped a written reprimand on his desk. It read: "... failure to notify supervisor of a request to consult with local police regarding a terrorism incident." Still, Gallagher didn't care. He looked at a live Joshua Jordan and his son, who was now laughing at a stupid TV show rather than lying in a million pieces. So he knew it was all worth it.

As he stood in the hospital doorway, Gallagher turned to say one last thing. It could have sounded perfunctory. It was probably said by all the agents to all the other families who had ever been traumatized. But this time, Gallagher meant it in a way he'd never meant it before.

"You know," he started to say. But right then he was surprised at how he had to fight a little to keep it together and not get choked up. "You people ... you're the real heroes here. Just wanted you to know that."

Then he gave a clumsy wave and left the room.

On the way down to his car, he was thinking about what he couldn't share with Joshua Jordan and his family. Classified information about Atta Zimler.

Of course, it was disturbing at first. The thought that Zimler had killed and tortured his way to the Jordan family, and then he terrorized them, yet had slipped right through the fingers of the large nest of NYPD officers at the scene. A clean escape. As if by some magic act.

□□□

Zimler knew that the airports and the roads would be watched. Getting out of New York City would be daunting. Which is why he'd planned all along, whether he was able to get the RTS documents or not, on the escape route he would use.

He'd spent an enormous amount of money in advance rigging his exit strategy from the United States. Zimler had prepared a large ocean-going container in the New York harbor and fitted it for human habitation during the Atlantic crossing. It had a chemical toilet, an air circulation system, a small solar-run generator, a satellite phone, and computer and plenty of freeze-dried food and water for the trip. From the outside, it looked like just another corrugated metal shipping container that would be loaded on a cargo ship bound for Rotterdam.

Once he landed in the Netherlands, he would connect with a member of the Muslim Brotherhood that he knew. He would go underground for a few months. Then he would start making his way to Cyprus where the initial fee that Caesar Demas had paid him was still waiting for him in an account.

And it was a smart plan.

Except that Petri Feditzch, in his shipping office in the Rotterdam port, got wind of it. He knew that Zimler had failed in his mission and that Caesar Demas had no more use for the assassin. So Feditzch made a call to some old friends in Moscow. Then, when the ship pulled into the harbor, and Atta Zimler's big metal container got unloaded, he had a greeting party waiting for him.

It was Vlad Levko and two other Russian FSB agents. They had two reasons to be there. First, they wanted to verify that Zimler hadn't confiscated the RTS documents himself, while pretending that his mission had failed. But they had a pretty good idea that, in fact, Zimler had returned empty-handed. The only exception to that was the fact that Joshua Jordan had been forced to email an executive summary of the RTS protocols. But it was questionable how useful that limited data might be.

But there was also another matter too. The business about Zimler assassinating several friends of Levko's in the FSB. That made it personal.

After the shipping container was lowered down on the dock, the Russians got ready.

Levko gave the signal to his two agents. They donned toxin masks, and one of them pulled out a radioactive aerosol. They would swing open the metal doors, and they would spray Zimler in the face. Then the Russians would lock him into the metal container from the outside. It would take Zimler about three hours of horrifying agony before he finally would lose consciousness. Two hours after that, covered with hideous radiation burns, he would be dead.

Laying his hand on the locking handle of the metal door, Levko lifted the handle and swung the door open. He shined a big flashlight into the container.

Levko took a step in. He was almost too wide for the narrow doorway. He stopped inside the big metal container, with his back to the agents. Then he turned, emotionless, and stepped back out into the sunlight.

After looking at each of the agents, Levko's face erupted into a purple rage. He made a fist and screamed several Russian profanities. One agent grabbed the flashlight and ran into the container, followed by the other agent.

The beam lit up the inside of the container nicely. They could see the chemical toilet. The generator. Some scattered bits of unfinished food rations. A few magazines.

But Atta Zimler had vanished.

SIXTY-NINE

"Your wife's an incredible person. We've all fallen in love with her here at the center. And she's done an excellent job with her recovery."

Margaret, Darlene Rice's counselor, was sitting across the desk from Fortis Rice. He had become a familiar face. He'd been traveling down to Tucson to see Darley on each of the visiting days at the Living Waters Recovery Center. He shouldn't have been surprised that her stay seemed to him to have been a long one. When he was a judge he would occasionally sentence a defendant to drug rehab as a condition of probation. He knew the routine. But back then it was a matter of cold, objective administration of justice. It was a case file on his bench. He'd issue the order and forget about it until the case came up again.

But this time it had intersected right through the center of his life. This time it was his wife. He was still trying to get his head wrapped around that fact.

"And your support for Darley has meant a lot to her," she continued. "I just know that's true, Fort."

Rice said, "She's different ... quite a different person. Not totally, of course. But in ways that a husband notices."

"That's what happens," Margaret said, "when a person encounters God. Your life changes. You start heading in an exciting new direction." She paused and then added, "I know you were cautious at first ... the fact that we were a Christian-based recovery center."

"Yes, I was." Then he thought about that for a moment. Fortis Rice had always been deliberative. Maybe that was what his professional peers meant when they talked about his "judicial temperament." Then he added, "But then I'm open to being proven wrong. In this case, I think I may have been overly suspicious."

Margaret smiled and stood up. She noticed Darley outside the glass door, waiting for her husband.

"There she is," the counselor said. "I'll let you go."

The two of them shook hands, and then Rice strode out into the lobby to greet Darley.

She had a big smile waiting for him, and she wrapped her arms around him and gave him a kiss, a hug, and then another kiss.

"Oh, Fort, it's so long between visits. You look like you've dropped some weight. I can't wait to get back home and make you some home-cooked meals. I'll make you that pot roast you love. With boiled potatoes. With that special recipe for the gravy."

She led him out to the glass-enclosed atrium, where they would usually visit. She loved it there. It was filled with huge cactus and blooming plants and had a panoramic view of the desert and the mountains.

They talked for more than an hour. Mostly about mundane things in their lives. But every so often Darley would say something, and Fort would zero in on it mentally, making a note to himself, though he wouldn't verbalize it right away.

As when Darley commented, "I'm responsible for my own changes that need to be done in my own life. I can't put that on you."

Not that Fort ever thought that he had been in charge of his wife's life, not in that way. It was just that he had just seen it as his job to manage things. Make decisions, that's all. Someone had to do that, right? But maybe there were changes that had to be made there too.

As Darley talked, Fort took the time to listen, really listen. And to study his wife. There was a glow in her face just then, and he thought back to how they first met. She was attractive and fun, and so full of life.

And she still was. Fort leaned over, put his arm around her, and said, "I love you. What you did here took courage. I'm proud of you. And I'm sorry that I couldn't see what was going on in your life. Not until it had gone too far."

Darley flashed a huge smile, rolled her eyes a little, and started tearing up.

When they were nearing the end of the visit, Fort mentioned that he needed to call Joshua Jordan.

"How's he doing in the hospital?" she asked. "That poor family. What a scary thing they had to go through." Then she added, "Tell Abby I got her letters. I love that girl. Can't wait to hug her to death and talk her ear off when I'm out of my anti-pill prison here!"

When they said good-bye, Darley cried a little and said how much she missed their home. And she asked how her houseplants were doing.

Out in the parking lot, Fort Rice dialed up Joshua Jordan, who'd just been discharged from the hospital the day before. The two men caught up on a lot of things, Joshua's recovery, the crisis at Grand Central Station, and, of course, the Roundtable.

"I sent you a package," Fort Rice said.

"It's sitting right here with all my other mail that's piled up," Joshua said. "But I haven't opened it yet."

"You'll want to read it. And share it with the Roundtable. It's a copy of a deposition transcript that was sent to me by a lawyer friend of mine. Long story short — it's part of a lawsuit brought by the families of several people who were killed in the melee in New York City when that talk-show host, Ivan Teretsky, blurted out over the air that Manhattan was about to be nuked. The suit is against Teretsky and his radio network. But you need to start reading at page one hundred and forty-five."

"Why?"

"It's the testimony of a guy named Lance Porteau. He was the live-in boyfriend of a Lana Orvilla, the White House chief of staff for Vice President Jessica Tulrude."

"Oh, this sounds interesting ..."

"The plaintiffs' lawyers were trying to figure out who telephoned Teretsky and spilled the beans about the North Korean missiles headed our way. So they looked at a list of the radio program employees. One of them was a radio engineer by the name of Reggie Orvilla. He's the brother of Lana Orvilla. It so happens that Lana was in the briefing room with the vice president when the missile alert went out. She panicked and called the radio station, thinking she was calling her brother to warn him, but it was the studio line, and Teretsky picked up and heard it all. Well, this gets better ... in the White House situation room, Lana Orvilla had heard the vice president say that she knew that the RTS system would be used. She didn't object to it at all. And Tulrude was yelling at the Pentagon brass saying that she was speaking for the president. That Corland supposedly approved of everything she said."

"That's a hundred and eighty degrees opposite of what the White House told Congress ... that they *didn't* authorize the use of RTS ..."

"Exactly."

"And this Lance Porteau guy ..."

"Lana Orvilla told him everything. So it can't be protected with executive privilege."

Joshua went silent as he was putting this all together.

Then he said, "We've got to get this out on AmeriNews."

"I figured that. I see your media plan is doing fantastically, everybody's talking about it ..."

"*Our* media plan," Joshua said. Then he asked, "But why was Tulrude speaking for the president during a national crisis?'

"That's the big mystery. Nobody knows. Not yet."

□□□

Later that day, in the nation's capital, a small, closed-door meeting took place in the West Wing of the White House. This was an unusual conference, perhaps even bizarre — even by Washington standards.

Hank Strand, President Corland's chief of staff, was confiding in the vice president. What he had to say was arguably a breach of ethics, certainly of protocol and probably illegal. But Strand was worrying about his political and professional future. In Washington, that often trumps everything else.

Strand appeared calm, but his voice was lowered and clearly stressed. "They finally have a diagnosis."

"And?"

"Something called 'transient ischemic attack.'"

"That's what causes the president's blackouts?"

"Right. Usually people with that disorder are really old. It's a little tough to diagnose. Which is why it took the medical gurus so long to figure it out. But in any case, the president really isn't old enough to fit the usual profile ..."

"So?"

"Well, there's only one other suggestion for why he's developed that condition."

"And?" Tulrude wanted the punch line.

Strand took a second to set the stage.

"You know, Madam Vice President, that the president would fire me in a heartbeat if he knew I was telling you this."

Jessica Tulrude leaned forward and patted his hand. "Don't worry, Hank. This is a safe place. I'll protect you."

Hank Strand had just heard the magic words. So he answered the vice president's question. Strand said, "Drug use."

Tulrude gave a startled look like she had just seen a protester enter her office holding a pie in one hand.

"Drugs? What kind of drugs ..."

"Nothing you can get from your local pharmacist, let's just say that."

A string of profanities flew out of Tulrude's mouth.

Hank Strand waited for the smoke to clear. Then he spoke up again. "I think, Madam Vice President, this can all be managed. You've already been doing a masterful job of taking over. Pulling the strings. I admire that. The president knows he can't run again. Not with this lurking in the background. You'll get the nod for the nomination. Now all we have to do — you and I — is make sure no one on God's green earth ever finds out about this drug thing. At least not until after the election. When you're elected the next president of the United States. And I'm your next chief of staff."

Tulrude was eying Hank Strand. She was nodding. He was smiling. Strand could see this was going fairly well. The two of them could do some very effective damage control together.

Strand was now thinking, *This just might be the beginning of a wonderful friendship...*

SEVENTY

Two Months Later

In the region called Krasnodar Krai, nestled in the foothills of the
Caucasus Mountains, three men had gathered in a well-guarded mansion belonging to the Russian Federation. In times past it had been one
of Stalin's secret neoclassical resort palaces, with a spectacular view of
the Black Sea. But in recent years Russia had been using it for discreet
meetings. Like this one. The men were now alone in an oak-paneled
library. All the doors had been shut.

One of them was Ivan Kranstikov, a silver-haired physicist, former
KGB agent, and the head of the Russia's tactical nuclear-assessment
unit within the FSB. Yet he didn't have the disheveled look of a scien-
tist. He was elegantly dressed. Nor did he have the tough bluntness of a
former Russian counterintelligence officer. But he was that too. All of
which made him a uniquely valuable asset in Russia's global blueprint.

The second man was dressed simply in a black suit with a collarless
white shirt. He was Hasan Rashmanadhi, the chief arms negotiator
for Iran.

Last was a short, stocky, humorless fellow in a bland uniform. Po
Kumgang was the political overseer of North Korea's nuclear program.

Kranstikov offered his guests some Russian tea. When they de-
clined he got down to business.

He described their meeting as an "extraordinary melding of common interests." Then he began reciting the current situation: Russia had been saddled with the Nuclear Nonproliferation Treaty and the Geneva and Lisbon Protocols. Under international pressure it had been forced to close — but did not destroy — its plutonium production facility. Russia still had an enormous stockpile of nuclear weapons, but they were all aging or obsolete, and all of them were under intense international scrutiny.

Then he turned to Po Kumgang. "It must be remembered that we supplied your country with its first nuclear reactor."

"Old history," the North Korean spit back. "That was decades ago."

"And your promises to us regarding weapons," Rashmanadhi pointed out, "have never been fully satisfied."

"Then it's good we three are talking," Kranstikov said. "To bind us together in a common pursuit."

"Which is what?" the Iranian asked.

"Russia has the technological experience and know-how in nuclear weaponry. But," he said with a sigh, "there are disadvantages to world leadership. There are many eyes on us. On the other hand, your countries, North Korea and Iran, have successfully played the game of cat and mouse. You have both begun admirable uranium-enrichment programs and plutonium production against all odds. You are to be congratulated. Yet you both have certain lacks. Iran lacks strong missile-delivery systems and is relatively new to this technology. Russia can help with that. North Korea cannot launch long-range nuclear weapons. Russia can provide that. In short, we can lend you both a high degree of technical assistance to bring your nuclear weapons programs to the highest levels."

"And what is it that Russia lacks?" Rashmanadhi asked.

The Russian smiled.

He knew what it was that Russia wanted. But he wasn't going to spell it out. Not yet. Rashmanadhi had already told him privately that Iran wanted to launch a devastating and decisive nuclear attack against Israel. Moscow knew that Russia's secret assistance with that deadly project would earn it the everlasting cooperation of all of the oil-producing Arab nations.

So instead of the unvarnished truth, Kranstikov gave them diplomatic platitudes but frosted with a tasty hint of the bottom line. "We want a nuclear partnership with both of your countries," the Russian said.

"What about Return-to-Sender?" Po Kumgang cried out, jutting his arms out to both sides.

Kranstikov understood his concern. North Korea desperately wanted revenge against the United States for the attack on its ship when it was decimated by its own nukes. It wanted to strike America, but it was still concerned about Joshua Jordan's RTS missile-defense system.

"There are ways," he said, "of accomplishing your desired nuclear aim against America without having to worry about the RTS shield."

Po Kumgang didn't smile. By all appearances he seemed incapable of that. But he arched his eyebrows and nodded vigorously. That was good enough.

The Russian knew that a successful strike against the United States would not obliterate it. But an East Coast nuclear strike at the center of commerce in New York and another at the seat of government in Washington could reduce America almost instantly to a second-rate country.

Which would then allow the Russian Federation to concentrate its energies and resources against the only competitor that stood between it and world dominance — China.

"So," Kranstikov said, "shall we talk frankly? About how we can move forward as partners?"

"Yes," Hasan Rashmanadhi said quickly, "let us move forward." There was a surprising urgency in his voice. Not even a hint of diplomatic masking or doublespeak.

Po Kumgang crossed his arms and nodded firmly. His leaders were anxious for revenge against the United States.

Kranstikov smiled. He had a remarkable epiphany.

This is going to happen even faster than I thought.

ㅁㅁㅁ

The whole Jordan family had come to Hawk's Nest early, before the next scheduled meeting of the Roundtable. They knew it would also do a world of good for Cal. Joshua was up and about, although he'd been warned by his doctor to avoid strenuous activities. He was told no horseback riding. Debbie was disappointed about that, but Abby was glad that her husband was trying to be smart about his recovery.

Still, Joshua had one thing already planned, and nothing, certainly not doctor's orders, was going to dissuade him. As soon as the Roundtable recessed, he and his son, Cal, were going backpacking for two days into the Rockies. Cal said he would carry the heavier pack with the tent, even with his finger in a cast, to give his dad's lacerated back some rest. And he was bringing some portable fishing rods so they could try fly-fishing for trout in the fast-running streams along the way. It would be a slow-paced hike, leisurely, no pressure.

Joshua said all that was fine. He just wanted the time alone with his son out there with the big sky and the mountains.

Now Joshua was standing outside the door to the large great room, which was used for the Roundtable meetings. Abigail was standing next to him. They could hear the voices of all the other members of the Roundtable chattering on the other side. Even Fortis Rice had come. He said he'd thought things over and had decided that his "conflict of interest" had disappeared. He now wanted back in. They were glad to have him.

Joshua turned to his wife. "Well, dear, are you ready?"

She smiled and asked him playfully, "Are you sure you can trust your wife as the newest member of this secret cabal?"

"I'll remind you," he shot back with a grin, "that Fort Rice said he'd come back only on one condition — that you head up the Roundtable's legal unit."

Joshua put his hand on the doorknob, but his wife stopped him.

"Hey, you still didn't answer the question!" she said still nursing a bit of a tease in her voice. "Can you trust me?"

He reached over and gave her a long, lingering kiss. "With my life," he whispered. Then he swung open the door.

As Joshua and Abigail entered the room, the members of the Roundtable were on their feet, giving both of them a standing ovation.

There were well-wishes and welcomes all around the table for a few minutes. But as much as he enjoyed it, Joshua had an urgent item of business to attend to. He called the meeting to order.

"I am going to address something that has just come to my attention," he said. "Forgive me for putting this ahead of the agenda. But when I explain, I think you'll understand why."

But before continuing, Joshua Jordan took a moment to lean back with his hands resting on each arm of the leather captain's chair. Out the window he caught a glimpse of the tall pines slowly swaying in the breeze. He yearned to be out there. In the fresh air. With the smell of the woods. But not yet.

There was a certainty in Joshua Jordan's posture and a look of ease as he directed his attention back to the group, to the dire business at hand. He looked across the big table, over to Abigail. For a moment they locked glances. There was the unspoken understanding between them that once again life was about to get complicated and very dangerous. Abigail knew exactly what it was that her husband was about to announce, that it was so explosive that some might even call it treason.

Yet when Joshua spoke, his voice was calm and unhurried. "I have received credible intelligence about two things," he said. He had to take a breath before he continued. "First, a nuclear attack is imminent. It will come against the United States. And also against Israel."

Then as he studied the faces of the members of the Roundtable, his trusted friends, patriots all, he continued. "The second thing is equally important. The current administration will dismiss this intel and will not take action."

After giving the group a moment to consider that astonishing announcement, he finished his thought. "Which means, my friends, only one thing," Joshua explained. For an instant he saw a fleeting image before him of the harrowing trouble ahead. But that wouldn't stop him. Not by a long shot.

"Our course is clear. Because the White House will not act — then *we* must."

An Excerpt from *Thunder of Heaven*
The Second Installment of The End Series
by Tim LaHaye and Craig Parshall

ONE

IN THE NEAR FUTURE

In a small warehouse in Howard Beach, beyond the border of JFK International Airport, Hassan was going over the details with his two partners. He stared into the eyes of Farhat, the young Turkish man who was fidgeting with his car keys. Hassan had his doubts about him, but had kept them to himself. The mission was too important to take a chance compromising it just because Farhat wasn't totally sold-out to the cause. Farhat's level of commitment had to be probed. Hassan was afraid that his young recruit was more concerned about his pretty girlfriend back in Istanbul than he was about the mission.

"Farhat," Hassan began, "the time has come. Are you with us?"

"Yes. Why do you doubt me?"

"I don't waste time doubting. I believe. I decide. Then I act."

Farhat nodded and looked over with a jerk, toward the third man, Ramzy, the Palestinian on loan from Hamas.

With his arms crossed, Ramzy looked a little disinterested. But then he said, "Fine. Then we start."

Hassan held a *sat-fone*, the newest generation of digitally encrypted satellite cell. He clicked it on and waited until the woman on the other end, inside the JFK terminal, answered his call.

"Talk to me."

"Flight 433 to Denver, Colorado, is fully boarded, waiting on tarmac. Clearance has not yet been given. I'll tell you when it begins taxiing down runway."

Hassan acknowledged it and said, "I will be waiting. Remember. We need two minutes lead time."

The woman said, "I will make you proud."

After clicking off the sat-fone, Hassan barked out to Farhat, "Recite your role in the plan again."

Farhat swallowed hard and spoke: "I wait inside the van. I do not start the engine until I see your text on my Allfone. I have ten seconds to read the text before it self-deletes. Then I turn on the ignition. Wait for you and Ramzy. If I see any police or security, I turn off the van and get out and walk over to tell you, but don't run. If the mission is completed, then we all get in and I drive exactly three miles per hour over the speed limit — no more, no less — to our destination. Don't run red lights. Obey all stop signs."

"The route?"

"Shore Parkway to I-278."

Hassan got close to Farhat, in his face. He said, "Good. Except, one correction. Not *if the mission is completed*. Get straight on that. We will complete the mission. We must not fail." Then, to put a final point on it, Hassan put a finger to Farhat's chest and said, "Sha-Ja-'a ..." Farhat wrinkled his brow. Hassan smiled. His one-word mandate to Farhat to have *courage* was meant to be a warning.

"*Allah Ackbar!*" Hassan yelled out.

Now they would wait. But not long.

Deborah Jordan settled into her seat, 14A — right next to the over-wing emergency exit door on the big 797 jet, which was parked on the tarmac of JFK International Airport. First class was all filled up, so she'd had to settle for coach on her JFK to Denver. Too bad her father's Citation X private jet was getting some security upgrades and wasn't ready yet. Otherwise she could have asked for a ride.

Flying commercial didn't bother her much. She didn't have a rich-kid attitude. The point was to get home to her family's sprawling log mansion in Colorado.

She studied the slow pack-animal parade of passengers as they came down the aisle and stuffed bags into the overheads.

Deborah put her purse, still open at the top, on the floor by her feet. As she did, she stuffed her hand into the embossed leather bag and pulled out a compact, little magazine called *National Security Review.* She left the big latch of the purse unhooked and the top flap open as she sat back. After buckling her seatbelt, she tried to focus on her reading.

A man in his early thirties shoved his carry-on into the overhead and then took the seat next to Deborah, flashing a smile. He was wear-ing a golf shirt, a little too tight, she thought. Maybe it was to show off his biceps, which, she had to admit, were impressive. A chiseled face but something interesting about the nose. It was a little off-kilter. Like it had been broken. Short hair. Blue eyes.

Uh-oh. He's caught me looking.

The man smiled again. Deborah tossed a tight-lipped nod in his di-rection and then turned her attention back to her magazine. When the jet was full, an airline attendant bent over in her direction. There was a courteous smile and the standard question. Was Deborah willing and able to activate the emergency exit door next to her if the need arose?

"Absolutely. No problem."

The attendant disappeared, and the man next to her leaned toward her slightly.

"You sure about that? I'd be glad to help out."

The grin on his face told her two things. First, he was taking a clumsy stab at flirting. Second, it was a lame attempt at an ice-breaker.

"Thanks, but I can handle it."

Still managing a smile he added, "I'm sure you can. Just trying to be friendly. I'll leave you to your reading."

ooo

On the other side of the country, things at LAX airport seemed normal enough. Flights mostly on schedule. A few backups. Although no one seemed to know why, the security status had been raised for the TSA workers who were screening passengers at the X-ray machines. But then that had happened before. So the security staffers in the dark blue shirts started increasing the random carry-on inspections.

Outside on the tarmac, a couple of uniformed airport cops were slouching against an LAX OPS police squad car. They were talking casually and squinting behind their Ray-Ban sunglasses in the glare of the California sun.

One block outside the LAX perimeter, two men were on the roof of an apartment building. One of the men was a Muslim ex-military veteran from Chechnya. Next to him was an American-born Arab recruit from the U.S. Army. The location was ideal. It was on the line between Highway 405 and the tall, rectangular airport control tower with the spiked exterior that looked like some kind of giant Lego construction. When everything went down, it would be a short drive for them to the 405 where they could then drop the hammer and merge into the crazy-fast traffic from Los Angeles and escape from the scene of the disaster. They would leave behind their signature: the exploding inferno and a mass of human fatalities.

TWO

The good-looking guy sitting next to Deborah kept glancing over at the magazine she was reading. She noticed that out of the corner of her eye. The next time she caught a glimpse, he wasn't looking at the magazine. He was making a side glance, taking in her pretty face, softly square with double dimples and dark eyes.

She braced herself.

Great. Okay, here it comes.

And it did. The man gave a head nod toward the publication she had in her lap, and said "So, national security stuff. You work for a defense contractor?"

Deborah had to make a quick decision. *Engage? Or activate avoidance measures?*

She decided that limited engagement was the safest course. Then she could get back to the article she was reading about "nuclear deterrence in an age of asymmetrical warfare."

"No, not with a defense contractor."

"Military detail then?"

Deborah weighed her answer. "Not exactly."

Then, without looking up from her magazine, she added, "Technically not."

"Intriguing. Okay. Then you're in one of the academies." He eyed her closer. "Air Force? Naw. I'm Air Force. You definitely don't fit the profile..."

Deborah tried to keep up the stone face on the outside. *Profile? What profile is this guy talking about?*

"Not Navy I don't think. Not reading that kind of stuff. So, that leaves one more. West Point, right?"

Deborah didn't realize that she was blushing. Her seat partner kept talking.

"Wow, direct hit. Oh, sorry. Didn't introduce myself. Ethan March. Formerly Lieutenant Major, United States Air Force. Now civilian. Glad to meet you, Miss..." He reached out to shake her hand.

Deborah threw him a side look and offered up a quick handshake. And a short explanation.

"You're right. I'm West Point."

"Graduated?"

"One more year."

"Congratulations. In advance."

"Thanks. And you, Mr. March?"

"I go by Ethan. Defense contracting. Until recently..."

That got her attention. "Which company?"

"Raytheon. Just got laid off. Part of defense downsizing from Washington. Go figure."

Deborah gave a nod that showed she was underwhelmed.

But Ethan March made a rapid recovery. "I've been lucky, though. Been around the block. With some of the best."

Now he had her attention. She couldn't resist. "Oh? Like who?"

"Well, for one ... I had the privilege of serving under the great Colonel Joshua Jordan."

Deborah dropped her magazine and broke into a grin. Which slowly lapsed into laughter.

Ethan flashed a look of disbelief. Then he said with some disgust,

"Army. Can't believe it. You folks don't know how to honor a true-blue Air Force hero like Colonel Jordan."

When she was able to stop laughing, she explained. "You don't understand. You said you served with the 'great Joshua Jordan' ..."

"Exactly. At McGill Air Force Base."

"Well, Joshua Jordan is my father. Which I guess makes me ... well, his *almost-great* daughter ..."

Now Ethan was the one blushing.

"Oh man. Plane going down. Mayday, Mayday ..."

Now they were both laughing.

She reached her hand over to shake. "Let's start this again. I'm Deborah Jordan. Good to meet you."

They shook hands again, but this time he held on a little longer.

"I'm really honored to be sitting with you. Figure that. Joshua Jordan's daughter."

THREE

Inside the cockpit of Northern Air flight 199 at Chicago's O'Hare airport, the copilot was reading off the preflight checklist. When he got to one item he paused.

Then the copilot read it out. "Primary countermeasures."

The pilot, Bob Blotzinger, a veteran of twenty years commercial flying, flicked the little toggle switch and the green light on the instrument panel lit up. He said, "Check."

"Secondary system."

"Check."

The copilot stopped again for a second. Then, after turning full around to make sure the cockpit door was closed and they were alone, he asked, "What is the deal with that?"

"With what?"

"The secondary. You know, the RTS?"

"Hey, I'm just the pilot. Ask National Airlines. I only work here."

"Come on Bob. Humor me. Did the FAA really approve the Return-to-Sender defense system or not?"

The pilot gave it some thought and tossed his first officer a tired look. Finally he spoke. "Okay. This is only what I heard. So don't quote me. Apparently the FAA clears the RTS for installation in commercial jets, right? But then Homeland Security gets involved and says whoa, whoa, wait a minute. This is national-security stuff. So it starts getting even more complicated. Like it always does. Now you've got a battle between two different agencies. So they finally decide, okay leave it installed. But each airline and each airport jointly can decide whether the system actually gets activated. Anyway, the FAA wants to see if having it physically installed jinxes anything in your avionics. Which it shouldn't, from everything I know. But that's their compromise."

"But you're not answering me. Are we able to use the RTS against a threat or not?"

"No. Not really. Not automatically. Have to call it into air traffic control. Give them the alert. Get their permission first. Ridiculous."

The pilot waved his hand toward the preflight log that the copilot was holding.

"Alright. So sign off on the preflight will you? I want to get to Dallas."

The copilot tilted his head as he listened in his headset to a message from the tower. He followed that with a nod. "Good news. They've moved us up. We're on deck."

By the time flight 199 started taxiing down the runway at O'Hare, across the country at JFK, Deborah's flight 433 to Denver was next in line for takeoff.

At LAX the flight from Los Angeles to Las Vegas was in the same position.

As the Chicago flight rolled toward takeoff, two men were hunched together inside the Ulema Salvage Yard in Schiller Park, Illinois, just outside of the perimeter of O'Hare airport. An Indonesian man was shouldering a FIM – 92 – A stinger missile. His brother was standing next to him reading the quick text messages from the other cell groups in Los Angeles and at JFK.

In the salvage yard outside of O'Hare the driver of the getaway van was behind the steering wheel with the engine idling, and he was watching the two-man stinger-missile team get ready.

The brother's sat-fone rang. He took the message and he became electrified. "Takeoff is confirmed for flight 199 to Dallas," he yelled. "It's coming …" A few seconds later they could hear the jet approaching off in the distance.

While flight 199 was taking off from Chicago, on the east coast, flight 433 out of JFK was slowly rolling down the runway. The 797 was being straightened in perfect alignment for takeoff. Deborah was fully engaged in conversation with Ethan March and wasn't paying attention to the usual sensations of a jet beginning to taxi.

Inside the cockpit, the pilot had his hand on the throttle and eased it forward on the computerized flight deck. The big jet started accelerating. Then the pilot powered it up for takeoff. The 797 started racing down the runway, and Deborah felt the familiar centrifugal force pulling her back into her seat. At that exact moment, her purse tipped over on the floor, spilling out the contents. Lipstick, compact, coin purse, Allfone cell, pens. Everything.

For a split second, she tried to fight the impulse. But she did it anyway.

Deborah quickly unbuckled her seatbelt so she could reach down and quickly stuff the contents back into her purse and zip it closed.

For Blotzinger, the pilot of Northern Air Flight 199 departing Chicago, it was the third time flying the new 797. He had a wife and three kids, two of them married with children of their own. There were eighty-eight souls on his jet that day, including the crew and the flight attendants.

Blotzinger piloted his big jet to lift off. The flight path took them over Schiller Park, Illinois, and Ulema Salvage. When the jet was directly over the salvage yard, the copilot noticed something. A blip on his radar screen. The blip was streaking right toward them. The attack warning bells went off in the cabin, and a yellow light started flashing. The copilot blurted out, "Bob, incoming ..." He hit the counter-measures button. The flares designed to detract heat-seeking missiles blew out from the underbelly. But they were not close enough to the trajectory of the stinger missile heading for the jet. The missile kept streaking toward its target.

Bob Blotzinger could see what was happening. "Fire the RTS!" he screamed.

The copilot hit the control for the RTS anti-missile system while Blotzinger tried to swing the big jet into an avoidance pattern.

Their eyes were riveted to the screen on the panel.

But for some terrifying reason, the linear blip kept coming. Closing in at a blinding speed. Heading right for the belly of the jet.

The RTS should have worked. Should have instantaneously trans-mitted a data-capturing/data-reconfiguring laser beam aimed straight for the guidance system in the missile. Should have reversed the flight path of the FIM–92-A stinger that was streaking toward the jet and turned it around. And sent it back where it had come from.

Something had gone horribly wrong.

The last sound on the cockpit voice recorder was a millisecond scream of the copilot when he got a glimpse of the long steel cylinder full of explosives momentarily flashing into sight just before it struck Flight 199 outbound from O'Hare.

There was an unearthly blast. And in one blinding explosion they were all gone.

On the ground, a man was walking his dog. He screamed out loud and jumped at the sound of the sky exploding into fire overhead. His dog howled and cowered on all fours on the ground. The man looked up and saw the fireball expanding in the air. Then he screamed again. Now he was seeing the charred pieces of fuselage, cockpit, and wing assembly of the jet plane falling from the sky all around him and crashing down on houses and streets in his Chicago suburb.

FOUR

Momentarily, National Airlines flight 433 out of JFK would be winging its way over the warehouse. Inside, Ramzy had the missile launcher on his shoulder. He was standing directly below the retractable skylight that was now open. Ramzy was looking through the clear pane of plastic on the sight of the launcher. Ready to line up the big jet within the rectangular lines of the sight. When the big 797 was inside the sight lines he would launch the missile.

Inside, as the plane was lifting off, Deborah had her seatbelt unbuckled and was bending down, quickly stuffing things back into her purse.

Ethan March, the former Air Force flyer, started to make a joke of it. "Seatbelt off? Leave it to an Army academy student to ignore flight regulations ..."

In the cockpit, the crew suddenly heard a shrill warning bell. The copilot pointed to a flashing light on the flight deck. They both saw an oblong object on the LCD screen streaking toward them.

The copilot blurted out, "Oh my G — "

The pilot thrust his finger down on the primary countermeasure button. A flare shot out from the underbody of the jet toward the incoming heat-seeking missile to detract it. But the FIM-92-A missile keep coming.

Alarm bells were ringing.

The security screen flashed: 7 SECONDS TO IMPACT.

The pilot punched his finger down on the button marked "RTS." A laser beam blasted out of a small orb on the belly of the National Airlines jet toward the incoming missile. The beam struck the guidance section right behind the missile's heat-seeking tip.

The pilot knew he had to put distance between the heat of his jet engines and the incoming missile. He banked the jet into a twenty-degree yaw to the left. The pilot frantically put the huge jumbo jet into an evasive turn and dive. Passengers screamed as magazines, jackets, and purses flew into the air.

In a millisecond, Deborah, who was still out of her seatbelt, felt herself lift up into the air. She would have been thrown straight up into the ceiling. Headfirst with the force of an automobile crash. But Ethan March had instantly reached over her when the jet started veering and blocked her with his arms holding onto her. Up front, a stewardess had hit her head against a bulkhead and lay unconscious in her jump seat.

Five hundred feet away from the jet, the RTS laser beam had triggered the guidance system of the missile into a mirror reversal of the trajectory.

Suddenly, the infrared head of the missile was deactivated. The stinger began its turning loop. Away from the jet. The missile was now on its deadly path back to earth at fifteen hundred miles per hour. Returning to the warehouse where it had been launched.

On the ground, Ramzy was trying to repack the launcher into the case. Hassan was waving to a cab driver from Lebanon, his backup for escape, who was roaring up to the warehouse with his taxi.

That is when Hassan, who was standing outside, thought he saw the glint of something up in the air. A thin metallic object streaking through the sky toward them.

It was the last thing he would see.

When the missile struck the warehouse, there was a flash and a deafening roar as the warehouse disintegrated in the enveloping ball of fire. Hassan, Ramzy, and Farhat were instantly consumed. Four workers on the loading dock of the neighboring building were taking a break. They never knew what hit them. The shock wave from the blast blew them in the air a hundred feet away from their building, which imploded behind them. Its windows sprayed broken glass in a shimmering mist as the walls buckled. The sonic blast from the explosion could be heard all the way across to the New Jersey shore.

In the cockpit of Flight 433 overhead, the LCD screen on the flight deck was flashing FIELD CLEAR, and the red light and the buzzer ceased.

The pilot corrected the jet's flight path.

Deborah found herself in a heap on Ethan's lap with his arms locked around her. She climbed back into her seat. Their hearts were banging in their chests.

Deborah threw a glance up to the ceiling of the plane, realizing what might have happened. She tried to manage a smile and turned to Ethan.

Thanks. Really. But a second later came her other thought. *What was that?*

In the cockpit, the pilot radioed the tower.

"Permission requested to use RTS secondary countermeasures per FCC rules. Over."

"Hey, what happened? What the — "

"Permission requested for RTS."

"Don't understand — "

"Look, I'll just take that as permission granted. Thanks, tower. Over."

Two minutes later, at the other end of the country, the men on top of the roof near LAX airport were monitoring the Los Angeles flight to Las Vegas that was just taking off.

They had already received an ecstatic voice message on their sat-fone from the Chicago cell group. "Plane down! Plane down! Allah be praised!"

Now the Chechen was helping the Arab missile expert shoulder the stinger launcher.

"Hear it? Listen. That's our jet!" he cried out. Then he added, "We have to bring it down like our brothers in Chicago."

The missile man aimed his launcher. The 797 was appearing off to the left. His aim would be exact. He pulled the trigger and the missile blew straight up into the sky leading the approaching jet perfectly in its approach.

In the cockpit, the bells went off. The copilot in the jet automatically slammed down on the countermeasures button. Two flares shot out, heading straight for the incoming missile.

The pilot next to him was yelling, "What is it? What is it?"

But before he could get a response from his copilot, he could see it all on the screen. The flares had diverted the heat-seeking missile off its trajectory slightly, but just slightly. Both the pilot and the copilot could see the missile for a split second. The pilot was praying out loud that the missile would not hone in on the heat from his jet engines.

"Get away from the engines!"

The missile shot past the jet with a trail of smoke. It kept traveling due west. It eventually fell harmlessly back toward earth, disappearing into the Pacific surf a half mile offshore.

Three hours later, a group of U.S. Navy SEALs and members of the L.A. bomb squad unit were able to locate the missile and defuse it. For some reason, the explosive charge never detonated.

The RTS system never had to be utilized on the LAX flight.

□□□

In the Rocky Mountains of Colorado, Joshua Jordan and his wife, Abigail, had been riding their horses. Earlier that day they had taken the pass that wound through the tall pines and eventually ended up at the barn near their log mansion. But the ride was over, the horses were stalled, and now they were inside their massive retreat house. Both of them were wondering when they would hear from their daughter, Deborah, who was expected to arrive at the Denver airport.

Joshua had already migrated to the big family room with the high timbered crossbeams and turned on the Internet television set. Then he took a few steps back and dropped into a cowhide chair. On the end table next to him there were some pictures from his years in the Air Force, before he started his own defense contracting company. One showed Joshua and a past president, shaking hands after his successful secret surveillance flight over Iran. Another framed photo of showed him with several members of the Joint Chiefs of Staff. But the third picture was his favorite. It showed his wife, Abigail, back when she practiced law with the DC firm, heading down the steps of the federal courthouse in Washington after having arguing a big case to the Court of Appeals. That would be just one of many that she would win.

Joshua's attention was drawn to the ticker scrolling at the bottom television screen.

NOA FLIGHT — FROM CHICAGO CRASHES ON TAKE-OFF. FEAR NO SURVIVORS. FLIGHTS FROM LAX AND NEW YORK TURNED BACK.

Joshua yelled out to his wife. Abigail ducked into the room. Joshua pointed to the screen and the message that was still scrolling.

A look of panic came over Abigail's face. "Flight numbers ... What flight numbers?"

"They haven't given any. What's Deborah's flight out of JFK? Where did you write that down?"

Abigail dashed out of the room to her study where her desk was.

Joshua was trying to make sense out of it.

Three flights in three parts of the country. One crashed. Two turned around. This is sounding terribly familiar ...

FIVE

Washington, D.C.

Mike Leaky was sitting at his desk eating a Cuban sandwich and slurping Mountain Dew from a plastic bottle. He was hitting "The Dew" because he needed an energy boost. Mike had been out late partying the night before.

His job at the U.S. Geological Survey, National Climate Change, and Wildlife Science Center was to analyze weather data. Specifically, data on global warming. But sometimes the endless stats all seemed to blur together. Like today. He chugged some more of The Dew while he was reviewing the latest printout.

Mike studied it. Then groaned out loud to himself in the empty computer room, "Oh no, man. No ..."

It seemed pretty clear that he had input the hundred-year average rather than the one-year average.

So he loaded into his computer the parameters once again. This time making sure that he was asking for the one-year average. He punched Enter. And waited.

Mike was bored and decided to wander down to the office of his supervisor, Dr. Henry Smithson. When he got there, Smithson and Ernie, his assistant, were glued to the little Internet television set.

When Mike started to ask what they were watching, Smithson put his finger to his lips and pointed to the screen. That's when he saw the footage of the smoking, charred wreckage that had landed in the residential neighborhood outside O'Hare.

Smithson said, "This is awful. No facts yet. The NTSB is investigating but isn't talking. Someone on the ground thought they saw an explosion in the air. Just to make sure, other flights are being canceled. You know anyone flying today?"

Mike shook his head.

"Me neither."

Smithson hit the search function on his remote, and on the right-hand column of the Internet TV screen, a series of weblogs and Insta-News articles appeared. They were all reporting the same thing. Smithson scrolled down. After fifteen other entries, all of them nearly identical, finally one looked different. It was from a new web and wire service called Ameri-News. It's headline read: MISSILE SIGHTED IN CHICAGO, HEADING FOR DOOMED PLANE ...

Ernie chirped out, "Hey, lookit that!" pointing to the headline on the screen.

But Smithson just grunted back, "Ameri-News? You've got to be kidding, Ernie. Bunch of crazies. Members of the flat-earth society."

He clicked off the Google search and then enlarged the TV footage on the screen. Mike hung around, watching the gruesome coverage of the Chicago crash on the television. Then he looked at his watch and figured that he needed to get back to his office.

When he arrived, he checked the screen. Then he hit print. After a few seconds, he collected the papers. Mike sat down with the earth-temperature average index and reached over to grab his Cuban sandwich. He took a big bite and savored the crunchy, thinly sliced dill pickle and the spicy meat. It was just the way he liked it. He chewed once. The side of his cheek bulged with his first big bite.

But then he saw it. At the bottom of the last page of the index.

Mike nearly chocked. He was coughing and gagging. He was so dumbfounded that he had forgotten to keep chewing.

This can't be right. No way.

He scanned every page, following the trail of data. Point by point. Until he got to the end. It made sense mathematically. It all fit. Except for the one-year average. That had to be wrong again. But it wasn't. It was correct. He had checked it. For a moment Mike felt like he was about to have an out-of-body experience.

"I must be going nuts."

Or else, it was something else. *The only explanation was that world-wide temperatures were climbing to dangerous levels. Catastrophic global warming had now kicked into overdrive.*

When Mike realized what it meant, he snatched the papers and sprinted down the hall like a maniac. His frenzied footsteps echoed off the linoleum floor as he ran. Until he reached Smithson's office.

When he burst in, Dr. Smithson and Ernie were still watching television. But Mike's frantic entrance made the Ph.D. of climatology and his research assistant whip around in their chairs.

Then Mike raised the papers in the air. His face had the stunned look of a pedestrian who almost got hit by a bus.

"God help us. It's happening ..."

SIX

In the conference room of the Eternity Church in Manhattan, the men who had gathered there for the day had a special custom for this kind of meeting. No cell phones. No wireless handheld devices. That meant they were temporarily cut-off from the news of the day. But it also meant that they could focus on the subject at hand with a hydraulic kind of intensity.

Today there was a palpable atmosphere of anticipation, though no one said it out loud. But they all felt it. Like being on the beach when the tide suddenly sucks backward toward the ocean and you know that a tsunami is about to hit.

The room was quiet. Except for the oldest man, Henry "Doc" Mc-Cowell, eighty-nine and nearly blind, who was clearing his throat until someone placed a glass of water in front of him to drink.

The chairman of the small, biannual conclave was Peter Campbell, the head pastor of Eternity Church, which occupied a historic brown-brick cathedral in downtown New York. Forty-three, athletic, with a calm kind of kinetic energy, his passion was the study of prophecies of the Bible.

The other six members of the group had the same emphasis. Two, Dr. Bill Rutledge and professor Jay Windom, taught at seminaries. Two were pastors of churches. One of them, Roger Ephraim, was the head of the Israel Study Institute based in Jerusalem. Doc McCowell was a retired president of a Bible college who had authored expositions on the books of Daniel, Ezekiel, and Revelation, and, during his long ministry had picked up a master's degree in archaeology as well as a Ph.D. in Semitic languages.

They had spent the last hour in prayer. Each had a nearly crushing burden for what they saw off on the thin line of the visible horizon.

Professor Windom led off.

"We've met here together for the last three years. Contemplating and debating. Wondering what we would do if this day ever came in our life time. And now it's here."

"And yet," one of the pastors said, "we all know the admonitions from our Lord. Standing on the Mount of Olives . . ."

Another pastor chimed in, quoting " 'Of that day and hour no one knows, not even the angels of heaven, but My Father only.' "

Dr. Rutledge had a point to make. The same idea that he had voiced before. "But remember what event it was that the Lord was referring to there. Not the events leading up to His coming. But rather, the actual occurrence of the His physical appearance. Which means that we might be able to identify the pre-appearing events, the stage-setting so to speak, with great accuracy. While still not knowing the actual day or hour of the Second Coming of Christ."

Doc McCowell was clearing his throat loudly again. The room grew quiet as he took a big swig of water from the glass. Then he removed his tinted glasses from his wrinkled face and put them on the table. He was a man not prone to speak quickly. Doc would choose his words, particularly on the weightier subjects, carefully. Like a sculptor cutting a face out of marble. With each blow calibrated just so. Knowing that every word, like a chisel on stone, has consequences.

Doc McCowell started talking. His voice was weak, with the tremolo of age.

"Great events cast long shadows. Can we deny that we see the shadows of these epochal events approaching? Some are even at our doorstep. Jesus upbraided the Pharisees. Didn't He? For failing to read the signs of the times? Will we be like them? Failing to tell the world the very thing that we see? While the world is saying it is a good day because it's morning ... friends, we realize that the sky is red. How can we stay silent about that?"

No one spoke for the length of a minute.

Finally Peter Campbell said it.

"I believe, just like the Apostles of old, that we have 'to declare what we have seen and what we have heard.' Tell the truth. Unvarnished. Then let the chips fall where they may."

No one dissented.

So it would begin.

SEVEN

After three desperate hours, Joshua and Abigail Jordan finally heard the voice of their daughter, Deborah.

Joshua and Abigail were both on the line. Abigail blurted out, "Deb, are you all right?"

"Our flight got shaken up a bit. I just have a few bruises. But I'm okay."

Abigail breathed a sigh of relief. "Thank you, God. What in the world happened?"

"Mom, I'm not sure. The plane took a dive. Things flew everywhere. Then we returned to JFK. They've been interviewing us nonstop but not giving us information."

As a former Capitol Hill lawyer, Abigail wanted the backstory.

"Who questioned you? Which agency? The NTSB?"

"Yeah ... National Transportation Safety Board. Right."

"Anyone else?"

"Guys in suits. Probably FBI. Gee, why don't I remember that for sure?"

That caught the attention of her father, and he pressed for more details. Joshua immediately asked, "Why'd they turn your flight around?"

"I don't know, Dad. One minute we were taking off, the next minute the plane goes into ... well, it almost seemed like evasive maneuvers, and then everything went crazy ..."

"Any talk about this being connected to the Chicago flight?"

"What?"

That was when Joshua realized that his daughter had been kept in the dark. She knew nothing about the crash of the commercial jet over Chicago.

He decided to drop it. "Never mind, honey. Just let us know how soon we can see you."

"They're putting us on two buses to Philadelphia today. Then they are flying all of us to Denver from there."

Joshua, a decorated Colonel in the Air Force and former spy-plane pilot, had cut his teeth on military flying, not commercial. But he knew something about flight-incident investigations. And his most recent stint as the premier anti-missile defense contractor with the Pentagon had also brought him into contact with a load of federal agencies: the NTSB, the FAA, Homeland Security, and the National Security Agency to list just a few. By now he already had a guess that his daughter's flight may have had some connection with the Chicago disaster.

Suddenly, Deborah changed the subject. "Oh, there's something I have to tell you."

She didn't give either parent a chance to process before she continued.

"I'd like to bring someone out there to Hawk's Nest. So you can meet him."

Abigail threw a look across the log-beamed living room to Joshua. He was sitting at the other end, by the five-foot-tall fieldstone fireplace. Even from across the room Joshua could read his wife's expression.

"Explain, dear," Abigail said in a tone freighted with a parent's expectation, "exactly who you are talking about?"

"Mom, this guy is former Air Force. And Dad, guess what else? He worked in defense contracting with Raytheon."

Abigail pushed a little. "How long have you known him?"

"Well, just a few hours ..."

Across the room Abigail was shaking her head. It wasn't adding up. Joshua tried to get to the bottom of it. "Sweetheart, this isn't making sense. You're probably shaken up."

"Dad," she began. They both heard the depth of emotion in her voice. "He saved me during the flight. Kept me from getting a broken neck, or maybe a fractured skull."

"Deborah, what on earth?" Abigail had had enough. Now she was going to launch into one of her skillful, impassioned cross-examinations. And Joshua could see that. But he waved his hand toward his wife has if to say — *not now. This is too sensitive for a phone conversation.*

In another family, that wouldn't have been understood. But in the Jordan household, it was different. After all they had been through as a family. And with the risks that she understood all too well, Abigail decided to pull back.

"Darling," she said, "just come home to us quickly. We love you so much, and we're so glad you're safe. Your brother's coming in a few days. Hopefully flights will be back to normal by then. Cal's in Boston right now. We'll all be together. I can't wait to hug you."

After they hung up, Abigail strode over to sofa where Joshua was sitting and dropped down next to him, grabing his powerful hand. She ran her hand through her hair with her other hand. Joshua, as usual, was doing the stoic thing. But she could see that he was carrying a two-hundred-pound weight on his chest. They both sat silently for a moment trying to absorb what their daughter just told them, scant as it was. Still, it sounded like something terrifying had happened during Deborah's flight. Abigail said she wanted her daughter with them "ten minutes ago." How frustrating it was that that their Citation private jet was down with repairs. But couldn't they simply charter another private jet to pick Deborah up?

Joshua shook his head. "Abby, I know what you're thinking. I'm there too. But by the time we lined up a charter, she could be heading home from Philly. Let her stick with the plan. Besides, I don't want to flag Deborah to the federal folks."

"You think there's something going on, don't you? Not simply a random crash of an airliner in Chicago ..."

"With all we've learned—with what we've seen—I think we have to expect anything."

They both disappeared into their own thoughts.

Then Abigail broke the silence. "Josh, what she said ..."

Then she finished it, but only after struggling with the words that caught in her throat. "She said someone *saved her* on that flight ..."

Joshua was rocked by the fact that his daughter's safety had been at risk on the flight out of JFK. But in the back of his mind, he was also thinking about Chicago Flight 199 going down. And the fact that the FBI had been interrogating Deborah and other passengers on her flight, which was four states away from the Chicago flight that crashed. And both were the big 797 jets. And he knew something about those jets.

He couldn't shake the feeling of catastrophe. And responsibility. As the designer of the RTS anti-missile system installed in the new 797s, he had a vested interest in commercial air safety. *For heaven sakes,* he thought to himself, *my daughter was on a National Airlines flight with my own RTS device onboard.* He had to find out why the Chicago flight ended in disaster. And right away. Pilot error? Equipment failure? Wind shear?

One thing he did know: there was one explanation for the crash that he was dreading. He wasn't a person who prayed, a religious type, like his wife. But what he said silently in his head sounded awfully similar.

Please, don't let it be that ...

The End Series

EdgeofApocalypseToday.com

#1 New York Times *Bestselling Author*
Tim LaHaye and Craig Parshall

EdgeOfApocalypseToday.com is the blog of Tim LaHaye and Craig Parshall, authors of the *New York Times* bestselling The End fiction series. Their blog not only regularly reports on current events that intersect the futuristic themes of their novels, but also analyzes those events that have a special relevance to prophecies in the Bible. Their blog will give you a perspective on the headlines of the day that you will be unlikely to find anywhere else.

Subscribe to the blog today to keep informed!

Joshua Jordan on Facebook

#1 New York Times *Bestselling Author*
Tim LaHaye and Craig Parshall

As a retired colonel in the US Air Force, Colonel Joshua Jordan wants to continue contributing to America's national security; protecting its ideals—such as freedom of speech, freedom of religion, and liberty and justice for all—from all assailants, foreign and domestic.

Colonel Jordan is married to the beautiful Abigail, an accomplished lawyer and best friend. They have two children: Debbie is a West Point cadet, and Cal is a student at Liberty University.

Colonel Jordan owns and operates his own company, Jordan Technologies, which is a leading provider of defense systems for the US government.

You can read about Colonel Joshua Jordan's harrowing adventures in the books *Edge of Apocalypse* (2010, Zondervan) and *Thunder of Heaven* (2011, Zondervan).

Follow Colonel Jordan on Facebook
for exclusive content and special offers.

ZONDERVAN®
.com

Share Your Thoughts

With the Author: Your comments will be forwarded to
the author when you send them to *zauthor@zondervan.com*.

With Zondervan: Submit your review of this book
by writing to *zreview@zondervan.com*.

Free Online Resources at

www.zondervan.com

Zondervan AuthorTracker: Be notified whenever your favorite
authors publish new books, go on tour, or post an update
about what's happening in their lives at www.zondervan.com/
authortracker.

Daily Bible Verses and Devotions: Enrich your life with daily
Bible verses or devotions that help you start every morning
focused on God. Visit www.zondervan.com/newsletters.

Free Email Publications: Sign up for newsletters on Christian
living, academic resources, church ministry, fiction, children's
resources, and more. Visit www.zondervan.com/newsletters.

Zondervan Bible Search: Find and compare Bible passages in
a variety of translations at www.zondervanbiblesearch.com.

Other Benefits: Register yourself to receive online benefits
like coupons and special offers, or to participate in research.

ZONDERVAN®

ZONDERVAN.com/
AUTHORTRACKER
follow your favorite authors